MW01014078

Legendary Hunts

SHORT STORIES FROM THE
BOONE AND CROCKETT AWARDS

Davy Crockett and Bear | *Acrylic*
by Boone and Crockett Club Member Bob Kuhn

COURTESY OF THE NATIONAL MUSEUM OF WILDLIFE ART, JACKSON, WYOMING

Legendary Hunts

SHORT STORIES FROM THE BOONE AND CROCKETT AWARDS

Presented by the Boone and Crockett Club Publications Committee
Chairman – Mark B. Steffen, M.D.

Compiled by the following individuals:
KEITH BALFOURD
MARK O. BARA
GEORGE A. BETTAS
ELDON L. "BUCK" BUCKNER
RICHARD T. HALE
ROBERT H. HANSON
RYAN HATFIELD
JULIE T. HOUK
MARIE PAVLIK
REMO PIZZAGALLI
JACK RENEAU
PAUL D. WEBSTER

Published by the Boone and Crockett Club

Missoula, Montana

2006

LEGENDARY HUNTS
Short Stories from the Boone and Crockett Awards

First Edition 2006
  Third Printing

Copyright © 2006 by the Boone and Crockett Club.
All rights reserved, including the right to
reproduce this book or portions thereof in any form
or by any means, electronic or mechanical, including
photocopying, recording, or by any information storage
and retrieval system, without permission in writing
from the Boone and Crockett Club.

Library of Congress Catalog Card Number: 2006929871
ISBN Number: 978-0-940864-54-2
Published September 2006

Published in the United States of America
by the
Boone and Crockett Club
250 Station Drive
Missoula, MT 59801
406/542-1888
406/542-0784 (fax)
www.booneandcrockettclub.com

THE MISSION
of the Boone and Crockett Club

*It is the policy of the Boone and Crockett Club to promote
the guardianship and provident management of big game
and associated wildlife in North America and to maintain
the highest standards of fair chase and sportsmanship in all
aspects of big game hunting, in order that this resource of all
the people may survive and prosper in its natural habitats.
Consistent with this objective, the Club supports the use and
enjoyment of our wildlife heritage to the fullest extent by this
and future generations of mankind.*

Executive Committee
Boone and Crockett Club

Photo from B&C Archives

Doug Johnson packs out the tremendous rack from the Alaska-Yukon moose taken by his father, John R. Johnson, near Tikchik Lake, Alaska in 1995.

Table of Contents

Legendary Hunts

Short Stories from the Boone and Crockett Awards Programs

Photo from B&C Archives

Musk Ox, Scoring 126–2/8 points,
Taken by M.R. James near Kugaryuak River, Nunavut,
in 2000.

Elk & Deer Continued...

Moose & Caribou 209

Horned Game 245

Photo from B&C Archives

Philip L. Wright served as the Records Committee Chairman from 1978 through 1986. Wright is pictured above at the 18th Big Game Awards Program with the well-known Chadwick ram – considered by some the greatest trophy ever taken by a modern-day hunter.

Introduction

By Robert H. Hanson

Boone and Crockett Club Records Keeping

BIG GAME RECORDS-KEEPING HAS ALWAYS BEEN AN IN-
TEGRAL PART OF THE BOONE AND CROCKETT CLUB'S
ACTIVITIES SINCE IT WAS FOUNDED IN 1887, BUT METHODS OF
MEASUREMENT, RECOGNITION PROGRAMS, AND OTHER ACTIVI-
TIES HAVE CONTINUED TO EVOLVE OVER THE YEARS. IN 1902,
THE CLUB'S EXECUTIVE COMMITTEE ASSIGNED THEODORE
ROOSEVELT, CASPAR WHITNEY, AND ARCHIBALD ROGERS TO A
SUBCOMMITTEE THAT WAS CHARGED WITH THE RESPONSIBILITY
OF DEVISING A SCORING SYSTEM TO RECORD BIOLOGICAL AND
SCIENTIFIC DATA ON WHAT WERE THEN THOUGHT TO BE THE
VANISHING BIG GAME SPECIES OF NORTH AMERICA. LITTLE
IS KNOWN TODAY ABOUT THE FRUITS OF THEIR LABORS, AS NO
WRITTEN RECORD OF THE WORKINGS OF THIS GROUP HAS EVER
BEEN FOUND. IT IS ASSUMED, HOWEVER, THAT THIS SUBCOM-
MITTEE CONTRIBUTED SIGNIFICANTLY TO THE SCORING CHARTS
USED IN THE 1932 AND 1939 EDITIONS OF *RECORDS OF NORTH
AMERICAN BIG GAME*.

The scoring systems used in those early days were rather
primitive and uncomplicated by today's standards. Most tro-

phies were scored by one or two simple measurements, and then ranked by the length of the longer horn, antler, or tusk. The only method of measurement that remained substantially intact, after the current system was adopted in 1950, was the one used to score the skulls of bears and cats. Otherwise, the methods employed for scoring all of the other categories were significantly changed.

Club members quickly realized that the scoring system used for the first two records books was inadequate. In fact, Grancel Fitz wrote a chapter in the 1939 book in which he urged that a more equitable system should be employed for the measuring and scoring of native North American big game. However, his recommendations were tabled until after World War II, largely because numerous Club members were involved in serving their country, in both military and civilian capacities.

Immediately after the War, Club members gathered with the intention of reinvigorating the Club's records-keeping activities. One of the first initiatives was the establishment, in 1947, of a program then called a "Competition," – designed to recognize the most outstanding trophies entered in a given calendar year. While the Club continued to work on devising a more equitable scoring system, the finest trophies in each category were invited to the first "Competition," held at the American Museum of Natural History in New York City, where they were certified by a Judges' Panel for Awards and Certificates.

The 1950, 1951, and 1952 Competitions were the first to employ the Club's copyrighted scoring system that was adopted in 1950. That system remains the universally recognized system for scoring native North American big game, with its emphasis on both symmetry and mass. With only periodic refinements and "tweaking," that system has endured to this day. More importantly, rather than recording data for animals that were originally thought to be on the verge of extinction, the Club's records-keeping activities now record the successes of conservation efforts and professional game management throughout North America.

The Competitions, previously held annually, were held on a biennial basis, beginning with the 6th Competition, which covered the years 1953 and 1954, and continued on this basis through the 13th Competition (1967-1968). The subsequent 14th Competition was the first trophy recognition program that became a triennial event, and also was the last to be referred to as a "Competition." Club members were of the opinion that it was inappropriate to refer to its recognition programs as "competitions," when the intent of such programs was to celebrate the outstanding trophies that were the by-products of sound conservation and game management practices. Accordingly, the "Competitions" became a part of history, to be replaced by "Awards Programs," to better reflect their purpose.

At the close of each Competition/Awards Program, the Club has historically published a poster or photo brochure which features each trophy sent to be rescored by the Judges' Panel. The so-called Place Award accorded to each trophy is mentioned, while the trophy winning the First Place Award is featured with a photograph. These photo brochures continue to this day, and are distributed at the Awards Banquet for each of the triennial Awards Programs. Until 1983 these brochures were the only written and pictorial publications of the recognitions programs that had taken place over the years. That would change a year later.

In 1984 the Boone and Crockett Club published a book titled ***Boone and Crockett Club's 18th Big Game Awards***. It was a modest beginning for what has become a hugely successful undertaking. The intent of such a publication was to provide a listing of big game trophies accepted into the Club's Awards Program for a specific three-year period – in this case the years 1980 through

1982. No longer would those with accepted trophies have to wait until the next edition of the "all-time" record book (published on a six-year cycle) to see their names in print. Moreover, every recipient of a Place Award, Honorable Mention, or Certificate of Merit at the Awards Program Banquet was invited to submit a short story relating the details of his or her successful hunt. Some 909 trophies were accepted as part of the 18th Awards Program, and 68 Place Awards, Honorable Mentions, or Certificates of Merit were presented at the Awards Program Banquet, held in Dallas, on July 30, 1983. Many outstanding stories appeared in *Boone and Crockett Club's 18th Big Game Awards*, several of which appear in this anthology.

It is the intent of this anthology both to include outstanding stories that have appeared in the eight Awards books that have been published to date, and also to chronicle the success of the Awards Program itself over the years since the 18th Awards book appeared in print. The stories themselves, represent the "best of the best," selected for the ways in which the successful hunters captured the essence of their hunting experiences, including their tenacity, their ethics, and their respect for the outstanding trophies they harvested. They are substantially unedited, in order to preserve the original story-telling of the authors, most of whom were more comfortable with a rifle or a bow than with a word processor. It is hoped that the reader will vicariously share with these authors the emotions felt by all hunters – the vagaries of weather, the torment of lung-searing climbs, the hours and days of frustration and disappointment, but ultimately the moment of joy and exhilaration accompanying the taking of an outstanding trophy.

But first, it is appropriate to detail the evolution and the growth of the Awards Program since the publication of the *Boone and Crockett Club's 18th Big Game Awards* book in 1984. In the early 1980s the Boone and Crockett Club was housed in modest quarters in Dumfries, Virginia, and had only a very small staff to support the operations of the Club.

Buoyed by the success of the 18th Awards publication, a major decision was made, effective with the 19th Awards Entry Period, covering the years 1983 to 1985. Henceforth, for the Awards Program only, lower minimum scores would be established for most of the big game species recognized by the Club. It was hoped that the establishment of these minimums would result in a greater number of entries, from those who would be able to see their names in print, for one time only, in the next Awards Program publication. More importantly, the Club felt that the submission of more entries would create a larger data base from which to assess game populations throughout North America, both in terms of quantity and quality. Effective with the 19th Awards Program, the Club added two more species to those it recognized – the Sitka blacktail deer and the Central Canada barren ground caribou. Partially because of these changes, some 1,383 entries were accepted for the 19th Awards Program, and 87 awards were presented at the Awards Program Banquet in Las Vegas – substantial percentage increases over previous Awards Entry Periods. Amazingly, the number of accepted trophies for the 20th Awards Entry Period increased once again by over 50%, to a total of 2,079.

In the early 1990s the Club moved its operations to the Old Milwaukee Depot, in Missoula, Montana, and occupies those facilities to this day. During the decade of the 90s, and into the early part of the 21st Century, the scope and outreach of the Club continued to expand, and the Records Program continued to evolve. New categories continued to be recognized, including non-typical American elk, tule elk, non-typical Columbia blacktail deer and non-typical Sitka blacktail deer. In connection

Photo from B&C Archives

Jack Reneau, pictured here at the 18th Awards Program, has been the Director of Big Game Records for the Boone and Crockett Club since 1983. Prior to that he handled the day-to-day operations for the Records Program for the NRA when they cosponsored the program with Boone and Crockett.

with each Awards Entry Period, the Club continued to invite outstanding trophies and potential World's Records to be sent to the site of the Awards functions for judging by panels of veteran Official Measurers. Until the turn of the century, the rules were fairly simple and rigid – the scores of the Judges Panel, up or down, were final, and a new World's Record could be determined only by a duly appointed panel.

For as long as the Club's present scoring system has been in place, there was a mandate that trophies could not be scored until they had air dried at normal atmospheric temperatures for 60 days. It was felt that during such a period any normal "shrinkage" would have run its course. Unfortunately, it was noted that many outstanding trophies were not being sent for panel judging, particularly those taken early in each Awards Entry Period. The Club surmised, correctly, that many trophy owners were fearful of their entry scores being reduced by the Judges Panel because of subsequent and additional shrinkage. Accordingly, under the leadership of C. Randall Byers, Chairman of the Records of North American Big Game Committee, substantial data was assembled, and the conclusion was reached that there was indeed additional shrinkage taking place after the original 60-day "drying period." As a consequence, and after considerable study and deliberation, so-called "shrinkage allowances" were developed, effective with trophies entered in connection with the 22nd Awards Entry Period, and Judges Panel are now permitted to accept an original entry score if they produce a lower measurement that falls within the bounds of the shrinkage factor. Initially, this procedure was not utilized with respect to potential World's Records, but subsequent discussion and deliberation accorded such treatment to those trophies, effective with the 25th Awards Program. Additionally, it was felt that a potential World's Record trophy should not have to wait until a triennial Judges Panel certified it as such, and on August 15, 2001, the Club assembled the first ever Special Judges Panel of four veteran measurers, who certified two new World's Records, at an afternoon session in Missoula. A subsequent Special Judges Panel was convened on May 24, 2003, to verify the World's Record status of two other trophies.

Finally, one of the enduring roles of the Judges Panel is its ability to determine that a specific trophy should receive the Sagamore Hill Award – the highest award that the Club can bestow. The Sagamore Hill Medal is given by the Roosevelt family, in memory of Theodore Roosevelt (Founder and first President of the Boone and Crockett Club), Theodore Roosevelt, Jr., and Kermit Roosevelt. It was created in 1948, and as noted, may be awarded by the Big Game Final Awards Judges Panel, if in their opinion there is an outstanding trophy worthy of great distinction. Only one may be given in any Big Game Awards Program. A special Sagamore Hill Award may also be presented by the Club's Executive Committee for distinguished devotion to the objectives of the Club, and since its inception there have been seven recipients of special awards. Since the publishing of the 18th Awards Program book in 1984, four trophy hunters have been recipients of this prestigious award – Michael J. O'Haco, in 1986, for his outstanding pronghorn; Gene C. Alford, in 1989, for his cougar; Charles E. Erickson, Jr., in 1992, for his non-typical Coues' whitetail deer; and Gernot Wober, in 2001, for his Rocky Mountain goat. Inside these pages the reader will not be disappointed when he relives the experiences of Gene Alford, who, by his own admission had been hunting cougars for over 40 years, finally taking the Number Two cat, along with the Club's highest award. Similarly, Michael J. O'Haco's taking of a World's Record pronghorn is a classic tale of the tactics involved in hunting North America's fastest land mammal.

So, as these words are written in mid-2006, to what level has the Awards Program risen? First, beginning with the 23rd Awards book, field photos were published in full color – a dramatic and striking improvement over earlier editions. One has only to look at the 25th Awards Book, published in late 2004, to see to what level, and standard of excellence, the Awards books have evolved. That book, encompassing 673 pages, and featuring many color photographs, details the 4,000 entries accepted into the 25th Awards Program, as well as the stories of the 118 award winners at the 2004 Awards Program Banquet in Kansas City, Missouri. Readers of this anthology will be able to read several outstanding stories selected from that book. The Club's 26th Awards book, covering the years 2004-2006, will be published in 2007.

That so many entries are contributed during a three year period is a testament both to the success and recognition of the Awards Program, and also to the successes of the various state and provincial wildlife agencies throughout North America. Their efforts are proof positive that sound game management can restore and maintain game populations at levels that are appropriate for the carrying capacity of the lands they inhabit. Moreover, it should be noted that the Boone and Crockett Club continues to recognize new World's Records as part of each triennial Awards Entry Period – demonstrating that these same, sound game management techniques produce high quality trophies as well.

Finally, it should be noted that several of the outstanding trophies featured in this anthology will live on, not only in the written words of those who took them, but also by virtue of the fact that they are seen by literally hundreds of thousands of people every year in Cody, Wyoming. It is in that northwestern Wyoming city that the Club's National Collection of Heads and Horns is housed, inside the Cody Firearms Museum, itself one of the five museums comprising the world famous Buffalo Bill Historical Center.

This author would be remiss if he did not recognize the extraordinary contributions of the many individuals who have contributed to the success of the Awards Program over these many years. First and foremost, is Jack Reneau, who has been Director of Big Game Records since 1983. Throughout these years Jack has tirelessly processed record book entries, trained hundreds of Official Measurers, answered countless questions relating to the scoring of big game trophies, and meticulously proofread the tables and text that make up both the Awards Program books and the All-time records book – *Records of North American Big Game*. Without his dedicated service, it is unlikely that the Big Game Awards Program would have risen to the level that it now enjoys, and received the accolades that it rightly deserves. The author also owes a huge debt of gratitude to Jack, and his encyclopedic memory, for having provided so much of the detail relating to the early years of the Club's records-keeping activities.

Additionally, the Club has benefited from the expertise and devotion of a number of Chairmen of the Records of North American Big Game Committee. Three of these Chairmen are no longer with us – Philip L. Wright, Walter D. White, and C. Randall Byers. The Club properly recognized the contributions of Phil Wright when it bestowed upon him the Sagamore Hill Award in 1996 for lifelong commitment to conservation, for dedication to the principles of fair chase, and scientific integrity with the records program. Today, the Records Committee is ably led by Eldon L. "Buck" Buckner, who continues the traditions of his predecessors by constantly displaying his expertise, enthusiasm, and wise counsel.

Finally, the quality of the Awards books, as well as other Club publications, has improved dramatically since the Club recognized the considerable talents of Julie T. Houk, when it hired her in 1993 as Publications Director. Julie has now reached the point where she is broadly recognized throughout the publishing industry as a first rank professional, and the Club is deeply indebted to her for her contributions.

Now, we invite the reader to sit back and enjoy the stories of those men and women who have taken outstanding trophies. We are sure that you will see, as has this author, that there are a considerable number of common "threads" that run through these stories. Yes, there is an element of luck associated with the taking of an outstanding trophy, but the author is reminded of the old saying "the harder I work the luckier I get." You will read of the tenacity of one hunter who pursued an individual buck over a number of years, until he finally downed him, and secured a World's Record. You will read the story of a dedicated bowhunter and of the meticulous preparation and tactics that resulted in his taking of an outstanding bull elk. You will share with the authors their recitals of rain, snow, sleet, and harsh conditions. Finally, and most importantly, you will see that each of these authors embraced the concept of fair chase, and for that they should be applauded.

ABOUT THE AUTHOR: Robert H. Hanson is the Secretary of the Boone and Crockett Club (1992-1997 and 2001 to present), and a member of the Club's Board of Directors. An Official Measurer, he is also a member of the Records of North American Big Game Committee, and served as a Panel Judge for the 24th and 25th Awards Programs. He is an avid North American and African big game hunter, and lives with his wife, Arlene, also a Club member, on their ranch near Wapiti, Wyoming.

Photo from B&C Archives

*C. Randall Byers, Big Game Records Committee Chairman from 1995–
2002, discusses the specifics of a particular measurement on a typical whitetail
deer at the 20th Big Game Awards. The captivated audience also includes,
from left, Eldon L. "Buck" Buckner (current Records Committee Chairman),
Walter H. White (Records Committee Chairman 1987-1994), and on the far
right bottom, Philip L. Wright (Records Committee Chairman 1978-1986).*

Entering Your Trophy

By Jack Reneau

Boone and Crockett Club

I F YOU ARE FORTUNATE TO HAVE TAKEN A ONCE-IN-A-LIFE-
TIME TROPHY LIKE THOSE FEATURED IN THIS BOOK, YOU OWE
IT TO YOURSELF, YOUR TROPHY, AND THOUSANDS OF HUNTER-
CONSERVATIONISTS TO ENTER IT INTO B&C'S PRESTIGIOUS
RECORDS BOOK. NOT ONLY WILL YOUR TROPHY RECEIVE THE
RECOGNITION IT DESERVES, BUT THE CONSERVATION RECORD
ATTRIBUTED TO THE EFFORTS OF HUNTER-CONSERVATIONISTS
IS INCOMPLETE WITHOUT IT.

In order to submit a trophy into Boone and Crockett Club's Awards Programs, you must first have it scored by a B&C Official Measurer. You can obtain a list of measurers in your state or province, as well as a list of minimum entry scores, by calling the Club's headquarters in Missoula, Montana, at 406/542-1888.

If your trophy meets or exceeds the minimum score for your category, the Official Measurer will provide you with a list of entry requirements and assist you in submitting it to B&C for listing in records book. This chapter includes a complete list of entry requirements with tips for streamlining the process.

SCORECHART

The most obvious and basic item needed to enter a trophy is a fully completed, current, original score chart, signed and dated by an Official Measurer appointed by the Boone and Crockett Club. Photocopies of score charts, as well as incomplete score charts, are unacceptable. Entries submitted on Pope and Young Club score charts, or on outdated score forms, are also unacceptable. When an entry is not submitted on the correct (and properly completed) score chart, all other processing steps must wait until a correct and accurate original score chart is received.

ENTRY FEE

A check or money order for $40 in U.S. funds must accompany each entry to cover the entry fee. If the entry fee is not included with the entry materials, or if the incorrect amount is tendered, the trophy owner is notified that the proper entry fee is needed.

ENTRY AFFIDAVIT

Another item of importance that must be submitted with each hunter-taken trophy is an original Entry Affidavit properly signed and witnessed. The correct Entry Affidavit is on the back of all current score charts. The hunter's signature on the Entry Affidavit needs to be notarized by a notary public, or witnessed by an Official Measurer. Once a trophy has been measured that makes the minimum score, the Official Measurer should give the trophy owner an opportunity to read the Entry Affidavit on the back of the score chart. Once the hunter is satisfied that he/she understands and meets all aspects of the Entry Affidavit, he/she should sign it in the presence of the Official Measurer who should then witness the hunter's signature by signing and dating it in the spaces provided on the score chart.

Please note that the Official Measurer's signature witnessing an Entry Affidavit on the back of the score chart is in addition to the Official Measurer's signature on the score chart verifying his/her measurement. The Official Measurer must actually be present and see the hunter sign the Entry Affidavit before the measurer signs it, or the Entry Affidavit is unacceptable.

The notary public is still required in cases where trophy owners have no direct contact with an Official Measurer. For example, measurers frequently do not meet trophy owners when they are scoring trophies for big buck contests, or when a friend, taxidermist, or other individual delivers a trophy to a measurer for the hunter. Canadian trophy owners only can also have their signature witnessed by an employee of a fish and game department, in lieu of the notary's or Official Measurer's signature.

PHOTOGRAPH REQUIREMENTS

All bear and cat entries must be accompanied with clearly focused, close-up photo prints (black and white or color) of the front, left side, right side, and top of the clean, dry skull. All trophies with antlers, horns, or tusks must be accompanied with clearly focused, close-up photo prints of the front, left side, and right side of the trophy, preferably with a plain background. Slides are unacceptable.

Field photograph submissions are highly desired but not required for trophy acceptance. We accept any submissions and publish photos showing the hunter with the animal in the landscape where the hunt occurred, excluding vehicles or structures. Please note that not all field photos will be published

Digital photographs, which were previously unacceptable for many reasons, are now acceptable in place of regular print photographs. The primary reason is technology to make and reproduce high quality digital photographs needed to guarantee and protect the integrity of the Club's archives is now adequate to meet our needs. Many digital photographs we receive are printed with poor resolution (less than 1,200 dots per inch) and/or are printed on plain copy paper. Such photographs are unacceptable because they cannot be reproduced in B&C publications and are highly susceptible to damage. The Club needs high quality photographs that will last forever with each trophy entry. The photographs, especially field photographs if available, need to be high quality to be reproduced in books and magazines.

Digital photographs submitted for acceptance into the Club's Awards Programs, must comply with the following criteria:

A. Camera quality - the resolution level of the image must be 2 mega-pixels and above.

B. Printer - digital photographs must be printed at 1,200 DPI or better.

C. Paper - digital photographs must be printed on glossy, photo-grade paper.

D. Photo size - 3"x4" or 4"x6" singly or three or four photographs per page on 8"x10" or 8.5"x11" glossy photo paper.

HUNTER, GUIDE, AND HUNT INFORMATION FORM

Each entry that was taken by a hunter must also include a completed Hunter, Guide, and Hunt Information (HGH) form, even if the services of a guide were not employed on the hunt. The hunter simply needs to complete the parts of the HGH form that apply to his particular trophy. The HGH form, and all other required forms, are available from the Official Measurer, and from the Records Office. The same forms can be downloaded from the Club's web site.

LICENSE AND/OR TAG

A photocopy of the appropriate hunting license (and/or tags, if applicable) must accompany each entry that was taken by a hunter. If a copy of the license and/or tags is no longer available, the Club will accept a statement from an appropriate Game and Fish Department official who will certify that a license (and any required tags) was possessed by the hunter at the time the trophy was taken. If the Game and Fish Department no longer has records at its disposal to verify the purchase of a license, a written statement, on official letterhead, from Game and Fish personnel stating the fact that the license information is no longer available is acceptable. The hunting license copy requirement will then be waived.

The last three items listed above, the Entry Affidavit, Hunter Guide and Hunt Information form and the hunting license copy, are only required for trophies that are known to have been taken by hunters. Trophy owners submitting picked-up trophies, trophies of unknown origin, or trophies taken by deceased hunters are not required to submit these items to complete the entry. However, entry materials of picked-up trophies and trophies of unknown origin, must now be accompanied with a narrative that tracks its origin and history.

In addition to all of the items previously mentioned, there are several other items or pieces of information requested for each entry. The first item is an accurate location of kill for each entry. In most cases the office simply needs the county or geographic location (e.g., river, mountain, etc.) and state or province where the trophy was taken. All trophies from the lower 48 states are listed in the records books by county and state, while all trophies from Canada and Alaska are listed by geographic location and state or province. Trophies from Mexico are listed by state and country. In cases where a trophy is harvested near a category separation boundary (e.g., mule deer/blacktail deer; grizzly bear/ Alaska brown bear; etc.) the exact location of kill, pinpointed by marking an "X" on a map, is required.

Finally, if available, the Club would like to obtain the age of each trophy entry if the age was determined by a competent authority. The Club also would like to record the rack or tusk weights (in pounds and ounces) for walrus, caribou, elk, and moose. Complete details for providing this information are given on the back of each Hunter, Guide and Hunt Information form that must be submitted with each hunter-taken entry. The age data will likely be useful in managing big-game populations for trophy animals, as well as supporting the case for trophy hunting. The rack and tusk weights can be used to make comparisons between various North American big-game species, as well as comparisons with their counterparts in other parts of the world.

Incidentally, up to four people can be listed in the records book as the hunter for a single trophy. However, in order to list more than one person, each hunter must submit a signed and witnessed Entry Affidavit, as well as a copy of his or her hunting license/tag, for the trophy being entered. There are no special requirements to list more than one owner.

RECOGNITION ITEMS

Once your trophy has been processed and passed the Club's due-diligence process, it will be accepted and you will be a sent a handsome acceptance certificate with an image of Theodore Roosevelt on it. In addition, your trophy will be listed in one issue of B&C's *Fair Chase* magazine, and a copy of the Awards Period records book, as well as the next edition of the all-time records book, if it exceeds the all-time records book minimum entry score. Finally, you can obtain several special recognition items to memorialize your accomplishment. These items include a shadow box, a laminated certificate plaque, a belt buckle, and a ring with the category and score of your trophy. 🦌

Bears & Cougar

BLACK BEAR

GRIZZLY BEAR

ALASKA BROWN BEAR

POLAR BEAR

COUGAR

Photo from B&C Archives

Black Bear, Scoring 22-8/16 Points,
Taken by Fred Peters in Gila County, Arizona,
in 1985 (pictured with the author's hound, Jake).

Lean, Raw-Boned Fighter

By Fred Peters

19th Big Game Awards Program

CENTRAL ARIZONA MAY SEEM AN UNLIKELY PLACE TO HUNT BLACK BEAR, BUT BEAR DO INHABIT THE BRUSH- AND CACTUS-COVERED MOUNTAINS AND CANYONS, AND AN INORDINATE NUMBER OF THEM REACH THE HUGE PROPORTIONS THAT HUNTERS DREAM ABOUT. MAYBE IT'S THE MILD WINTERS AND ABUNDANT FEED, OR BEING ABLE TO REACH A RIPE OLD AGE IN AN ISOLATED AREA, BUT FOR WHATEVER REASON, THERE ARE SOME ENORMOUS BEARS IN ARIZONA.

Ingrained in the Southwest is a long and deep tradition of hunting bear with hounds. Many of the greatest of the lion and bear hunters, men like Ben Lilly and Monteque Stevens, Uncle Jimmy Owens and Homer Pickens, the Goswicks, the Evans, the Lee brothers, and many others, did their hunting in the rugged southwestern mountains. Teddy Roosevelt made numerous trips to Arizona and Colorado to hunt bear and lion behind a pack of local hounds. And even today, there is some fine bear hunting within sight of Zane Grey's cabin, where the author wrote many of his western novels, and chased bear and lion with hounds. A man riding these hills today is following in some famous footsteps as he pursues his elusive quarry.

My own pack of seven dogs is a mixture of redticks and blueticks, out of the big game hounds of Clell and Dale Lee. I was fortunate to have hunted with Clell and Dale, and I learned by their example the meaning of persistence and long rides, of fair chase, and true hounds. Bear hunting from horseback, using dogs in the dry and rocky southwest, is an uncertain and sporting proposition.

I live in Show Low, Arizona, and have hunted for bear and lion with hounds for the past 16 years, mostly on the White Mountain Apache Indian Reservation. This 1.7 million-acre reservation is famous for the trophy elk taken annually from the high, aspen- and pine-covered ridges, and there is also good hunting for deer, bear, lion, and javelina.

One day in October 1984, my son Joe and I decided to hunt some of the pinyon-juniper country that borders the Salt River Canyon, where I had found a particularly large bear track the previous spring. Cut a small section out of the Grand Canyon and drop it in central Arizona, and you'd have a fair replica of the Salt River Canyon. It is this type of ruggedness that discourages hunters and, we hoped, had allowed some bears to grow both old and big.

The third day we hunted, the dogs trailed a giant bear track into an impossibly rough, rocky canyon where the bear whipped the dogs and escaped. Joe and I, our horses and our hounds, were physically beat as we limped back to camp by moonlight. But, we resolved to regroup and try that big, mean bear another day

In the spring of 1985, despite numerous hunts in the Salt River area, we were unable to locate the big bear. The weather had been relatively dry, so we did most of our scouting near sources of water. At one of the cattle water catchments we found the big bear's impressive tracks. We did not find enough sign to know his exact habitat, but at least he was still alive and in the area. Not far from the water catchment was a suitable campsite with an old corral and water for our horses. The road into camp was difficult and steep, but we figured we could pull the horse trailers in by using four-wheel drive if the weather stayed dry. We made our plans for a three-day hunt in early September. I would hunt the first day alone, and Greg and his son would haul in additional horses and camp gear for the next two days.

It was cool in the early morning darkness as I loaded my hounds and horses. Show Low is over 6,000 feet in elevation, but our campsite, 45 miles from town, was about 1,000 feet lower and much warmer. In September it is sometimes too warm, as the hounds run out of gas quickly in hot weather, leaving only the cool, early morning hours to hunt effectively. By the time I arrived at our campsite, dawn was breaking. I hurriedly saddled my big brown horse, while the dogs whined impatiently in their boxes. The first place to check was the cattle tank where we had found the big bear's tracks in August.

The dogs detected no scent at the tank; so, we continued down the crooked ravine that drained from the cattle tank. A mile or so down the ravine, we climbed out and headed across a series of ridges and canyons. As I rode into one particularly rugged canyon, the dogs started drifting ahead with their heads up and noses quivering, as they searched the air currents for the scent of bear. Just as they reached the bottom, my big redtick hound (Bart) announced with a bellow that he had found a bear. Immediately, the other six hounds joined in. With an excited chorus of barks, the dogs roared up the twisted canyon. These canyons are also inhabited by Coues' whitetail deer and javelina, which my young dogs will sometimes chase, so I leaped off my horse to try to find a track. In the gravel where the dogs had barked was a single large, flattened-out area. Not really much to go on, but it was a bear, and a big one, and the dogs were going in the right direction.

By the time I had remounted and urged my horse forward, the baying of the dogs had faded into the distance. My big horse, a veteran of many bear hunts, dodged between rocks and trees as he rushed after the dogs. For a long time, my goal was simply to hold on and not get wiped off by branches or brush. At the same time, I tried not to lose the distant sound of the baying hounds.

I would ride rapidly for a quarter-mile or so, then stop and listen for the dogs. This stop-and-go procedure continued for quite a while, until one of the times I paused to listen I thought the dogs sounded louder. Then, within minutes, I could hear clearly the excited barking, mixed with angry growls. The dogs had jumped the bear, and he was headed back down the canyon in my direction. I quickly dismounted, and withdrew my Model 99 Savage in .250 caliber from its scabbard.

As the furious sound of the hounds came closer, I searched for movement. Finally, I saw him, a huge black bear running easily ahead of the dogs. But, before I could get the rifle up, he was hidden by juniper trees and then was gone on down the canyon, the dogs thundering behind him. From my brief glimpse, I could tell that he was indeed a big bear. But, he was more of a lean, raw-boned fighter, not a fat, roly-poly butterball. He was remarkably tall, and he ran effortlessly. This could be a long chase.

Again my horse carried me at a fearful rate between boulder and branch as we plunged down the canyon after the bear and hounds. For a time, we held our own; but, it gradually became apparent that we were falling farther behind. Despite our best efforts, the bear was getting away and the dogs would soon be out of hearing. From a high vantage point, I could barely discern some faint echoes as the dogs and bear were swallowed-up by the immense Salt River Canyon. And then, when all appeared lost, there was a strange silence. For a long minute, I strained to hear above the breeze, until finally a solitary bark emanated from the distant chasm. Then, there was another bark, and another, until there was a thunderous roar from the depths of the canyon; the bear had treed!

I couldn't believe my good fortune! I rode rapidly to get closer. From a promontory, I could see a solitary ponderosa pine in the canyon bottom. The excited chorus was coming from it.

About 400 yards from the tree, I dismounted and, leaving my horse, approached the tree from downwind with a cartridge chambered in my rifle. When approaching a treed bear, it is best to keep out of sight and smell until you can dash under the tree; this helps keep the bear up in the tree. There can be real havoc if a bear comes down into a pack of dogs who are trying to impress their owner. It's the bear who usually makes the biggest impression.

Luck was with me that day, as I was able to approach within 40 yards undetected, then rushing under the tree before the huge bear could decide what to do. He was standing on his hind legs on a limb about 15 feet off the ground, and he would occasionally emit a low rumbling growl and snap his cavernous jaws. Immediately, I knew that this bear was one of the big boys. Even though he was not fat, there was no doubt that he was a tremendous bear with an awesome head and neck, and formidable, pile-driver front feet. He appeared to be an old bear, well past his prime, but still in good shape and the obvious kingpin of this area. I had a momentary impulse to tie the dogs and let this old warrior go. But, this was the bear of a lifetime, so I raised my rifle.

After he was dead, I sat for a while and admired him, alone with my dogs and my thoughts. I was feeling proud that I was able to catch this old monarch. But, I was also melancholy that my sons weren't here to share this moment, and that by killing this old bear, there would be a void in these hills and canyons. Perhaps we, as hunters, need to dwell more upon these things. Happily, there were to be many more hunts with my sons, and bears to take the place of Old Big Boy. 🦌

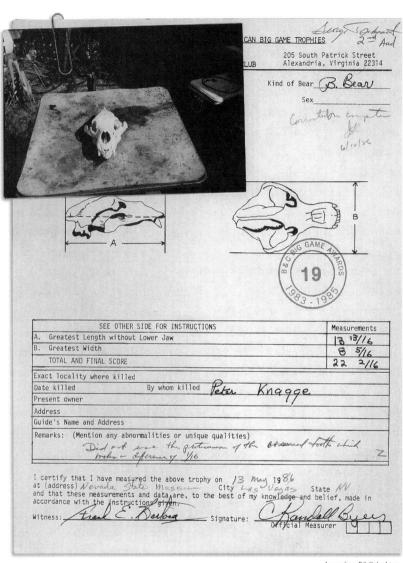

CAN BIG GAME TROPHIES

Serge ?????
2nd And

205 South Patrick Street
Alexandria, Virginia 22314

LUB

Kind of Bear **B. Bear**

Sex

Correction compute
_JE_
_6/10/86_

A

B

B&C BIG GAME AWARDS 1983-1985
19

SEE OTHER SIDE FOR INSTRUCTIONS	Measurements	
A. Greatest Length without Lower Jaw	13	13/16
B. Greatest Width	8	5/16
TOTAL AND FINAL SCORE	22	2/16

Exact locality where killed	
Date killed	By whom killed _Peter Knagge_
Present owner	
Address	
Guide's Name and Address	

Remarks: (Mention any abnormalities or unique qualities)
Did not see the premolars of the observed tooth which broke a difference of 1/16 Z

I certify that I have measured the above trophy on _13 May 1986_
at (address) _Nevada State Museum_ City _Las Vegas_ State _NV_
and that these measurements and data are, to the best of my knowledge and belief, made in
accordance with the instructions given.

Witness: _Frank E. Derboa_ ___ Signature: _Randall Byers_
Official Measurer

Image from B&C Archives

*Black Bear, Scoring 22-2/16 Points,
Taken by Peter C. Knagge in Graham County, Arizona,
in 1982.*

Terrified

By Peter C. Knagge

19th Big Game Awards Program

I HUNTED BEAR IN THE GALIURO MOUNTAINS FOR SEVERAL YEARS, BUT SEPTEMBER 9, 1982, WAS TO BE A DAY THAT I WILL NEVER FORGET. IT BEGAN VERY MUCH LIKE ALL MY PREVIOUS HUNTS. AFTER TWO DAYS OF CALLING WITHOUT SPOTTING ANY BEARS, AND TWO UNFRUITFUL STANDS ON THE THIRD DAY OF THE SEASON, I SET MY CALL ON THE GROUND AND BEGAN TO LIGHT MY PIPE.

A hunter needs to be alert after calling, but the lack of success had my guard down. When I heard the faint sound of an animal walking through the small pebbles on the ridge, I was surprised. My first thought was that the sound was a fox since it was so soft. A few seconds later, more stones crunched under foot of the animal. Looking around for the sound, I saw a black object moving toward me. From behind the large rock I was using for cover, the critter moving through the thick brush looked like a black Angus cow that was nearly starved to death. The animal appeared to be nothing but a bag of bones.

When I finally recognized the animal as a bear, I was not very excited. I was sure this bear was not the bear that left the huge track I had been following for so long. This bear was in such bad shape, and so skinny, he could not possibly last through another winter.

Watching the bear come in, I tried to decide whether to shoot. I caught a glimpse of the bear as he passed through the brush. I could see the hair hanging from his belly, which indicates, just as with cattle, a male. I knew that a boar was necessary to make the 22-inch official score that I wanted. I had called in at least 30 bears, most of them sows and cubs and a few small boars. After five frustrating years of calling so many bears, and not getting a single shot at a big boar, the temptation to shoot grew.

When the bear cleared the brush at 35 yards, I drew my 82-pound pull Laser Magnum bow. I held the 30-yard pin on the top of his scrawny back as he presented an excellent front-quarter shot. At this time I decided to take the bear.

In my entire life, I never imagined I could experience the fear that soon hit me like an avalanche. I had been through some tough times as a rancher, and as a Marine in Viet Nam, but none of those experiences led to the fear that would soon consume my mind and body.

When I drilled the 2219 arrow with a four-bladed Satellite shaft into his chest, the bear rolled on his back, twisting to grab at the shaft of the arrow. But then, he ran straight toward me! Terror overpowered my body. I stood frozen to the spot, since I thought he was coming after me! But, he was not aware of my presence until he hit my scent at about 12 yards. Then, he stood on his hind feet, swinging his front legs wildly as he growled. My feet felt as if they were glued to the ground. "My God! What do I do now?" I thought.

I hesitate to say it, because you won't believe it, but that bear looked like he was over eight feet tall. Many times you can expect a black bear to run the other way, but a big, dominant boar who has been king of the mountain is not afraid of anything.

He will avoid danger, but when he is provoked, he will not back down from anything.

My advice to other bowhunters about calling bears would be, "Don't do it alone!" Have a fellow hunter there to back you up, preferably with a big bore like a .44 Magnum, in the hands of someone who can shoot accurately under extreme pressure. I would not want a .357 Magnum behind me, since I've heard too many stories about the number of shots it takes to drop a bear with this gun. *Just do not hunt them alone, or it might be the last time you do anything.*

In 1977, a rancher friend told me that he had seen a big bear track in the same country where a big buck pronghorn lived. Numerous trips failed to produce even one sighting of the trophy pronghorn, but I did see the tracks of a huge bear. I knew immediately this was the bear I wanted. A number of scouting and hunting trips were fruitless until 1979. I finally saw the big bear, after following his tracks from Aravaipa Canyon to the Muleshoe Ranch. The entire Galiuro Mountain range was his home.

Since bear tracks are fairly easy to see and follow, especially those of a big bear moving uphill or down, I found his sign marking the areas he frequented. I followed his tracks in manzanita berry country and lower on the mountain, in oak country. Usually, during the season when the manzanita berries are ripe, bears can be found higher on the mountain, so I concentrated my hunting efforts there.

In the summer when prickly pear pods are ripe, bears will drop into the desert to enjoy the intoxicating fermented pods. But, there were not many prickly pears in this country, so the adage of "the bears are in the pears" did not apply to my hunt. I believed that persistence would eventually give me my chance, so I continued calling in the ripe manzanita berry country.

Five years of hunting with only one sighting would discourage many a hunter, but I believe that luck is part of every hunt. A hunter can force that luck through knowledge and skill, so I was within a few hundred yards of my big bear. I felt confident that I would call him within bow range.

Every time I stopped to call, I looked for characteristics that would provide a good set up. Generally, I look for things that indicate good bear country, watching especially for high concentrations of foods currently being used by bears. Next, I look for an area that has either lots of dry oak leaves or small rocks, so that I can hear any animal approaching. I also look for an area that provides enough visibility for a shot. I used to look for visibility out to a few hundred yards so that I could see them coming in. But, experience taught me that even when I could see them early, I could not do anything until they were closer. Now, as long as I can see within my accurate shooting range, I have all the visibility I need. I prefer to shoot within 25 yards, so that I can be totally confident with my shot placement.

Another characteristic that I look for is an area that has no fresh tracks. Fresh tracks tell a hunter where a bear has been, not where he is now. When I find an area that has good (and current) feed, lots of leaves, visibility with good shooting lanes within my accuracy range, no fresh tracks, and good cover, I know that I have a good calling spot. Finally, I make sure that I set up behind a large rock or thick bush. I need the cover in front of me to hide any movement while drawing my bow. I don't worry about what is behind me, since my scent would alert any bear that might move onto my back trail.

With bears and lions, a hunter will almost always have plenty of time to get off a shot, since they tend to stand and look, trying to figure out what has invaded their territory. Deer and turkey move out when a hunter moves, but bears will stay around long enough for a shot if the hunter uses some cover to partially conceal movement.

Since I believe only one out of five bears that hear a call will come, either out of curiosity or hunger. I am not frustrated by calling stands that do not produce a shot. I also believe that a bear that hears a call from a long distance is less likely to respond so I do not call loudly. I keep my calling soft and make each one softer as I repeat calls from the same stand. I always hope that I have set up within a few hundred yards of a bear that is feeding or has bedded for the day. Of course, I always keep the wind in my face, whether I am moving to a calling stand or on stand. Any human scent, and the bear is gone.

During my five years of chasing the big bear's track, a typical day would find me walking 10 to 12 miles. Within each day, I would call about 10 times. I would walk for 20 minutes to get into country that was beyond my last call, then move to the best vantage point I could find. Whenever I made a stand, I would call for 30 minutes. Some hunters have success calling bears from long distances and waiting much longer, up to two hours. But, my approach and experience has led me to believe that calling will be more productive with soft calls made from more spots, with less time on each stand. I have been known to cover as much as 25 miles in one day, but usually I try to circle out for five or six miles, then work back to where I began.

Some experts say that bears are nocturnal; others say that they feed a few hours in the early morning, then bed for the day. Somebody must be right, but I figure it doesn't make any difference with my hunting style. Whether a bear is "laid up" or not, he will respond to a call. My problem is to get on stand, when there's bear in the vicinity that is within range of my soft calls, without him knowing I am there. That is why I often call into side canyons.

Once on stand, I will normally call from 30 to 45 seconds, wait for 10 minutes and call again, softer, for about 30 seconds. I then wait another 10 minutes, then repeat the cycle using a jackrabbit single-reed call. I do not think the sound made by the caller is that critical; a variety of sounds and calls have successfully called in bears.

I imagine a few bears have been collected by chance where someone stumbles blindly into a bear. To me, that is not bear hunting. Bears are not like other big game animals that have a limited home range of a few square miles in which they live their entire lives. Not only will a bear use an entire mountain, like my bear used the Galiuro Mountains, but they will travel from mountain range to mountain range. Consequently, a bear hunter has to be willing and able to cover ground, especially if he is pursuing one particular bear like I was.

On that eventful day in 1982 when my big bear finally responded to my call, my persistence paid off. The fear still haunts, and the details of that day linger. As he charged, it was little relief when I saw the red, bloody froth gushing from his mouth. As he came closer, all I could think was, "Get your knife. You've got a fight on your hands." I knew this bear was bigger than I first thought, but I was not excited yet, only terrified. I knew that I could not outrun his 35-mile-an-hour speed. I knew climbing a tree was out of the question since the tallest one around was a six-foot juniper. Anyway, I figured climbing a six-foot tree would put my belt buckle right at his nose. I wanted no part of that, so I stood my ground thinking, "Now, why did I do this?"

As he advanced on his hind legs, closing the last 12 yards, his growls contained a few gurgles. At five yards, the bear fell and rolled on his back, paws in the air. It was then, for the first time, that I realized I had shot the big bear that had left his tracks all over the Galiuro Mountains. Excitement began to mingle with the fear that overwhelmed my whole body.

His claws, just five yards in front of me, were huge. The bear stood and charged again, but fell and rolled over. Since he was on a slight incline, the bear lost with each fall the ground he gained with each charge. But he continued to struggle to get me! After five or six attempts, he fell for the last time, spread-eagle over a clump of Spanish dagger. Yet, he clawed forward, trying to reach me, refusing to give up. Even though he was a bag of bones, this king of the mountain fought, clawing forward, until his last breath. If I had not hit my bear solidly through the lungs, I probably would not be telling you this story.

It is not important what the final score of my bear was, or what rank in any book my bear maintains. The important thing is that I took the best bear I could hope to take. The value of records book programs is the objective picture they paint of the size of all animals in the field. A specific score is irrelevant, and who shoots the animal is even less important. I was hesitant to enter this bear in the various programs because of the false assumptions that are sometimes drawn and of the ego that is too often involved. I sometimes wish the trophy books did not list the hunter's name. Yet, I finally decided that the animal deserved his place in the books, and the validity of the listings would be more accurate if all trophy animals were listed including my bear. Only then will a true picture be painted of what size a big bear can and does obtain, making accurate comparisons possible. 🐾

Photo from B&C Archives

Grizzly Bear, Scoring 27-2/16 Points,
Taken by Roger J. Pentecost near the Dean River in British Columbia,
in 1982 (pictured with his son, Jason).

World's Record Grizzly

By Roger J. Pentecost

19th Big Game Awards Program

JASON, MY SON, WAS THEN 12 YEARS OLD; THIS WAS TO BE OUR FIRST "REAL" HUNT. HE HAD HUNTED SINCE HE WAS SEVEN YEARS OLD, AROUND OUR RANCH IN SOUTHERN BRITISH CO-LUMBIA. WE HAD DECIDED ON GRIZZLY. I HAD ALWAYS WANTED A TROPHY GRIZZLY. I HAD RANCHED SOME YEARS BEFORE IN THE ANAHIM LAKE AREA. WE HAD FRIENDS THERE, AND WE KNEW THERE WERE LARGE BEARS IN THE AREA.

With weeks set-aside, we packed our guns. Jason chose a single-shot Savage Model 219L in .30-30 caliber, with a four-power Weaver scope. I chose my .270 caliber Husqvarna with a 2.5-8 power Bausch & Lomb scope.

After arriving in the Anahim Lake area, we spent a few days visiting and talking about bears, and hunting moose. We contacted Wayne Escott, who had worked for me in the early 70s and was now a commercial bush pilot for Dean River Air. We made a deal to rent the floatplane from Monday, October 11th until the 16th. We had heard the stories of big bear down on the Bella Coola River, but some of the Indians talked of "good bear" along the nearly inaccessible Dean River mouth where it meets the Dean Channel.

On Monday morning, we left Nimpo Lake and flew south-west over Charlotte Lake, then heading west to Lonesome Lake, circling to take photos of the very impressive Hunlen Falls that drops straight down about 1,000 feet and flows into the Atnarko river. I had wanted to see these falls for a long time.

We then headed north, stopping for lunch so Jason could fish at Squiness Lake, named after an old-time Indian family of the area.

We arrived late that afternoon in the Dean Channel. Pull-ing up on a sandbar at the river mouth, we unloaded the plane and made camp right there. We had already found tracks, so our excitement was starting to build. The next day we moved the plane along the river bank about 300 yards and on the south side, so as to be next to our camp. Starting out, we crossed the river and worked our way up the shoreline. Wayne knew Felix, an 80-year old Swedish recluse, who had been living in near isolation for many years there.

We took Felix a moose meat roast as a gift, and got into a long conversation with him about life, bears, etc. He told of mushroom hunters landing there by plane and picking up to $1,000 per trip, each, with the mushrooms being sold in Japan. We scouted that area quite a bit, finding sign of bear but not seeing any of the real thing.

The next morning Jason and I left early, ready for bear. We went south, down the channel, finding sign again, but no bear. The banks along this channel were steep and made the going really tough. We saw seal out in the water, and a lot of eagles, but no bear. We worked our way back inland, arriving about a half-mile upriver from camp, where we found really promising sign and country, but that was all.

Thursday the 14th was cold and damp, but not yet freezing. We had made up our minds that we would go up river on the south side. Wayne, our pilot, was going to come along, having fiddled enough with the plane the day before. The going was really slow and tough. It seemed that for every 10 feet forward, we would also go 10 feet sideways, first down into the river edge, which was usually covered with masses of tangled logs, then up along the very steep banks above the river. There we were, climbing over dead trees and inching our way along. The thought never really occurred to me as to how I would get back with a bear, if we got "lucky."

About mid-morning, we stopped to snack. Jason had found a simply enormous bear track in a sandy bay area tucked into the river edge, and we speculated over lunch at the size of the bear that made that track. It was surely a "good bear." We could not see up or down the river more than 100 yards.

About then, we heard a Super Cub drifting low and slow, as they are so good at. For a brief moment, it flashed in front of us, coming downstream and passing out toward where our plane sat. I cursed under my breath, thinking that I had come all this way to have any bear spooked right out of the area by people when we were 100 miles from a village and even farther from a town.

With a little more uncertainty, but still the same enthusiasm, we started off, crossing a small side channel and soaking ourselves for at least the tenth time (or so it seemed). After a while, I decided to move away from the river's main course. Soon we were walking in a succession of semi-clearings, under some enormous cedar trees that shut out most of the direct sunlight. The flickering shadows across the leafy carpet gave a shady, peaceful look to the area.

Suddenly, off to our left, about 70 feet away and partly obscured by a cedar, something started to move slowly up out of the ground. It was a massive head in profile, followed by an enormous shoulder bump. We froze. Here was what we had come all this way for — a good bear. But really, I never wanted it quite so close. As I readied my Husqvarna, I heard Jason close his gun.

For what seemed to be a long time, I had an excellent side shot. I squeezed the shot off. But, the bear, instead of falling over dead, rose up out of the hollow in the ground and turned towards us. Here it was, coming right at us. I aimed at his shoulder, still hardly believing he wasn't down. This next shot hit his side, I had gut shot him. This turned him, and he plunged off sideways into a really thick area of alders, windfalls, and devils club. As he was going in, I placed a third shot.

All hell seemed to break loose in that small wooded area. It was too thick to see what was happening, but boy, could we hear the bear snorting, growling, grunting, and gasping. It was a simply enormous and rather frightening sound. I looked back at Jason and Wayne. They looked as apprehensive as I felt. I knew a grizzly could explode out of that cover like an express train, with none of the bush slowing him down at all, and leap 15 feet in a bound.

I indicated to the others that I was going to circle around, hoping I could get to a point for a fatal shot. Using some of the larger trees as cover, I circled from tree to tree in the best John Wayne style, but without his air of confidence. Jason and Wayne were following me. All of us were feeling very vulnerable, only knowing where the bear was by that noise. At last, I could see part of the bear's rear.

At this point, I swapped guns with Jason for the final shot as I had used three of my five bullets. He still had all six that he carried. I was finally about 20 feet away from the bear, feeling, to be honest, quite scared, before I could place the fatal shot into his neck with Jason's .30-30. As it lay dead, I could see that we had a very good bear indeed. But why had my first shot not killed it?

When I skinned it out later, I could see the bullet hole in the exact spot I had aimed, but the Nosler bullet had shattered before getting deep enough in such a large bear. I also found a tight, leather radio collar around his neck. It was well into his fur, and had rubbed sore marks on either side of his neck. I felt bad now, knowing that the bear I had shot was part of a study. But, what was it doing here, 50 miles from any closed area? Thinking back on this, I did not see the collar, even when close to the bear. Plus, with us walking up on him, I don't know if the bear would have given us the choice of letting him, or us, walk away.

We started the task of skinning, still in awe of this great trophy bear. The skinning went slowly, and we were only about half-finished when Wayne pointed out that it was about an hour before sunset. So, with great apprehension, we left the partially finished bear. With some knowledge of the best route back, we made it to camp just at darkness. We had nervously picked our way, expecting to meet another bear at every turn.

That night, I had many mixed thoughts. Some were good and some terrible. I'd really shot a good bear, but there was the matter of the number of shots, the collar, and worst of all, leaving him there. What if a coyote, fox, wolf, wolverine, eagle, etc. got to him? All these "what ifs" kept coming back to me. We consoled ourselves that at least another grizzly would not eat it.

That night, we had entertainment of a nature that we didn't need. It started with some splashing and grunts that sounded all too close. Were they just trying to find salmon carcasses, or were they looking for us? We built the fire up high, and in the light of it, pulled in some more of the washed-up logs scattered around real close. Supper was welcome, but the food seemed to dry out and stick as it went down my throat. Even Jason noticed the tension. Normally, good food and sleep would be the only thing on his mind by now, but that night he was making sure he could sleep in the middle of the tent.

It seemed that all through the night, the bears were getting closer. Wayne and I agreed that we would take turns to keeping fire going. Morning drifted in, as a cold, damp blanket of mist, leaving everything dripping. Jason walked toward the river, about 20 feet from the tent area where we were preparing breakfast and coffee. His face told us that he had seen something.

"Look! Quick, over there in the river are three more bears, not 200 yards from our camp," he said.

They were poking around in the river, looking for their breakfast. We could have shot any one of them, with one looking as big as ours, right in camp!

We didn't discuss it, but I was feeling worried as to what would await us back at the bear site. Soon, we had the pack board, rope, and some lunch ready, and we were off. Wayne felt he should carry his .30-30 Winchester — just in case. We set out up the river, with the three bears noted earlier no where to be seen. We tried to make quite a bit of noise and took our path out in the open as much as possible. Things had taken a 180-degree turn from yesterday. I really hoped that our furry friends would stay away today.

A couple of ravens flew up as we approached the bear, but no eagles were in evidence. A quick examination showed the hide to be perfect, so we got down to work. Only then did the size of this bear really impact on me. Just lifting his paws and looking around at the havoc he had wrought, made me even more respectful of the grizzly's massive power.

I had skinned out many moose while I was guiding, and also cows on the ranch, but trying to turn over and move 1,000 pounds of grizzly is tough. We pushed, pulled, shoved, and did just about everything we could think of to turn him over. Boy, what a job. I had cut the skull off at the neck joint, and the paws at the wrist bones, thinking that I would do the rest in Anahim Lake the next day. We rolled up the skin, with the feet, paws, and head inside, and proceeded to rope it onto the pack board.

Then I tried to lift it and get it on my back. That didn't work. Wayne and I carried the pack board over to a large cedar, lifted it up to shoulder height, and with Wayne's help, I swung it on. Hell, it just about swung me down with it. I tightened the waist belt, and with Jason carrying my .270, we started back.

Things went well, until we came to the first downed tree. As I tried to get over, the pack and bear skin pulled me backward. It was no use, I couldn't hike out with this massive weight. I decided the only way was to skin the head and paws out, and generally flesh-out the hide. Two hours later, we were ready to continue. We had lost at least 50 pounds from the load, and when re-packed, I felt that I could at least manage it. Boy, what a journey back to camp. I was glad we were only three miles in.

After a quick lunch, we broke camp and loaded the plane. This is when our next excitement began. The tide in the inlet was down; consequently, the river level at the mouth had fallen. It was too shallow for take-off with all the weight, so we unloaded the plane. I waded out into the river, holding the plane straight up stream as I stumbled around in the icy water. With the plane as light as possible and the motor warm, Wayne gave it full throttle. My heart was in my mouth as Wayne, in his expert manner, bounced the plane up the river, until first one and then the other float lifted, and he disappeared round the bend. Moments later, we were pleased to see the plane lift up above the trees, as it wheeled round grabbing for height to get over the trees. It was then I realized my legs were damned cold; I was still standing out in the cold, rushing water.

Wayne landed out in the channel, then taxied in to the sand-bar that we had started this hunt from. Packing our equipment on the plane went well, as I thought of warm baths and scotch whiskey that was waiting at Anahim Lake. A half-hour later, we were skimming over the lake infested timber. We landed at

Nimpo Lake. We were soon at Darcy Christensen's village store, where we related the story for the first of many times.

Darcy, our host, had a country butchers shop out back, and a 500-pound scale with a meat hook hung high. Two of us hoisted up my grizzly and watched as the needle pointed to 148 pounds. Next, we weighed the undressed skull; it was 45 pounds, so we assumed that with the paws, etc., the hide had weighed over 200 pounds. No wonder it was so impossible to pack any distance over that rough going.

We got to work, spreading out the bear and then working coarse salt into the hide. From the measurements we took, we determined the bear stood over 10 feet, 6 inches high and could have reached over 13 feet. The rug has a 9-foot, 6-inch spread, with claws longer than my fingers.

This was far more of a grizzly than I had ever dreamed of getting. As we retired that night, we went over bear stories such as the Anahim Lake rancher and neighbor, Cony King, who had been attacked by a grizzly sow and now sports a blank eye socket and massive scars from this near fatal encounter.

It was April 1983 when I got an excited phone call from Helmut Schold, a young German émigré taxidermist who had impressed me with his skill and artistic ability. He had been so shocked by the finished size of the skull that he had taken it to Helmut Cofmeister, a Government Wildlife Technician. They had measured a skull length of 17 inches and a skull width of 10 5/16 inches, giving a total score of 27-5/16, putting it well over the existing World's Record. On June 21, 1983, Jack Graham a Boone and Crockett Official Measurers, met with grizzly and me for an official measuring.

Jason and I have reflected on this hunt on several occasions, still only half believing that his first major hunt could end this way. For us, it simply remains "our grizzly hunt." 🦌

Image from B&C Archives

Original score chart for Roger J. Pentecost's World's Record grizzly bear, which scores 27-2/16 points.

Photo from B&C Archives

Grizzly Bear, Scoring 26-7/16 Points,
Taken by Jon D. Seifert near Lone Mt., Alaska,
in 2000.

Perfect Hunt

By Jon D. Seifert

24th Big Game Awards Program

ALL HUNTING TRIPS ARE SPECIAL — SOME FOR THE QUAL-
ITY, OR QUANTITY OF GAME TAKEN. SOME FOR THE
GRANDEUR OF THE SCENERY OR THE CAMARADERIE; FRIEND-
SHIPS MADE OR STRENGTHENED. STILL OTHERS FOR THE
HARDSHIPS ENCOUNTERED AND ENDURED. MOST OFTEN,
HUNTS ARE A MIXTURE OF THESE ELEMENTS. EXPERIENCED
HUNTERS DON'T EXPECT PERFECTION. THE PIECES OF THE
PUZZLE ARE TOO NUMEROUS AND THE OPPORTUNITY FOR POOR
WEATHER, MISHAP, OR JUST PLAIN BAD LUCK TOO GREAT. SO
IT IS THE RAREST OF TIMES WHEN EVERYTHING FALLS NEATLY
INTO PLACE CULMINATING IN THE "PERFECT HUNT." I WAS
FORTUNATE ENOUGH TO HAVE SUCH AN EXPERIENCE — THE
RESULT OF WHICH WAS THE HARVEST OF ONE OF THE LARGEST
GRIZZLY BEARS EVER TAKEN.

For 15 years my friends and hunting companions, Tim
Crombie, Troy Auth, and I had dreamed about hunting Alaska.
Troy's first cousin, Rod Schuh, is one of the proprietors of R&R
Guide Service operating out of Anchorage. Rod had encouraged
Troy to bring his buddies up for a hunt for years, but school,

work, and family had always won out. Finally, in the fall of 1998, the three of us decided the time was right and we booked a hunt for September 2000. We would be hunting bear and moose. The months passed slowly as we read books about the game we would be hunting. We watched videos, reviewed gear lists, and spent long hours at the range. Unfortunately, a few months before the trip, one of Troy's sons was diagnosed with a medical condition that required his attention. Troy's hunt would have to wait a season or two. My wife Tracey and daughter Rachel escorted me from our home in Pepin, Wisconsin, to the airport in Minneapolis. Tim and I boarded a flight bound for Anchorage on September 9, 2000.

I've always considered myself to be pretty lucky. Whether it's hunting whitetails, bear, or turkeys back home in Wisconsin or meeting my lovely wife, things always seem to work out. But the next few days would be more than even a lucky man could expect. Skies were clear and at 30,000 feet we had a panoramic view of the Rockies from British Columbia over the Yukon and into Alaska. Once on the ground, Tim remembered that an old friend of his had moved to Anchorage ten years earlier — the last time Tim had seen him. His friend's name is John Hanson, and Tim decided that, since we had a day before leaving for base camp, he'd give his friend a call. Turns out that John lived two blocks from our hotel. Better yet, he had the next day off and wanted nothing more than to give us a guided tour of the city. We video taped moose in the woods along the airport, and saw salmon and huge rainbow trout running in Ship Creek in downtown Anchorage. We picked up last minute supplies and made mental notes of all the hot spots to tour upon our return. John even invited us to his cabin north of Anchorage for a float-fishing trip if we had time after the hunt. So far so good; things would only get better.

The next morning the hotel shuttle dropped us off at R&R's hangar. The weather was poor — low ceiling, overcast, and raining. Rob Jones, the other "R" in R&R Guide Service, was flying in from base camp this morning to pick us up. By mid-morning Rob had fought his way through the clouds and made it to Anchorage. Before the whine of the 206's engine had died, Rob leapt from the Cessna and greeted Tim and me. He was a man on a mission. There was no time for pleasantries or long conversation about our trip. The weather was bad. We had supplies to round up, a plane to load, and clouds to beat before they shut down the passes. Time is always precious to men who make their living during the short months of hunting season, but there was another reason for urgency. The day before, a moose-hunting client had spotted a big grizzly guarding a wolf-killed cow moose. If we could get through the Alaska Range (you don't go "over" the Alaska Range in a 206 Cessna) in time he might still be on the kill. Part of Rob's rush — I would be the only hunter in camp booked for grizzly.

We headed for Rainy Pass, which seemed appropriate as a steady drizzle streaked the windshield. Between mouthfuls of cold pop-tart that substituted for breakfast and dinner, Rob continually checked with other pilots in the area to determine if we would make the pass in time. We didn't. When we were close enough to see the V formed by the mountains guarding Rainy it looked like someone had opened the door to a giant steambath on a cold day — no chance. We had to backtrack. Rob figured Merrill Pass might be worth a try. It would mean flying the hour and a half back to Anchorage then swinging North. As we flew up the pass the slot narrowed around us. Rob kept easing the 206 closer and closer to the rock faces to the East while peering at the tiny triangle formed by the upper reaches of the pass and the clouds squeezing down against them. Finally I had to ask, "Aren't you getting a little close over here?"

"Got to," Rob yelled over the drone of the engine. "If the clouds close the pass before we get to it, I'll need all the room I can get to turn this thing around. Look down there. Those are the guys who waited too long to make up their minds."

Looking out the window we could see the mangled wreckage of at least a dozen light aircraft scattered along the upper end of the Pass. I had been intermittently taping the scenery, but since my wife was certain to see the video I chose not to add the wreckage to my little documentary. I might want to come back some day! We slipped through. For a few minutes the sun shone brightly on the backside of the Alaska Range illuminating the Big River Drainage, home to R&R Guide Service.

Once the plane hit the strip things didn't slow down. Half a dozen guides and packers converged on the Cessna like an Indy pit crew. Gear out; fuel in. First to welcome us to base camp was Scott Christian, "Chris." Once again this outfit proved to be all business. Chris instructed me to get my gear stowed in the comfortable two-man guest cabin set aside for Tim and me, pack my backpack, grab a bite to eat at the cook shack, and meet him back at the strip. The pilots would be flying Chris and me out to spike camp before dark. If we could get in on the Middle Fork of the Kuskokwim River northeast of Lone Mountain before dark, the big grizzly might still be on the kill the next morning.

Rob had traded the workhorse 206 for a nifty little 150 Super Cub on tundra tires. He and Billy Ray Vollendorf in his black 150 Cub, the "Dirty Bird," dropped Chris and me in on a gravel bar about two miles upstream from the moose kill. The "runway" was strewn with rocks the size of basketballs and other assorted river trash. Fortunately the pilots operate the Cubs like flying go-carts, and we landed without incident. I helped Chris make camp, a comfortable four-man "bomb shelter" tent on the gravel bar. Chris has 25 years of guiding experience, 10 with R&R. If the "griz" was still there he assured me, we'd get him.

That night we cooked over a mountain climber's stove and Chris told me bear stories. The air turned crisp as the sun went down and the cool breeze in the golden aspen harmonized with the flowing river. The anticipation, as I sat there cross-legged in the tent door under the glow of the Coleman was like a thousand opening mornings on my deer stand or in my duck blind. Somewhere out there in the fading light was a big boar grizzly guarding a kill, and in the morning we were going looking for him.

Before turning in, Chris lay a loaded Smith & Wesson Model 29, .44 Magnum, on the gear box between his head and mine. "If you hear anything wake me up," he said. "Oh, you don't sleep walk or anything do you?"

"No," I replied.

"You have to be able to sleep before you can sleep walk!" I must have slept some but I was up two hours before the sun, ready to head out.

Chris was up too, making coffee and frying pop-tarts. "How far are we going to go before it gets light?" I eagerly inquired. The .44 was already in the breakfast chefs' shoulder holster.

He smiled and said, "We don't go anywhere in grizzly country in the dark." After only a moment's reflection, that made perfect sense. We set out at first light.

The Middle Fork is a braided stream this time of year as glacial melt slackens. We made good time the first mile or so crossing and recrossing the thigh deep rivulets. We weren't certain where the bear was. We knew he was on the West bank just below a jack pine snag that jutted out 90° over the river. The moose hunter and his guide had told us the kill was right on the bank and the bear had hauled up a big pile of sand and mud to bury his prize. They had walked to within one hundred yards before they spotted him lying ominously atop his cache. They didn't stick around; there's a lot of good moose country in Alaska. After the first mile or so we slipped into the brush on the East bank. We made half-moon loops out to the edge to glass as far down the opposite side as we could.

The brush was thick, and it was tough going. We had all day though, and we were moving cautiously. As we passed two and a half hours into the stalk, it hit 9:30 a.m. The sun was high, and I figured the bear would feed at first light then lie-up until afternoon. Our strategy was to find the kill and set up an ambush from our side of the river. If that didn't work, we'd look for him in the thick brush near the kill. I'm sure you understand why that was plan B. At about 10 a.m. and after a half dozen half-moons, Chris eased out to the edge of the river. He scanned up, down — then stopped. By this time I was certain that we were just looking for the kill, not the bear.

All Chris said was, "He's on it."

Boom! Instant adrenalin rush. I was light-headed as we maneuvered to the thin brush on top of a cut-bank. There he was, 150 yards distant, diagonally across the river. He was standing on the kill, angled away from me.

I was using a Ruger No. 1 Tropical in .375 H&H Magnum. I knew I would have to place my single shot perfectly and in part, that's why I opted for this rifle. I'd practiced hard and had the bruised shoulder to prove it. As I slid into a half kneeling position I found a stout sapling with a convenient fork.

The bear looked huge through the Swarovski 30mm tube. As the crosshairs settled behind his right shoulder I knew the angle should take the 300-grain Failsafe bullet straight through the joint on the far side. It was classic "*Field & Stream*," the kind of mental image that rivals the covers of outdoor magazines. There stood a mammoth boar grizzly over a moose at just the right angle 150 yards away across a beautiful Alaskan river. The crosshairs had stopped moving.

I squeezed the trigger. The recoil of a .375 H&H Magnum does not allow you to watch for bullet impact. When I relocated the bear, he had spun back toward us and was favoring his left leg. He lunged up the bank on three legs and disappeared before I could reload.

Chris called the shot. "Looked good, broke the offside shoulder." We waited. Chris had a smoke and I a chew. I dug out my video camera and did a bit for the folks back home. After a half-hour we crossed the river, and as we neared the place where we had last seen the bear, Chris provided one of the most memorable moments of my hunting life.

I had met Chris only 18 hours earlier. He didn't know me. I didn't know him. But standing on that gravel bar, for better or for worse, we were going to become a team engaged in some potentially very tricky business. "I'll go first," Chris said.

I thought, so far I like this plan. "You follow 10 yards behind, move when I move, stop when I stop. I'll be looking for sign, you'll be looking for the bear. Look ahead of me 45 degrees on both sides then behind us. It's awful thick in there and he might try to backtrack on us." The thought of a wounded grizzly sneaking up behind me dissipated the enthusiasm I had first felt for the scheme. "If you see the bear," Chris continued, "don't yell, don't point, just shoot." As he gave these directions Chris was staring me straight in the eye as a man does when he wants to emphasize his point. "Don't yell, don't point, just shoot. I'll hit the ground at the shot and locate the bear. Got it?"

I nodded and hoped the old bear was dead. We moved slowly up the bank. Chris was looking down for blood. My little prayer had been answered. The bear lay stone dead ten yards in.

He was a tough customer in bad shape. His spine was clearly visible, like someone had draped a bearskin rug over a sawhorse. His hipbones stuck out six inches. His hump was exaggerated and made his long frame look out of proportion. After a congratulatory handshake we looked him over more closely. His teeth were all but gone. Both lower canines were broken off and three of the upper incisors were hanging by a shred of gum. We later learned that he had an abscessed molar in his upper jaw. The infection had eaten a quarter-sized hole through his palate and into his sinuses. This torment must have been with him for several years. As if that wasn't enough he was missing a toe and a testicle. The Fish and Game biologist in Anchorage estimated his age to be between 20 and 25.

His hide measured nine feet from front paw to front paw and was eight-feet two-inches long making him close to a nine-foot square interior grizzly. We taped the skull at 10 inches wide and 17 inches long, bottom jaw included. The official score was 26-7/16 points; tied for 13th place all-time as of the close of the Boone and Crockett Club's 23rd Big Game Awards.

We made the long hike back to camp and settled in with a few "Swift River screwdrivers," vodka and Tang. The first day of my hunt was over, but not the trip by a long shot. I also took a decent moose and a nice black bear.

Like I said, all hunts are special. I've hunted harder and not seen game. I've had opportunities and missed. I've spent days in the back of a truck snowed-in in the Bighorn Mountains of Wyoming. They are all good memories in their own way. This time everything came together. The timing of the hunt, the weather, the skill of the pilots and the guide, the wind, the quarry, and the shot. I'll remember these things as my "Perfect Hunt." 🐾

Image from B&C Archives

*Original score chart for Jon D. Seifert's grizzly bear, which scores
26-7/16 points.*

Photo from B&C Archives

Grizzly Bear, Scoring 26-14/16 Points,
Taken by Eugene C. Williams near Kala Creek in Alaska,
in 2001.

Dark Timber Grizzly

By Eugene C. Williams

25th Big Game Awards Program

LOOKING INTO THE FOREST SHADOWS, I COULD SEE A FORM THAT LOOKED OUT OF PLACE AGAINST A BACKDROP OF THICK SPRUCE. I SHOULDERED MY RIFLE AND PEERED THROUGH THE SCOPE. THE IMAGE OBSERVED THROUGH THE RIFLESCOPE ELECTRIFIED ME AS I REALIZED I WAS ONLY YARDS FROM THE MONSTER GRIZZLY — AND I WAS CLEARLY THE FOCAL POINT OF ITS ATTENTION.

This hunt started days before, on April 28, 2001, when local area Alaska Department of Fish and Game biologist Glenn Stout and I went on a snow machine ride into the Kaiyuh Mountains south of Galena. Our day's adventure was driven by the notion that we wanted to see some new country. Spring thaws had settled the heavy mountain snow pack, opening up some backcountry that is rarely visited. We each carried rifles with us on this occasion, just in case we spotted a distant wolf or possibly a bear, though it was a bit early for bears to be emerging from hibernation.

Breaking out above the line of timber and onto the open alpine tundra, we were met with snow flurries and low clouds that blanketed our intended destination with a thick carpet of white — so dense that to press on would risk getting us lost or driving off a cliff.

Backtracking to lower elevations near the upper tree line, we came across a several-days-old track of a large grizzly bear. The bear had moved up out of the timber of one drainage and slipped down into the head of another. We guessed the bear's destination to be the bottomlands along the Yukon River, approximately seven miles to the northeast, where the monster would likely stalk and pull down a moose to feed what had to be a ravenous post-hibernation appetite.

As the day's plan was no longer workable, we elected to satisfy our immediate curiosity in the enormous track by following it a short distance into the heavy timber. Glenn joked that he would defer any bear shooting that day to me, as I was carrying a .30-06, and he was packing his .223 varmint rifle. The direction taken by the bear put it on an intersecting course with the Yukon River. Curiosity in the tracks quickly vanished as the deeper, unsettled snows of the steep timbered slopes caused our snow machines to bog down and us to perspire freely and often in digging out mired machines. With the excitement of this game now gone, we retreated back the way we had come.

Thoughts of the monster bear haunted me for the next two days. On the evening of April 30, I gave Glenn a call to see if he was up for another trip to the bush to look for the bear. He declined, electing not to waste a day of his vacation time to pursue my fanciful notion of finding a large bear in the thousands of square miles of roadless wilderness south of Galena, Alaska, where we lived.

My wife was reluctant to allow me to go on my own, fully understanding the risks of snow machine failure, weather, and terrain — not to mention risks associated with confrontations with bears. What probably worried her more than anything was the notion of me crossing the Yukon River on a snow machine this time of year. It was spring. Snow pack was melting. River ice had to be thawing. She signed off on my plan for the solo trip, but only after I promised to wear a life jacket while on the river and grilling me as to the contents of my day pack in case I had to spend a night in the woods. I left her a topographic map, on which I defined the area where to look for me should I not return. She was also advised that Glenn would know where to begin to look for me if need be.

I left the house at 6 a.m. on May 1. The temperature was 10°F. With six extra gallons of fuel and a pair of snowshoes, I headed out on my snowmobile. My plan was a simple one. I would follow an abandoned, decades-old dozer trail that started on the south bank of the Yukon River upstream from the village of Galena. One branch of the trail led through the hills and then cut down to and across Kala Creek, about two miles off the Yukon, and terminated at an old military radar site on Ketlkede Mountain. The other branch led up to and across the Kaiyuh Mountains to an inactive mining claim. As Glenn and I had taken the west fork to access the Kaiyuh Mountains on the earlier trip, I decided to travel the east fork of the dozer trail down into Kala Creek. This was new country I hadn't been in. I reasoned, too, that this course had the potential to put me in a position to intercept the trail of the bear discovered earlier, or at least possibly into the country where the bear might be.

It didn't take long, once leaving the south bank of the Yukon River, to travel the two miles of old dozer trail into the bottom of Kala Creek. To my amazement and delight, there in the frozen slush atop the creek ice was a lone set of very large bear tracks headed away from the Yukon and back up into the mountains.

There was no way to gauge the age of these tracks. The slush, or "overflow" as it is called locally, could have been the result of any of the freeze/thaw cycles of the several previous days. Overflow can be a trap for unsuspecting snow machiners or dog mushers. The condition typically is hidden under an undisturbed surface crust of snow, where seepage from snow melt, springs, or adjacent wetlands collects. Breaking through the surface crust into several inches (or several feet) of slush/water can ruin your day, particularly if aboard a 600-pound snow machine. As temperatures had dropped into the single digits the previous night, and coupled with settling from the recent warm weather, the overflow here was frozen hard clear to the creek's surface ice in most places.

I followed the bear's trail up the creek on the snow machine out of curiosity, with little thought about the possibility of a bear in the last tracks on the other end. But after 200 yards of following the creek, with open water peeking through and gurgling sounds below, I thought more about cold wet feet and the dreadful notion of pulling a waterlogged snow machine out of a hole in the creek ice. I retreated.

Returning to the first point of intersect with the tracks, I headed off on the old dozer trail toward Ketlkede Mountain in search of more tracks. The run to the mountaintop didn't take long and no other tracks were discovered.

I returned to the creek, electing to follow the bear track on foot as a form of morning entertainment. The weather was crisp and the skies clear. Winds were light and variable. I was intrigued by the meandering course the bear had taken upstream. It was interesting to note, as I followed its path, what objects or odors caught its attention. Occasionally, the bear would turn at 90° angles and moving off a few feet to investigate something in its surroundings. At one point, its nose told it there was a shed moose antler buried under two feet of snow, which the bear dug up and bit into. The heavy print of the bear was obvious and easily discernible well ahead along the creek's course. Occasionally, it broke through the crust into the intermittent overflow or soft snow beneath. In contrast, I was leaving little evidence of where I had been.

After two hours of fanciful pursuit on foot, I decided I should return to the snow machine, as going overland with the machine to this point on the creek was an easy option. I would also be that much closer to a ride home when I elected to call it quits. I returned with the machine, and struck off again on foot on the tracks of the grizzly.

The bear was still sticking to the creek bottom. I told myself that if it stayed in the bottom or turned east into the tundra/open scrub black spruce stands, I would follow. That was, of course, providing the snow crust would carry me. If the bear turned west into the timbered slopes of the Kaiyuh Mountains, where snow was deep and soft, I would give up the pursuit.

The grizzly regularly cut across the points of land in the creek's many meanders, but sometimes would stick to the creek channel and follow it around the bend. If the bear took the shortcut and I could see through the timber to the other side, I would follow. If it took a shortcut through the trees and visibility was poor, I would follow the meandering channel around and pick up the track on the other side.

Over the course of the morning's trek, it became apparent to me that the grizzly's trail here had been made since the temperature had plummeted late the previous evening. Where the animal had walked on snow-free southern bank exposures, it had tracked dirt and spruce needles out onto the clean snow. Had the dirt been tracked out onto the creek the day before, the tracks would have been melted out by the sun's warm rays being absorbed by the dark material. These tracks were not. I now knew I had a chance for this bear.

I removed my shooting glove, checked my firearm, and ensured myself that my scope was on low power. I was carrying a .300 Magnum Browning BBR, a companion on countless previous hunting trips.

The game of simply following a track in the snow had transformed into a cautious pursuit. The pursuit remained much the same as the previous three hours — in and out of the timber along the course of Kala Creek, going upstream. The sun was still low in the clear eastern sky and morning shadows were long. Once more, I followed the grizzly's shortcut across a narrow point of land at the bend in the creek channel. I had broken with the morning's discipline of not following the track into the timber when I couldn't see bear tracks in the snow in the creek on the far side. The point of land here, though narrow, was of higher elevation. There was very little plant understory.

I felt secure, and assumed the bear had simply returned to the open channel on the upstream side. The giant bear had not! Once in the trees, the grizzly had come across a maze of moose tracks along the far bank and elected to follow them — and travel by stepping into the tracks left by the moose!

I no longer had a clear picture of where the bear was. I scanned the creek channel upstream and downstream — no bear tracks. My attention turned to the moose tracks at my feet. I couldn't discern which direction the bear had gone. I looked to my left and spotted a form that didn't fit with its surroundings. I shouldered the rifle and peered through the scope at the strange form. It was the grizzly! The bear was facing me head-on, while standing with front feet atop a downed tree. It was huge! The bear's intent stare told me it had seen me before I saw it. The grizzly was too close! I knew full well it was a mere few seconds away. A charging, running bear can outrun anything afoot in these parts.

As the safety came off and my finger found the trigger, my mind was asking the question of what would happen next. Would the bear turn and run at the shot, or would it come for me? The rifle fired and I quickly worked the bolt to chamber a fresh round. As if in slow motion, the bear reared up, roared, threw its head back with front paws high in the air and tumbled over backwards. Then all was quiet. The grizzly got up momentarily behind the blowdown timber and then sank out of sight. It remained quiet!

As it turned out, the bear had been napping behind some blowdown timber along the creek bank, in a bed it had prepared for itself by scratching away the two feet of snow and ice down to bare earth. Remaining hidden through my approach, it had heard me approaching, or possibly caught my scent in the variable breeze that was blowing, and got up.

I looked at my watch. It was 11:45 a.m. I waited a full 10 minutes before walking in a big semicircle around the bear on the creek side. The grizzly had tumbled backwards down the bank into the creek channel. I approached cautiously. When close enough to lob in some tree branch projectiles, I did so, to ensure the animal was dead. As I got close enough to use the gun barrel, I poked the grizzly with it to ensure no life was left. The bullet had struck the bear at the midpoint of its sternum and traveled the length of the body, stopping just under the hide of its right hip. The 200-grain bullet had done its job.

The animal was in excellent physical condition, but with very little body fat remaining. It was an old bear with some long-ago healed dental problems, likely created by an encounter with a flying moose hoof. I had been on the track since 8:00 a.m., having followed it for over five miles on foot.

There was a healthy bounce in my step as I returned to where I had last parked the snow machine. I carefully guided the snowmobile up the creek from where it was parked and was able to maneuver to where the grizzly lay. Skinning the animal was easy, other than the two feet of soft snow, which made it difficult to turn the animal over.

It was an interesting ride for the two of us on the snow machine during the trip home. The distance to my home's back door from where the bear fell was 35 miles.

This was my first grizzly. At this point, I knew I had harvested a nice trophy, but had no idea how big the bear really was!

I called a taxidermist in North Pole to tell him what I had. Charlie Livingston of Alaska Wilderness Arts and Taxidermy was skeptical, at best, as I described the size of the animal to him. "How big? You have to be kidding!" he said.

Mr. Livingston had worked with scores of grizzly trophies and had not seen anything like I described. Unofficially green-scored by Glenn Stout, and subsequently by Mr. Livingston, it was pointed out that it may be within a few sixteenths of the World's Record grizzly.

The news that I had taken a big grizzly passed through Galena quickly. Galena, a traditional Native Athabaskan community, consists of about 650 people. Though half white now in cultural mix, many Natives still adhere to a lifestyle dependent upon natural resources. The interior grizzly is respected and typically not hunted alone. Many were in awe of the notion that I went out on a solo bear hunt.

I returned to the kill site the following weekend to reflect on the last moments of this hunt. I collected the moose antler the grizzly had dug up and chewed on. I measured the distance from where I was standing when I shot to where the bear was located at point of bullet impact. It was only 38 yards!

I am certain that it was this bear that had left the large tracks Glenn and I had spotted earlier. There aren't that many big grizzlies out there. Most larger interior Alaska grizzlies taken by hunters measure six to seven feet in length. This one measured 8 feet 3 inches! This animal clearly is a trophy of 10 lifetimes.

To be able to step out and hunt from one's back door and do a day-trip grizzly hunt is easy enough to do when living in rural "bush" Alaska. To cross paths with a Boone and Crockett bear is an entirely different matter. Mr. Livingston advised me, "My friend, you will not outdo this monster ever again."

Photo from B&C Archives

*Alaska Brown Bear, Scoring 29-14/16 Points,
Taken by Cindy L. Rhodes on Alaska's Aliulik Peninsula,
in 1997.*

The Granny and Andy Show

By Cindy L. Rhodes

23rd Big Game Awards Program

M Y HUSBAND, DOUG, AND I HAD BEEN APPLYING FOR ALASKA BROWN BEAR PERMITS FOR SEVERAL YEARS. I WAS LUCKY ENOUGH TO DRAW A PERMIT IN THE EARLY 90S, BUT WAS UNSUCCESSFUL IN GETTING A BEAR. THESE PERMITS ARE NOT EASY TO COME BY. A LOT OF OUR FRIENDS HAVE APPLIED FOR MANY YEARS FOR VARIOUS HUNTS AND HAVE NEVER DRAWN. WE ALL WAITED ANXIOUSLY FOR THE NEWSPAPER TO COME SO WE COULD READ THE PERMIT SUPPLEMENT. THIS LISTING SHOWED ALL THE PERMIT RECIPIENTS FOR EACH HUNT: GOAT, SHEEP, BISON, BEAR, ETC. THIS PARTICULAR YEAR, WE RECEIVED THE PAPER LATE AND IN THE MEANTIME, SEVERAL OF OUR FRIENDS HAD CALLED TO SAY WE HAD NOT DRAWN A PERMIT FOR ANYTHING. NEEDLESS TO SAY, WE WERE FEELING EXTREMELY DISAPPOINTED, AGAIN.

Over coffee the next morning, I scanned through the list again. There it was, my name under brown bear. I sat looking at the paper to make sure it was really me. My husband walked into the room a minute later to hear a very fast-talking wife telling him how all our friends were crazy and, "Look! Here's my name under the brown bear permits." We were both very excited. Later that day our good friend and Master Guide, Andy Runyan of Exclusive Alaskan Hunts, called with congratulations. He offered to take me on a 14-day spring bear hunt, which even got me more excited. We've known Andy for many years and his ability and expertise is unsurpassed. He has had the same hunting area for over 30 years. The next order of business was planning the trip.

We decided to fly to Kodiak a couple days before the hunt. Even after six months to prepare, I still needed a little time to get my mind focused on the task ahead. We arrived in camp on April 14, 1997. The flight over from Anchorage offered spectacular scenery. Andy and his assistant guide, Craig Rose, were on the beach waiting for us when we landed. Andy has a real cozy cabin, and we all sat around the table discussing what we would do the next day. I recall being anxious, excited, nervous, and sleepless all at the same time.

The next morning came with sunshine and little wind. We loaded into the skiff and motored down the bay three miles to a lookout point where we could sit and glass. I started glassing and I spotted this huge rock bear. I watched him for awhile and then pointed him out to Andy. Andy looked at mine and then showed me a bear he had been watching for some time. Oh my God! It was huge and bigger than the one I was looking at. Okay, now I knew what I was looking for. Doug was giving his eyes a rest when he looked down. There was a bear on the beach below us. He pointed it out to Andy who said, "Oh, that's a beach bunny." She was small and rubbed badly. Andy said she looked like Abe Lincoln with leg warmers. He obviously knew the bears in his hunting area very well.

Doug and I own the Brown Bear Rhodehouse in Glennallen, Alaska, and we are used to 12 to 14 hours on our feet, so all this sitting around was getting to me. I stood up to stretch and let out a groan. Doug said, "What's the matter Granny, you getting stoved up?" (We have six beautiful grandkids.) Well, Andy thought that was really funny and from then on we were known as "The Granny and Andy Show."

On the fourth day we went back to the lookout. We had seen bears every day and today was no exception. We were glassing the facing mountainside and spotted two bears, both of which were a good size. They were in the high country, heading over the mountain. I was hunting for a big male with a good, clean hide. You don't run across one of these every day. We glassed until just before sundown and those two bears were the only ones we saw.

On day-five we awoke to heavy cloud cover and lots of wind, but by midmorning it had cleared. The weather had treated us well so far; in fact, I had one heck of a sunburn on my face. This was unusual since the weather in April is notoriously bad on Kodiak.

Andy took us to another spot where he had taken several good bears in the past. We climbed the mountainside for a mile and a half and began glassing. After a few hours, Andy spotted a really good size bear on the facing mountain. We watched him for a while until he started heading over the other side of the mountain. Andy said he knew where he was going to come out, so down the mountain we went. On the way down, I saw the grass moving. All of a sudden I was looking into two big black eyes! It was an otter, and I was delighted to see him, but I don't think the feeling was mutual. He took off through the grass heading for the ocean. I got a real kick out of that. When we reached the skiff, we traveled about halfway back to camp, landed, and headed up the mountain again to the spot where Andy said the bear was going to show. Sure enough, about an hour later, here he came over the side of the mountain. Andy hates to be right.

He was a big bear, and we watched him zigzag back and forth across the mountainside before he disappeared in an alder patch. We never did see him again.

On the sixth day the weather was still holding, but I wasn't too sure about myself. All the hiking up steep terrain and mountain climbing was getting to my legs. We went back to the same spot as the day before and glassed all day, not seeing a thing. We still enjoyed the day. It was very peaceful listening to the ocean.

The next morning at breakfast we decided to go back to our original lookout point. We spent two more days at this spot and saw bear, but they were either females or rubbed. The weather was starting to get ugly — clouds, rain, and cold wind — so we decided to head back to camp. Andy told me he knew of another good spot and that we would head that way the next morning. On our way back to camp we saw plenty of deer and fox. We had a good dinner and went to bed early because Andy said tomorrow was going to be a hard day.

It was a three-mile ride in the skiff to where we tied up and started walking. We walked for awhile and then started up the beach. There were boulders the size of pickups littering the beach. It was tough going. We came to a spot where a freshwater creek was flowing, filled our water bottles and took a short break. When we started walking again, Andy stopped and looked straight up. I looked at him like he was crazy.

He said, "Yep, up there." We started climbing up the side of the mountain without much to get a foot-hold on. It was steep, with lots of sand and clay. We made it about three-quarters of the way up to an alder patch where we stopped to take a short break. Being only 4'11", the brush was slapping me on the face pretty good. I was having a hell of a time, and my Ruger 7x57 kept getting hung up. I was resting in the crook of the alders and wondering just where in the hell Andy was going. I'm 40 years old and Andy is 68, so I was thinking it can't be too much farther or neither one of us will make it. We took off again, climbing straight up. Finally we reached the top, to a spectacular sight of mountains, ocean, creeks, and gullies. It was breathtaking.

Once we got situated and started glassing, it wasn't long until we spotted a nice bear meandering on the mountain straight ahead of us. The weather was now getting really bad. We hunkered down and kept watching as the bear started up over the other side of the mountain. We spotted another bear that was doing the same thing, wandering up the mountainside. We decided we had better start heading back to camp because of weather, and it was getting late in the day. Just as we stood up, Andy and I both looked over to our left.

Oh my God! Here he came and he was huge! We looked at each other and Andy said, "Let's go Granny!"

We started running down the mountain trying to keep that bear in sight. When we reached the base of the mountain, I needed to stop and catch my breath. I also needed to shed some clothing. Once I got my wind back, we started walking again, crossing several creeks.

After crossing the last creek, Andy turned and said, "Do you see him?"

"No," I said. Then Andy pointed to a little tuft of fur and we quietly crept through the last creek and got into some tall grass. Like I said earlier, I'm not very tall. As I knelt in the grass I couldn't see anything. We sat quietly for a minute and Andy motioned that we should move closer. When we started to move, the bear threw his head over his shoulder and stared at us. He was wallowing in a deep mud hole and here he came.

I've always been told to shoot a bear so far below his hump. Unfortunately, Mr. Bear was not turning for the proper shot. I waited and waited for him to turn.

Finally, Andy said, "Cindy, ARE YOU GOING TO SHOOT THAT BEAR?"

This guy was coming, and fast. I had no other choice but to shoot him between the eyes. My mind was reeling. Andy said once more, "Cindy, SHOOT THAT @#*& BEAR!" I had my rifle up and all I could see was fur through my scope. I squeezed the trigger and my Ruger 7x57 with the Leupold scope did its job. The Barnes, 160-grain bullet hit home right between his eyes and I quickly had another one on the way. All my friends kept saying that I should have a larger caliber, but my 7x57 had been modified to fit me perfectly. As far as I'm concerned, shot placement is a lot more important than caliber.

Andy had his range finder with him. It was 22 yards from where we stood to where the bear dropped. Andy looked at me and asked, "Are you okay Granny?"

He said that when I looked at him to answer, my mouth was a little circle and my eyes were huge. I said, "Uh huh." Then I started shaking. I couldn't believe how close he came and how awesome he was. When I got up the courage to go see him up close, I was amazed at what a beautiful animal he was. He was muddy and soaking wet but I was still able to tell he had a beautiful hide with no visible rubs. His claws were six inches or better and in excellent shape. I was so excited and overjoyed. This was the experience of a lifetime and I will never forget it. With much respect and admiration, I thank you, Andy, from the bottom of my heart.

My bear green scored 29-15/16, and after the 60-day drying period scored 29-14/16. The hide squared 10 feet 6 inches. 🦌

OFFICIAL SCORING ... GAME TROPHIES

Records of ... 250 Station Driv
Missoula, MT 5980
(406) 542-188

Kind of Bear: *Alaska Brown*

2nd Award

CLUB

B&C 23 1995 - 1997

SEE OTHER SIDE FOR INSTRUCTIONS	Measurements
A. Greatest Length Without Lower Jaw	18 9/16
B. Greatest Width	11 14/16
FINAL SCORE *Kodiak Island, Alaska (02)*	29 14/16

Aliulis Pgn.

Ennot Leaaliny Whare Hill... *Klavak Point, Aliulik Pen., Kodiak Island*

Date Killed: April 23, 1997   Hunter: Cindy Rhodes

Owner: Cindy Rhodes   Telephone #: 907-822-3663

Owner's Address: P.O.Box 110 Glennallen, Ak 99588

Guide's Name and Address: Andy Runyan, H.C.O.-1 Box 1702 Glennallen, AK 99588

Remarks: (Mention Any Abnormalities or Unique Qualities)

   Bullet hole in skull, but otherwise undamaged.

I certify that I have measured this trophy on _____ *July 8th* _____ 19 *97*

at (address) *7950 Rovenna St.* City *Anchorage* State *AK.*
and that these measurements and data are, to the best of my knowledge and belief, made in
accordance with the instructions given.

Witness: _____ Signature: _____

B&C Official Measurer | D | 0 | 3 | 9 |

I.D. Number

Copyright © 1997 by Boone and Crockett Club®

Image from B&C Archives

*Original score chart for Cindy Rhode's Alaska brown bear, which scores
29-14/16 points.*

Photo from B&C Archives

Alaska Brown Bear, Scoring 29-3/16 Points,
Taken by Robert M. Ortiz near Deadman Bay, Alaska,
in 2001.

Monarch of Deadman Bay II

By Robert M. Ortiz

25th Big Game Awards Program

I SPENT MANY EVENINGS ADMIRING THE PHOTOS OF THE MAG-NIFICENT TROPHIES AND READING THROUGH THE RECORDED ENTRIES THAT WERE IN THE 11TH EDITION OF THE BOONE AND CROCKETT CLUB'S *RECORDS OF NORTH AMERICAN BIG GAME*. AFTER AWHILE, I TOLD MYSELF, "I'M GOING TO HUNT ALASKA, AND I THINK I'LL START BY HUNTING THE BIGGEST AND MEANEST BEARS AROUND."

It was the fall of 2000, and I set my sights on an area in the southwestern part of Kodiak Island called Deadman Bay. After a few phone calls, I got in touch with Alaskan Guide Tom Kirstein to inquire about hunting Deadman Bay for Alaska brown bears. Tom caught me off guard by responding, "Well, I actually have an opening for this coming spring. You interested?"

I guess I must have been. On April 29 of the following spring, my companion, Tonya Buxton, and I found ourselves in Kodiak, Alaska, some several thousand miles away from our home state of New Mexico.

The next day, and after several hours in the air just above Kodiak's rugged, snow-capped peaks, we landed via floatplane at the headwaters of Deadman Bay. Upon our arrival we were greeted by guide Tom Kirstein, assistant guide Jeff Poor, videographer Doyle Moss, and hunters Jim and Angie Ryan. Everyone was very courteous and sincere in welcoming us to the great hunt. After the formal greetings and so forth, our gear was carried over to the bear camp, which sat nestled in the thick alders several hundred yards away.

The camp consisted of three aged wooden structures. The largest of the three was considered the main cabin, and it had two rooms. One room contained a kerosene stove, sink, dining table, and some shelving, while the other contained a few sets of bunks for sleeping. The main cabin was a place that lent warmth to our bodies at the beginning and at the end of each hunt day. It was also the place where we enjoyed our early morning breakfasts and our end-of-the-day dinners, not as guides and hunters, but as newly-made friends.

The two other cabins were small 7'x7' wooden structures. Each contained a set of bunks, two shelves, and a small heater. Tonya and I would house in one cabin for the next several weeks. Jim and Angie would house in the other. For some odd reason, Tonya was not buying my "it doesn't get any better than this" story.

After unpacking our gear, I proceeded to check the accuracy of my rifle one last time. Several shots later, I was confident that my rifle would perform if and when it was summoned to do so. On this particular hunt I was using my .30-378 Weatherby, equipped with a 3.5-14x 52mm Leupold scope, and shooting my favorite bullet, the 180-grain Barnes X. As always, my rifle was set to shoot dead-on at 300 yards. This setting is one that had proven to be deadly accurate in the past, and one that would ultimately have the chance to prove itself again.

Word was that Tom Kirstein ran a good bear camp, especially with the assistance of folks like professional hunting guide Jeff Poor. Tom was very outspoken and there was no doubt that he knew most all there was to know about bear hunting. On the other hand, Jeff was very quiet and kept to himself most of the time. Nonetheless, Jeff proved to be one of the best guides and hunters with whom I have ever had the pleasure of hunting. It was agreed early on that Tom would guide Jim and Angie, and that Jeff would guide Tonya and me.

During the early evening of the first day we arrived at camp, I sat alone on the shale-covered shoreline looking westward at the majestic snow-capped mountains that sheltered the bay and its inhabitants from the rest of the world. As the sun's rays pierced down through the clouds and onto the bay's waters, I immediately felt God's grace and blessings.

Following dinner that first evening, Tom shared some of his bear hunting adventures with us. He also told us a little about the history of the island and of Deadman Bay. He went on to mention that there was a good book on the cabin's shelf titled, *Monarch of Deadman Bay*, and that it told the story of a mighty Kodiak brown bear that once roamed and ruled in Deadman Bay. Before closing for the night, I chose the faded brown-colored book from the many that lay on the cabin's shelf. I decided to make it my evening read for the next several days.

The *Monarch of Deadman Bay* was indeed a book that shared an early tale of a mighty Kodiak brown bear that once roamed and ruled in Deadman Bay. In the story, the Mighty Monarch inhabited and ruled the area for many years, and it did so despite the fact that one-half of its right front paw had been bitten off in a battle to the death with another great, but less fortunate, Kodiak bear. As I eagerly read page after page of the tale, I could only imagine what it might have been like to hunt a creature as great as the Mighty Monarch. As fate would have it, however, I soon too would cross paths with the mighty half-pawed Monarch, who had returned once again to roam and rule in Deadman's Bay.

During the springtime, the bears on Kodiak prefer the hillsides and the cover of the alder and willow bushes. As such, hunting them requires many hours of glassing and spotting. Luckily, we came prepared with 10x50 Swarovski binoculars, a 20x60 Swarovski spotting scope and a lightweight tripod. Additionally, hunting the drainages on Kodiak during springtime also means snow melt, deep rivers, and fast running water. To deal with these obstacles, we equipped ourselves with waist-high Gore-Tex waders, as well as wading boots that could be utilized both in the water and on land hiking comfortably for many miles over the rough terrain.

The weather changes on Kodiak are phenomenal. I can recall leaving camp one morning under a clear blue sky, bright sun, and warm weather. Two hours later, it rained cats and dogs. Then about an hour after that, the sky turned deep black and the winds blew hard enough to easily capsize a medium-sized boat. Then about an hour after that, it calmed, started snowing for a while, and then the sun came out again. No doubt, we were pleased that we had the proper all-purpose weather-proof clothing, a definite "must have" on Kodiak.

On the first day of the hunt, we spotted two bears that were approximately two miles away from us on the other side of the bay, and near the top of a 4,000-foot, snow-covered hillside. We stayed watching the bears until they disappeared into a deep drainage. We also spotted a group of mountain goats on the same hillside and just below the area where we had initially spotted the two bears. The second day of hunting was dreadfully windy, making it very difficult to hold our binoculars steady enough to glass any particular area meaningfully. Nevertheless, we were able to spot several different bears that were hanging out just below a rock-faced hillside about a mile away. The circular blowing wind, however, rendered the thought of any stalk on these bears null and void.

The third day of the hunt proved worse than the second. I swore that I had never been in wind so fierce in all my life. So much for our "all-purpose" clothing on that particular day, as it seemed as though we had none at all.

The fourth day, however, started off like a gem. The skies were clear blue, the sun was shining bright, and the weather was nice and warm. Needless-to-say, that was the day that I learned that the weather on Kodiak can instantly change, that is, from one extreme to the next. Despite the nasty weather, we did spot two medium-sized bears that particular evening. Neither one, however, was the type of bear we were after.

It wasn't until breakfast on the morning of the fifth day that our luck changed for the best. The past four days we had hunted down-bay and Tonya couldn't bear the thought of spending another one just sitting and glassing. She was eager to exercise and suggested that we hike upstream. Jeff seemed favorable to the idea, so we decided to hike to an area upstream where several of the rivers commenced their journey down to the bay. After about a six-mile hike and crossing several deep and fast-running rivers, we elected to stop and glass for awhile. It was no surprise that the wind proved once again just how relentless it could be.

We glassed on and off for about two hours, when Tonya and I decided to take some shelter from the cold wind. We were just over the hill from Jeff when he came running frantically over the top shouting, "Bear!"

Jeff had spotted a bear on the other side of the drainage about 600 yards away. The bear had been sunning out of the wind in an area that made it almost impossible to see it. We studied the 9-footer for about 25 minutes, when for some reason, the bear quickly got up from where it was lying and commenced to travel up the draw. That particular draw ultimately led to a deep canyon. It was then that we realized why it was rapidly moving out of the area. About 100 yards behind it in the brush moved a very large dark brown-colored creature. When the creature became visible, it was without a doubt the largest and most impressive bear that I had ever seen, dead or alive!

The enormous creature was most likely pursuing the 9-footer for an afternoon challenge to the death, or for its next meal, or maybe both. Whichever it was, the next thing I heard was Jeff saying, "Let's get a movin'!"

It immediately became apparent to me that the bear was headed straight for the canyon, and that we only had a couple of minutes to try and get to a point that would enable us to get a shot. Within seconds, we had our packs and rifles slung over our backs, and we were traveling through the brush as if it never existed. Somehow during our run, I was able to reach over to the top of my barrel and remove the balloon I had placed over it to keep it free from debris. Nothing, and I mean nothing, was going to stop my shot at this bear. But, maybe I spoke too soon. As we were proceeding in the direction of our would-be vantage point, we ran out of mountain. Two feet in front of us was a 60-foot straight down drop. I knew that this was it; I could either shoot from there, or let the bear get away.

Off came the packs. I immediately piled them in front of me to create a shooting rest. I then turned the adjustable objective on my scope to somewhere between 300 and 400 yards, and loaded one in the chamber hoping that the big brown bear would give us a shot. Fortunately for us, the 9-footer had traveled to the corner of the drainage which was 350 yards away, and then traveled down and into the canyon. We could only hope the large creature that followed would do the same. Just then, out of the brush came the big brown following its predecessor's trail over to the same drop-off point. Jeff quickly ranged the point at 350 yards.

When the big brown reached the edge of the rim, it looked

down and then raised its nose in the air attempting to scent its prey. All I kept thinking was, "What a monster!"

It was then that I laid the crosshairs on the bear's right-front vitals and pulled the trigger. I knew it was a hit, as the bear had picked up its right front leg off the ground, turned around, and started back in the direction of the brush. Then, in mid-stride, the bear turned to its right and ran in a direction directly away from us. As everyone who hunts big bears knows, follow-up shots are highly recommended, so a few more were taken to make sure the job was finished. This time it slowly made its way about 20 yards into the brush and collapsed. We waited for about 45 minutes, as this was not a wounded bear that we wanted to meet up with in the brush on that day, the next day, or on any day for that matter.

After convincing ourselves that the big brown had expired, we proceeded to find a way to get to the bottom of the canyon, cross the waist-high, ice-cold river, and then climb up the other side and over to where the bear had last lain. As we cautiously neared the big brown, I began to realize how incredibly big this bear truly was. Its head was so massive that I couldn't wrap my arms around the sides of it. The widths of its forearms were an easy 26 inches. Its coat was long and a beautiful chocolate-brown color with cinnamon highlights, and not a single rubbed area.

After the excitement of the handshakes and picture-taking, we began the tenuous skinning process. When I lifted the bear's right arm, my eyes froze in amazement as I stared at the bear's paw. At that moment, I could not believe what I was seeing. One-half of the bear's right-front paw was missing, just like in the story of the Mighty Monarch. Suddenly, the same special feeling of that first evening's sit on the shale-covered shoreline ran through my body. Upon realizing what had just happened, I bowed my head and thanked God for bringing back the Mighty Monarch, to once again roam and rule in Deadman Bay. 🐾

Photo from B&C Archives

Polar Bear, Scoring 27-3/16 Points,
Taken by Robert B. Nancarrow on Banks Island, Northwest Territories,
in 1997.

Polar Bear Number 9

By Robert B. Nancarrow

23rd Big Game Awards Program

I HAD JUST BEEN THROWN FROM THE SLED, WHEN JOHN, MY GUIDE, PREMATURELY THREW OUT THE ANCHOR BEFORE THE SLED HAD SLOWED ENOUGH FOR A SAFE DISMOUNTING. I LANDED ON MY CHEST, WITH MY RIFLE UNDER ME, SLIDING ACROSS THE ICE IN THE SNOW. WE HAD TRIED TO INTERCEPT A LARGE BOAR THAT HAD BEEN PURSUING A SOW, WITH TWO YEAR-OLD CUBS. WE JUST WEREN'T QUICK ENOUGH. THE BOAR HAD REACHED THE NEW ICE, AND WAS QUICKLY ON ITS WAY TO THE ROUGH ICE.

Hunting polar bear by traditional means, using dog sled and Inuit guides, is without question one of North America's greatest challenges. We were using a team of seven dogs, solely for transportation. John didn't believe in chasing polar bear with dogs. His exact words were, "We will 'hunt' the polar bear with dogs." That's exactly what we were doing, the sixth day of my 15-day hunt.

At 180 yards, I quickly rested my .300 Winchester Magnum on the nearest block of ice, placed the crosshairs on the bear's shoulder, and pulled the trigger. At the report of the rifle, the bear stopped running and stood up. I was surprised I had not hit the bear, but now I had a standing shot. I squeezed the trigger a second time, again with no results. I shot a third, followed by a fourth and final shot, still with no results. I quickly checked my scope to see if it was loose, and inserted four more shells. By this time, the bear had started to run to the rough ice. I fired two more shots, and did not touch the bear. My guide looked at me with disbelief, but with calm reservations that we would see another bear and maybe get another shot. Not finding the scope loose, I blamed myself in my excitement for just plain poor shooting, never thinking that my gun was at fault.

That night it was very difficult to sleep, because I knew I had just lost a trophy of a lifetime. John was reassuring, and I was able to finally fall asleep. The following day we started our hunt where we left off the day before. The tracks were still there, and the mistakes I made were still fresh in my mind. We then took to the huge track and started to hunt again. By noon, we came up against a wall of ice. John decided we would hunt in the direction of our main camp, 10 miles back. Not feeling as though I was going to have the good fortune of seeing a bear of that magnitude again, I sat in the dog sled with mixed emotions. John stopped and climbed a large block of ice to look for bear. He quickly motioned me to join him, and when I got there, he was pointing a quarter mile in the distance to a very large bear, eating a bearded seal. The bear was on new ice, approximately four to six inches thick. The wind was coming from the north, and was starting to pick up. We were 22 miles west of Banks Island on the Arctic ice flows. I asked John if he would stay with the dogs, so they would not bark. I would make the stalk alone. He agreed and wished me luck.

I was now on my own, crawling the entire distance since there was nothing but smooth ice between me and the bear. On my belly, I was instantly aware that the ice was rolling under me. It seemed to intensify as the wind became stronger, but all that mattered was that I was getting closer to my trophy. I was now within 180 yards, and although my heart was hammering, I elected to take my shot from that distance. As I calmly squeezed the trigger, expecting to hit the bear, the horror of the day before became real once more. I fired the second, third, and fourth shots, all with the same results. I could not hit the bear at this distance and had to come up with a different plan. My guide was too far away to get his rifle and the bear had now become nervous, moving further away. The one thing in my favor was the constant cracking of the ice, which sounded as loud as the report of my rifle. The only two options I had were to give it up completely or get within bow range, and hope for the best. I chose the latter.

I had waited for too many years, and spent more money than I could afford getting this far. Only a hunter could understand my decision. As I crawled to within 70 yards, I could truly see the bear's tremendous size. My heart was pounding out of control and I was actually starting to feel fear. At approximately 60 yards I decided to shoot, not knowing what to expect. As I pulled the trigger, I can honestly say I did not know what the results would be. I had the crosshairs on the shoulder of the huge bear, and the bullet struck three feet back from his front shoulder. The bear let loose a tremendous roar and started diagonally toward me. Seeing that the gun was that far off, I had to force myself to aim off the bear, in order to hit him again. It worked! The next bullet struck the bear in the chest. The bear turned sideways, going in the opposite direction, so I aimed at his hip, striking the bear square in the shoulder. I was out of bullets and the bear and I were now only 35 yards apart. The bear got up again. Knowing there was nothing I could do, I laid with my face on the ice, hoping he would not see me.

After what seemed like an eternity, the bear finally expired. By that time, I was so exhausted from fear, that I almost could not raise up to look at my monstrous trophy. The bear was the ninth bear seen on my hunt — truly, the most fabulous creature I have ever seen. Later I discovered that my gun barrel was blocked with ice and had split at the magna-porting when I was thrown from the sled, causing its inaccuracy. 🐾

Photo reprinted from *Fair Chase* magazine

Gene Alford and his faithful hunting companions, Scratch and Kelly, in Idaho's Selway-Bitterroot Wilderness where they spent countless months together tracking cougars.

A Long 27 Years

By Gene R. Alford

20th Big Game Awards Program

FOR 40 YEARS, I HAVE HUNTED COUGAR WITH HOUNDS; AND, HOPEFULLY, MY 1988 HUNT WILL NOT BE MY SWAN SONG. THE LAST 30 YEARS, I HAVE HUNTED IN THE SELWAY BITTER-ROOT WILDERNESS IN IDAHO EACH WINTER, TRYING TO KILL A BOONE AND CROCKETT LION. EACH WINTER FOR THE LAST 20 YEARS, I HAVE HIRED A SKI PLANE TO FLY ME, MY DOGS, AND CAMP, INTO THE BACKCOUNTRY WHERE I HUNT FOR A MONTH OR LONGER. I PREFER TO START HUNTING ABOUT THE FIRST OF FEBRUARY, AS THE WEATHER TENDS TO IMPROVE RATHER THAN DETERIORATE AFTER THAT TIME.

That was my thought on February 3, 1988. The day dawned clear and cold, and since I had loaded my pickup the day before, all I had to do was to phone the local commercial fly-boy and make arrangements for the flight. I called Frank Hill, of Hill Aviation in nearby Grangeville, and told him I was ready to go.

After a 30-mile drive, I arrived at the airport around 9 a.m. and started loading my gear into a 180 Cessna ski plane. I'd done this many times, so I had a pretty good idea of what I was doing. When the load got to within a foot of the headliner, I stuffed my two hounds on top and we were ready for takeoff.

The airstrip we were using was long and black, so there was no problem getting airborne. The strip we were going to, however, would be different.

Forty-five minutes later, and 100 miles east, we came to the snow-covered, 900-foot, private airstrip with a double dog-leg. Frank extended the skis below the tires and powered-in around the ridge to the final approach, and we splashed down in 18 inches of fresh snow. My work was just beginning.

After unloading the plane, I packed all my gear 200 yards to the campsite. I had to clear snow for a place to set up my tent, then get the stove in place, and cut a good supply of wood. It was dark by the time I was finished, and the stars were out. The night was going to be really cold.

I'm 65 and have been a senior citizen for 10 years already. While I spend most of my life outdoors and take long summer and fall pack trips with my horses and mules, I wasn't ready to run up and down the mountains as I once did. Consequently, I spent the first week getting in condition and breaking the trails. The first three weeks, my dogs treed several lions, one of them a big tom and the rest females. None were big enough to consider taking. I was enjoying the action and the solitude.

Then came the morning of February 26th. It was clear and cold, and the snow was hard and crusted. After a good breakfast, I turned the hounds loose and headed for a saddle in a ridge a mile from the river. My dogs reached the saddle first and had a track started by the time I got there. But they'd trailed-off the other side of the ridge, down into the canyon, then up the other side and over the end of a ridge that came down from the high country. Not knowing if they were trailing forwards or backwards on the track, my only choice was to try to stay within hearing of them. In the steep Selway Bitterroot, that's not always easy. I headed up, staying on top of the ridge they'd crossed. From there, I could hear them well enough to know the direction they were going.

Three hours of uphill climbing later, I found where the dogs and lion had crossed the ridge that I was on. After another hour of steep climbing on snow that was getting soft, I could hear the dogs barking treed. They were still a long way off.

When I finally got to the scene, I found the cougar treed on a steep, north-facing hillside, in a tree that had fallen downhill and was not lying in the tops of others. When I saw it, I realized for the first time that my dogs had treed the cougar that I had spent most of 30 years looking for. It had been a long time since 1961, when the lion I killed that year had challenged Teddy Roosevelt's record cougar. I would take this cat.

The big lion was nervous and wanted to get out of the tree. I was nervous and didn't want him to jump. I had already gone farther down the mountain than I'd wanted, and I did not want him to jump and go even farther down into the canyon. It was already going to be a long trip out.

Light conditions for picture taking were very poor, but I tried a few photos anyway, while the cat was still in the tree. Then I tied up my dogs in case I had a cripple, a situation that can get dogs hurt or killed. The shots were at close range and the two slugs in the ribs from the Smith and Wesson Model 19, .357 Magnum pistol put an end to the excitement.

Skinning the heavy cat on the steep hillside in two feet of snow was no small job. An hour later, I had his hide and head on my back and had started up the mountain. In another hour it was growing dusk and I was only on top of the first ridge. Camp was still miles and hours away.

I can only estimate the cat's live weight, but from experience and the size of the hide (laid-out on a log, it was 9 feet, 7 inches long) I'd put it at 225 pounds. While I would later find that the hide and head weighed 42 pounds and my backpack 18 pounds, the entire load felt like it weighed 100 pounds.

It was dark when I hiked into camp three hours later and the stars were out again. It had been a long 27 years. 🦌

NOTE: This outstanding trophy, taken on an excellent example of the epitome of a fair chase hunt, was awarded the coveted Sagamore Hill Award at the 20th Big Game Awards. While at the Awards, in the spirit of sharing this exceptional trophy with all sportsmen, Gene Alford donated this skull to the Boone and Crockett Club's National Collection of Heads and Horns, with the collection on continuing display at the Buffalo Bill Historical Center, Cody, Wyoming.

Final 1st Award
GRB

IG GAME TROPHIES

P.O. Box 547
Dumfries, VA 22026

Kind of Cat *Cougar*
Sex *M*

SEE OTHER SIDE FOR INSTRUCTIONS	Measurements
A. Greatest Length Without Lower Jaw	9 8/16
B. Greatest Width	6 11/16
FINAL SCORE	16 3/16

B&C BIG GAME AWARDS 20 1988-1988

Exact Locality Where Killed:

Date Killed: By Whom Killed: *GENE R Alford*

Present Owner:

Address:

Guide Name and Address:

Remarks: (Mention Any Abnormalities or Unique Qualities)

I certify that I have measured the above trophy on *30 April* 19 *89*

at (Address) *N.M. Natural History* (City) *Albq* (State) *NM*

and that these measurements and data are, to the best of my knowledge and belief, made in accordance with the

instructions given.

Witness: *Dennis L. Shirley*   Signature: *C. Randall Byers*

B&C OFFICIAL MEASURER   B 0 4 8

I.D. Number

Image from B&C Archives

Original score chart for Gene Alford's cougar, which scores 16–3/16 points.
The tom was taken in Idaho County, Idaho, in 1988.

RICAN BIG GAME TROPHIES

Serge Torkant
2nd Aud

205 South Patrick Street
Alexandria, Virginia 22314

CLUB

R

Kind of Cat _Cougar_

Sex _____

Updated
_6/10/86_

B

A

B&C BIG GAME AWARDS
19
1983-1985

SEE OTHER SIDE FOR INSTRUCTIONS		Measurements
A. Greatest Length without Lower Jaw		9 9/16
B. Greatest Width		6 8/16
TOTAL AND FINAL SCORE	_Idaho Co., ID_	15 8/16
Exact locality where killed _Idaho Co., Idaho_		
Date killed _1-1-1982_ By whom killed _Jerry J. James_		
Present owner _Cabela's RR-3-220d_		
Address		
Guide's Name and Address		
Remarks: (Mention any abnormalities or unique qualities)		
		_Z_

I certify that I have measured the above trophy on _13 May_ 19 _86_
at (address) _Nevada State Museum_   City _Las Vegas_   State _NV_
and that these measurements and data are, to the best of my knowledge and belief, made in
accordance with the instructions given.

Witness: _Randall Byers_   Signature: _Frank E. Bertoca_
Official Measurer ☐☐☐☐

Image from B&C Archives

Cougar, Scoring 15-8/16 Points
Taken by Jerry J. James in Idaho County, Idaho,
_in 1982._

Determined

By Jerry J. James

19th Big Game Awards Program

MY COUGAR HUNT BEGAN IN THE SPRING OF 1979 WHEN I FIRST DECIDED TO GO ON A HUNT. I WROTE LETTERS TO GUIDES, AND THEN EAGERLY AWAITED THE MORNING MAIL FOR THE REPLIES TO COME. I WAS ABLE TO NARROW MY GUIDE SELECTION, AND AFTER CALLING SEVERAL REFERENCES, I FINALLY DECIDED ON BOB SMITH OF KOOSKIA, IDAHO. I HAD READ ABOUT IDAHO'S REPUTATION OF HAVING LARGE CATS, AND THE SELWAY-BITTEROOT AREA HAS YIELDED NUMEROUS RECORD-BOOK CATS.

My enthusiasm was brightened, when upon arriving in Lewiston, Idaho, I was informed that they had a fresh snow in the high country. My enthusiasm was quickly dampened, though, when my hunt began the next day and the weather turned extremely warm. The snow quickly melted, and the possibility of finding a fresh track was just about nil. Bob and I spent a week walking in the high country with no luck. I returned home, but I was determined to try again.

The next year was a repeat of the first, with no snow. I

planned my trip for two weeks later, but little did I know that Idaho would experience a snowless winter. When you consider the number of miles that guides cover when there is snow to cut a fresh track, you can imagine how lucky you would have to be to jump a cougar under non-snow conditions.

My plane trip home was once again a long ride back to Minnesota. But, I was even more determined than ever to get a cat. I vowed that my third trip would only happen if snow conditions were perfect, and I planned on staying until I was successful, or Bob sent me home, whichever came first.

Finally, in late December 1981, I got the call. Bob said that they had 18 inches of snow in the high country, and more was expected. My first night after arriving was spent in renewing acquaintances and preparing my equipment. I shoot a 60-pound Bear Alaskan bow, with Bear Magnum arrows and Satellite broadheads. My equipment has accounted for numerous whitetails and two bears, and I knew that this would be adequate medicine for cougars.

The hunt began with Bob and I driving the back roads in his four-wheel-drive truck, along with his two best cat dogs, Chief and Ralph. Chief is an Airedale and bluetick hound cross, and he has been involved in more than 100 cat kills. Ralph is a pit bull and Walker hound cross, with a big hate for cats and bears. It was really a switch, driving back roads through more than a foot of snow, compared to our first two years. I was really amazed at Bob's ability to determine what kind of tracks there were along the road. I had never seen a cougar track, so I had Bob stop several times for tracks that I thought were those of a cat that he called elk, etc. And, he was always right.

As we drove along, Bob told me about different cougars he had taken over the years. I told him that I wasn't fussy after two unsuccessful trips; all I wanted was a cougar, and he did not have to be a record-book cat. Bob told me that if I got a cougar, more than likely it would make the book, as the cats in his area all seem to have large heads and every mature cougar would make it.

About 10:00 a.m., we cut a day-old cat track crossing a bridge and heading up the side of the mountain. We took to the trail, with Ralph on a leash while Chief was allowed to run ahead. The cat headed straight up the mountain, Bob and I following in a foot of snow. Bob told me that Chief did not have to be leashed because he would only run the trail if Bob gave the command. Once the command was given, Chief would run the trail silently until he jumped the cat. Then, the hound would take over and he would bark like crazy. Ralph was leashed so that he would not take the trail. Because of Idaho's remoteness, Bob does not want to turn his dogs loose until the trail is fresh, as his dogs could be gone for days. Four hours later, the track was not getting any fresher. My legs were suffering from cramps from climbing the mountain, so we decided to quit. I was dog tired and soaking wet as we slid down the mountain to the Bronco.

That night, about a foot of snow fell which made it impossible to go back and follow the old track, and we found no new tracks that day. For me, it was a welcome relief, as I was still tired from the first day. That night it snowed again, and next day we cut another cougar track on the road. The cat had crossed the river and headed up the mountain. Bob was really excited, as he thought the cat was a big tom with skull measurements that would easily exceed 15 inches. The track looked as big as a pie plate in the snow.

We started up the mountain again, with Ralph on a leash and Chief following the trail. After climbing about a mile, we came to some rock bluffs where the dogs went wild. The cat scent was strong in the rocky area, and both Chief and Ralph were barking like crazy. Bob sent Chief on the trail and turned

Ralph loose, and the chase was on. The trail paralleled the river for about a mile, then headed downhill straight to the river. We tried to keep up with the dogs, but it was impossible as the snow was more than three feet deep, and we did not have snowshoes.

We could hear the dogs barking down by the river, so we raced down the mountain. Unfortunately, the cat swam the river. After that, our daily equipment list included a boat, and we hunted both sides of the river. I doubt that we could have followed the cat anyway as we were both tired and it was getting late. Bob also thought that the cat had crossed the river before he had even turned the dogs loose, as the cat had made a lot of tracks down by the river.

That night, it snowed again. We decided against taking a boat across the river and following the cat. The track would have been over 36 hours old, and the cat could have been 15 miles away. We drove up one back road where a tree had fallen across the road. We turned around before we got to the fallen tree, since we did not have a chain saw to remove it. That night, it snowed again. As we headed up the road the next day to where the tree had fallen, I joked to Bob that there probably was a cat track just beyond the fallen tree. Sure enough, there was a track only 100 yards on the other side of the tree! Needless to say, a chain saw was added to our equipment list after that. The cat had crossed the road and walked up the fallen tree and then up the mountain. The track was already over 24 hours old, but we decided to follow it anyway, hoping the cat had made a kill on the mountainside. Unfortunately, the cat had not, because he continued to climb the mountain. Soon we were wading in four feet of snow. After about four hours of trailing, we headed back to the Bronco totally exhausted. I didn't think I was ever going to get my cat.

The sixth day, we did not cut any tracks. This was just as well, as I was still too tired from the day before. I saw more hills in Idaho in one day than I have seen in Minnesota in a lifetime. The scenery was beautiful beyond description; and during the day's hunt, we continually saw numerous deer and elk.

The seventh day was a perfect day for hunting; we had two inches of fresh snow. We stopped at a cafe to have a cup of coffee, and we were told that a truck driver had seen a cougar right next to the road two days before. We went to where the cougar had been sighted, and then spent some time in the area listening for ravens which might indicate that the cat had a kill. His track was too old to follow, so we decided to cover our daily route.

After some time, we found the track of a large cat that had crossed the road and headed up the mountain. The track was filled with snow, but we knew that it had been made during the night. We hoped that the cat was not too far away. We started our usual procession of Chief leading the way, with Ralph on a leash, and me bringing up the rear. We headed up and then paralleled the mountain, when the cat track turned and headed into a small canyon. All of a sudden, Chief, who had gotten out of our sight, started barking as though he had jumped the cat and was following the trail. Bob turned Ralph loose and he headed down into the canyon. After days of walking, I was finally listening to hound music.

The chase was short; soon both dogs were barking that the cat was treed. We hurried over to the tree, and there was the most beautiful sight that I have ever seen. The lion looked golden brown against the green pine trees, and it was obviously a big tom. Finally, the moment I had worked at for the last three years was about to happen. Bob tied up the dogs as I positioned myself for a shot with my bow. I only had a small hole to shoot through as I released my arrow. The arrow deflected on a small branch and hit the cat on the side of the head. The cat started snarling, and he knocked off every branch as he started down the tree. I nocked another arrow, and took another quick shot before the cat was halfway down the tree. The arrow hit him right behind the front leg. The cat died before he could go 20 yards.

I beat the dogs to the lion, but I remembered what Bob told me about not touching the cat until the dogs got there. I knew what he meant when Ralph hit that lion wide open. I am sure he would have chewed on me too, if I had been holding that cat. Chief gave the cat the business too, but he knew he had done his job, just as he had done dozens of times before.

Later, we laid the hide on the floor. The big tom measured 8 feet, 7 inches long. Bob joked that we could stretch him a lot further, especially if we used two pickups. Needless to say, I was elated. After hunting 22 days over a three-year period, walking at least 200 miles, sliding down mountains, and crossing icy rivers in a rubber boat, I had finally taken my cougar.

Fortunately, this is not the end of my story. I received a phone call from my taxidermist in the middle of July. He had sent the skull to the University of Minnesota to have it cleaned in a bug-box. After receiving it, he had taken the skull to a Pope and Young scorer who gave it an official score of 15-11/16. My cougar was recognized as the new World's Record at the Pope and Young Club Awards Banquet on April 9, 1983, in Milwaukee, Wisconsin. It also was awarded Pope and Young Club's prestigious Ishi Award, which is the highest form of recognition given by the club. The Ishi Award is presented only when a truly outstanding big game animal is taken, and the award criteria are similar to those for the Boone and Crockett Club's coveted Sagamore Hill Award.

Never in my life did I believe this could happen to me. I called Bob Smith and thanked him for a tremendous hunt, as it had been a real experience to see Bob and his dogs work. I also reminded him about the big cat that swam the river and got away from us. There is no doubt that cat was larger than the one I shot. I am sure when someone gets him, Bob Smith and his dogs will also be there.

Photo from B&C Archives

Cougar, Scoring 16 Points,
Taken by Brian K. Williams in Archuleta County, Colorado,
in 2001.

Lock Tail

By Brian K. Williams

25th Big Game Awards Program

MY MOUNTAIN LION STORY BEGAN A LONG TIME AGO WHEN I WAS JUST A BOY. I GREW UP IN SOUTHERN OKLAHOMA WHERE I HUNTED COONS, BOBCATS, SQUIRRELS, AND RABBITS WITH MY DAD, DAVID K. WILLIAMS, OUR FRIEND, CHARLES "COTTON" RUSSELL, AND MY UNCLE, MARK GILLHAM, WHO WERE ALL HOUNDSMEN.

My family moved to Colorado in 1979. My dad raised and hunted with a few bear hounds the first couple of years we lived in Pagosa Springs, until he became a government trapper near Grand Junction. He hunted with Larry Sanders and Jeff Brent, the state bear and mountain lion men, for a couple of years. I accompanied them a few times in the summer after problem bears that were killing the local ranchers' sheep.

I attended high school in Pagosa Springs where I met Mike Ray, his dad, Dick Ray, and Dick's brother, Sam (owner and operator of Bear Paw Outfitters), and Dick and Sam's brother, Rodney. I started guiding for Dick, owner and operator of Lobo Outfitters, just after I finished high school.

The Rays had a lot of good dogs then, as they do now. About four years after I began working for Dick, I went to work for his brother Sam. I acquired some dogs from Sam; I even traded him a crazy old horse for one. I hunted bear and lion with him for several years; those were the best years of my life. I raised my own hounds for a little better than 10 years, then the constant barking of eight hound dogs started to wear on my neighbors, so I reluctantly decided to sell them. I called Mike, and he and Dick agreed to buy my dogs. Four of my dogs were really proven. Charlie, Andy, and Pebbles I got from Sam. Doozie, a female, I bought from my old friend, Cotton, in Oklahoma. I also had a few pups. I told Mike that Snoopy, one of the females, was going to be a good hound.

After that I didn't lion hunt much until I booked a hunt with Lobo Outfitters in January 2001. This would be the hunt I would never forget. A little before daylight on the morning of the first day of my hunt, Mike and I took off on snowmobiles in search of a big tom track that Mike believed was in the area. We had gone about two miles when Mike stopped dead in his tracks, and as sure as the nose on your face, there was a huge track in the two-day old snow. We tried to cut the track again by circling the area. Not finding it again, we knew it had to be in that area.

We went back and picked up the dogs, but by then it had warmed up and the dogs could only cold trail. But to hear my old dogs, Andy and Pebbles, trailing again was music to my ears. I was kind of glad that they didn't tree a cat that day because my hunt would have been over too soon.

We hunted a few more times in February and also in March, but I was unsuccessful during those times. Other hunters with Lobo Outfitters, however, took a good many lions that season. Some were huge, with one scoring 15-6/16 Boone and Crockett points.

It was a long summer and fall. Then, on December 1, 2001, after a good six-inch snowfall, I resumed my hunt with Lobo

Outfitters. Harold Thompson, a local dentist and a good friend of the Rays, was my guide that day. Harold went out early to beat the rush of other lion hunters in our area. I had overslept that morning and was rushing around trying to find my tire chains. By the time I arrived at Mike's, he was loading dogs in the truck. He said that Harold had gone ahead of me. Mike told me to take Andy, Jube (a dog Mike and Dick had raised), and Snoopy. Mike was taking a hunter to a different area. I was glad to hear that I would find Harold in the same place that Mike and I had spotted the big tom track nearly a year before.

When I found Harold, he had already found a track not far up the road, so by the time we figured out that it was a female, the other lion hunters had hit the other roads in the area. Harold and I made a different plan. He was going to go to the end of the road, and I was going to make sure the other hunters hadn't missed anything.

I called Mike on his cell phone and he told me they had found a good tom and all but had it treed. I told him where Harold had gone, and Mike said that it was a bad area and Harold was probably stuck. We hung up and I went to check on Harold. To my surprise, he wasn't stuck. He informed me that he had found a dandy track near the end of the road. He had already called Dick, and Dick told Harold that we might as well try it. We went back to where Harold had found the track and turned the dogs out. It was 11:30 a.m., and my thermometer read 26°. We had a chance!

Harold and I got our packs together and added extra food and supplies, knowing that we might have to spend the night. We were going into some of the roughest country I knew of, and we were also off to a late start. I turned the three dogs loose, and they were out of earshot in a hurry. I cannot speak for Harold, but I was excited in a scary kind of way, knowing we had some dangerous cliffs and ledges to climb through. In some places we even had to take off our packs and crawl through narrow ledges.

About 3 p.m., we could hear the faint sound of dogs in the distance. The going got a little easier and we could see that the big tom knew exactly how to maneuver through the rough terrain. We had two pistols; mine was a 9mm and Harold had a .357. I asked Harold if he wanted to take the tom. He had taken a huge tom a few years back, so he declined my offer, saying he just loved the chase. I was wondering how big the cat was because I had already killed three lions in the past, two of which had skulls 14 inches in size. I thought to myself that I couldn't believe I was actually the hunter this time, and not the guide. We found scrapes in the trail along the way, indicating that this was a large tom, but its track didn't seem overly large. I did note that the tom had an extra-long stride.

We eventually made our way to where the dogs had the cougar treed. We saw the back half of the lion in the tree first. Harold asked, "What do you think?"

I gave him a thumbs up. I was grinning when I saw the front half of the lion. Harold tied up the dogs while I readied for the shot. I took aim and jerked the trigger like a greenhorn, not knowing the pistol was on safety. Realizing just how excited I really was, it was a struggle to stay calm. I took a deep breath and squeezed the trigger. This time the result was a good lung shot.

When the mammoth tom hit the ground, it ran down the side of the mountain about 25 yards. I followed right behind it. When I whizzed by Harold, I asked if I could borrow his .357. He handed me the pistol while continuing to hold Andy. Unfortunately, we had only taken two leashes. I rounded the brush and rocks, thinking the tom had gone quite a ways, but to my surprise, it was sitting on its hind end in some boulders not 10 yards away. The tom turned and faced me. It couldn't go through the boulders, and its only escape was to go through me.

Now, I have been in some tough spots with lions before. I have seen a lion crush a dog's jaw and legs. An angry lion on the ground can do a lot of damage to a pack of dogs, not to mention what this tom could do to me. I had a pistol in each hand ready for the battle.

The lion snarled at me, not like any old lion would snarl at you, but like the fourth biggest lion in the world would snarl at you. As the legendary Ben Lily would say, I got the "lock tail" and ran backwards as fast as my cowardly body would carry me. For those of you who don't savvy "lock tail," it's when a dog is in the scared retreat mode and has its tail tucked tight between its legs against its belly.

Well, I made it back to Harold and the ecstatic hounds. We decided to just let the fatal shot take its toll and wait a few minutes. It worked; when we went back, the monster had perished. I wanted to move it to a rock to take some pictures so Harold grabbed a front leg, and I grabbed the other front leg. Failing to pull in sync, the lion didn't budge. We had to put our backs into it and pull together to get it to the rock. I told Harold I was going to try to lift it for a picture. He chuckled. I guess I still had a little adrenaline left, because I managed to barely hold it up for a couple of quick shots. I was still so excited; I had no idea the trophy I had.

Mike and his hunter had taken a good tom, also. Later, Mike came looking for us. He could hear the dogs and cut across the canyon. It was an easier route than what we had taken, except that he had to cross a deep and frigid river. He had taken some small logs and made a footbridge. I was glad to see him as he walked up to us. He said that my cougar was the biggest lion he had ever seen. Mike is very conservative when it comes to judging the size of an animal, so I thought he was teasing me. When we arrived back at Mike's house, Dick said that the lion was the widest he had ever seen. That's when I realized Mike hadn't been teasing me.

Mike and Dick very conservatively measured the huge skull. It was over 16 inches. After the 60-day drying period, it officially scored 16 B&C points. It is now the new Colorado state record. The prior state record had been held by President Theodore Roosevelt since 1901. His cougar scores 15-12/16.

I would like to thank Mike and Dick Ray of Lobo Outfitters and Harold Thompson for giving me the hunt-of-a-lifetime. I thank God for watching out for us lion hunters out in such treacherous country. I want to give a special thanks to the dogs, Andy, who is about 10 years old now, Snoopy, who is in her prime, and Jube, one of the best young dogs I've ever seen. 🐝

Photo from B&C Archives

Elk & Deer

American Elk

Roosevelt's Elk

Mule Deer

Columbia Blacktail

Sitka Blacktail

Whitetail

Coues' Whitetail

Photo from B&C Archives

Non-typical American Elk, Scoring 430-2/8 Points,
Taken by William D. Deweese in Rio Blanco County, Colorado,
in 1888.

Ten Days Among the Elk

By William D. Deweese

25th Big Game Awards Program

T HE STORY ON THE FOLLOWING PAGES WAS WRITTEN BY
WILLIAM DALLAS "DALL" DeWEESE IN 1888, OVER 115
YEARS BEFORE HIS ELK WAS EVER SCORED FOR THE BOONE AND
CROCKETT RECORDS BOOK. IT IS NOT SIMPLY A RECOUNTING OF
THE STORY OF HIS HUNT; IT IS ALSO A PRICELESS LOOK INTO THE
PAST OF OUR HUNTING HERITAGE. EVERYTHING IN THIS STORY
TELLS A TALE, WHETHER IT'S THE HUNTING SLANG OF THE DAY,
THE THINGS THEY SAW, OR WHAT COMMON THOUGHTS AND
ACCEPTABLE PRACTICES WERE IN THAT ERA.

The year 1888 was amidst the infancy of conservation. The
roots of the Boone and Crockett Club (North America's oldest
conservation organization) had been planted only one year previous. Game laws were noticeably absent, as were general public
concerns for the future of our wildlife populations and welfare.
Very few people in that era thought about "fair chase" or ethics
in the field. Those concepts were all but non-existent. Hunting
was a simple act — reduced to possession, cook, and eat.

The fact that Dall DeWeese even took the time to write of
his adventure is amazing in itself. It also shows, however, that
even in that day, people had an appreciation for wild things and

places. There are also references in this story that show evidence of the beginnings of people's changing views. At points in the story, he references the fact that they waited for a clear shot, as to not wound cows and calves. He also mentions, "We saw dozens of fine fat deer at close range but killed none, as we were not out to see how much game we could slaughter and let lay in the mountains — as is too often done." This exact sentiment is one of the founding principles of why the Boone and Crockett Club was established, as well as North American wildlife management as a whole.

Some of the content of this story would be, by today's standards, unethical and irresponsible. Back then it was not only acceptable, it was commonplace. We have chosen not to sanitize the story, nor correct the grammar. This story is an education, as well as a glimpse into past realities. It also shows that even in 1888, there was a true romanticism of wild places. The original words and language leave these pages authentic. Dall DeWeese's story appeared in the *Canon City Clipper* on October 31, 1888.

Successful Hunters!

Ten Days Among The Elk, Bear, and Deer.

A Former Tipp Boy's Successful Hunt After Big Game in The Rockies.

Camp Big Horns, Colo., Sept. 1888.
Messrs. Bowman, Clark Bros., Williamson, Hawver, and Huber:

My Dear Nimrods – Your letters were received in due time stating that it was impossible for you to join me this fall in an elk hunt in the Rocky Mountains. I regretted much to receive this word and think you "tender-feet" will regret sending it after reading of our grand time.

Mr. J. E. Brown, Mr. L. E. Franck (county treasurer), both "old-timers" here, and myself took train September 3d, crossed the Rockies to the mouth of Eagle River where I had saddle horses and pack animals (jacks) awaiting us. There are no toll pikes in this country but simply a jack trail leading here and there up into the cedars and pinons, then up to the quakenasps, thence higher to the spruce-covered mountain tops and timber line peaks, and into the very heart of the Rocky Mountains. We soon packed our bedding and supplies on our jacks and took the trail leading up Sweetwater (Turret Creek.) We reached Sweetwater Lake the same evening and camped for the night. The lake is one mile long and half a mile wide, located in a canon between two great mountains; its waters are full of the beautiful speckled trout and our jointed rods, lines, leaders and flies were quickly adjusted and seventeen of the speckled beauties were landed and prepared for supper.

The next morning the bright face of Old Sol found us in the saddle and two miles up the steep ascending trail. What fresh invigorating atmosphere and how grand the scenery of this forenoon ride! We climbed higher through groves of quakenasp and the grassy mountainsides until noon when we reached the "flat tops," or summit of the range. I wish I could picture this landscape for you so you could imagine the grand surroundings of our camp, but I can only say that these flat tops are timbered with dense groves of the stately spruce and are broken here and there with open parks which are covered with a luxuriant growth of the tall gramma grass. Notwithstanding the altitude is 10,000 feet, fine springs, small streams and lakes are everywhere. Turret Peak and Shingle Peak tower up to 12,000 feet – 1,000 feet above timber line – and on their North sides lays perpetual snow. From these peaks you can see forever! You can see into Egeria Park, the head waters of the Grand, Piney, Eagle, Roaring Fork, Muddy and Bear Rivers, and at their base heads the great White River. This was the Ute Indians' paradise for summer and fall hunting, and here is the home of the elk, mountain sheep, silver tip grizzly and cinnamon bear, and the gamey black tail [mule] deer. Three o'clock p.m. found our jacks and horses unpacked and picketed out in the rich grass, dinner over, tents up, hunting equipments in place, and then we started out after fresh meat for supper, although we had a goodly supper of bacon.

Sundown found us all back in camp with three deer packed in and hung on the spruce [in] back of the tent. I killed a big buck that weighed 260 pounds, fat an inch thick over the rump, horns in the velvet which makes for a fine trophy.

Having all the camp meat necessary the next day was spent in looking for elk sign through the spruce forests on the North and shady sides of the breaks on the flat tops. Our notes compared favorably on our return at night, and after camp-fire stories we retired fully convinced that we were in the land of the "wapiti," and believing that our desire to kill a bull elk would soon be gratified.

The next day we discovered quite a chain of small lakes about six miles Northward, with no end to elk and bear sign in their vicinity. We saw dozens of fine fat deer at close range but killed none as we were not out to see how much game we could slaughter and let lay in the mountains – as is too often done. We returned to camp early that day, boned our meat, salted it down in the hides under the spruce trees where the sun never shines and covered it up with boughs. Then we folded our bedding, packed some supplies on our jacks, saddled our horses and made a branch camp at one of the newly discovered lakes by 8 o'clock the same evening.

After we had retired we heard a bull elk "bugle" – probably a half mile distant – and he came nearer and nearer until he was ack of the tent. I killed a big

SUCCESSFUL HUNTERS !

Ten Days Among The Elk, Bear And Deer.

A Former Tipp Boy's Successful Hunt After Big Game In The Rockies.

CAMP BIG HORNS, Colo., Sept. 1888.

Messrs. Bowman, Clark Bros., Williamson, Hawver and Huber :—

MY DEAR NIMRODS—Your letters were received in due time stating that it was impossible for you to join me this fall in an elk hunt in the Rocky Mountains. I regretted much to receive this word and think you "tender-feet" will regret sending it after reading of our grand time.

Mr. J. E. Brown, Mr. L. E. Franck, (county treasurer,) both "old-timers" here, and myself took train September 3d, crossed the Rockies to the mouth of Eagle River where I had saddle horses and pack animals (jacks) awaiting us. There are no toll pikes in this country but simply a jack trail leading here and there up into the cedars and pinons, then up to the quaken-asps, thence higher to the spruce covered mountain tops and timber line peaks, and into the very heart of the Rocky Mountains. We soon packed our bedding and supplies on our jacks and took the trail leading up Sweetwater (Turret Creek.) We reached Sweetwater Lake the same evening and camped for the night. The Lake is one mile long and half a mile wide, located in a canon between two great mountains; its waters are full of the beautiful speckled trout and our jointed rods, lines, leaders and flies were quickly adjusted and seventeen of the speckled ——

morning. I had not and went to th where they should have been. Gone "bugle"—probably a half mile and he came nearer and nearer was within 200 yards of the cam he bugled and repeated, strikin note in the staff in a loud, clea whistling tone that echoed from woodland. It was indeed a gra nade, but we were so eager for his elkship that we did not awai clusion. Hastily kicking aside t ets we hurriedly dressed and tried a march on him. There being no was quite dark, and we stole a edge of the spruce near the open he was crossing. We could hear h ing and down we crouched near of willows. All was still as death rustle of the tall grass at his feet casionally a musical bugle, but he ing at right angles from us and within 80 yards—close enough to breathe. But alas! we could n out the outline of his "darned old and he gained the shelter of the and bugled again. I tried to ans but my "bugle" was evidently a ure, or else he heard one from congenial mate, for he bugled us "good-bye" or "some other evening grew fainter and fainter, and s with cold we crept back to bed m an emphatic good-night to bull elk

In the morning we were out ea all keeping together we followed high ridge near the lakes. Fresh s seen on all favorable ground and a sharp lookout. Presently the sp of water near at hand attracted ou tion and looking down we disco band of elk in a little lake just be

Image from B&C Archives

The article written by William D. Deweese about his hunt for this great non-typical American elk first appeared in an 1888 edition of the Canon City Clipper. The story is reprinted here in its original context.

❦ 125 ❧

within 200 yards of the camp. Here he bugled and repeated, striking every note in the staff in a loud, clear, shrill, whistling tone that echoed from park to woodland. It was indeed a grand serenade, but we were so eager for a crack at his elkship that we did not await its conclusion. Hastily kicking aside the blankets we hurriedly dressed and tried to steal a march on him. There being no moon it was quite dark, and we stole along the edge of the spruce near the open park that he was crossing. We could hear him coming and down we crouched near a clump of willows. All was still as death save the rustle of the tall grass at his feet and occasionally a musical bugle, but he was going at right angles from us and passed within 80 yards – close enough to hear him breathe. But alas! We could not make out the outline of his "darned old carcass," and he gained the shelter of the spruce and bugled again. I tired to answer him but my "bugle" was evidently a sad failure, or else he heard one from a more congenial mate, for he bugled us a loud "good-bye" or "some other evening" that grew fainter and fainter, and shivering with cold we crept back to bed muttering an emphatic good-night to bull elks.

In the morning we were out early and all keeping together we followed along a high ridge near the lakes. Fresh sign was seen on all favorable ground and we kept a sharp lookout. Presently the splashing of water near at hand attracted our attention and looking down we discovered a band of elk in a little lake just beyond a grove of spruce. The wind was against us, and silently we stole around to the opposite edge of the timber. Here a grand sight met our eyes – a band of forty elk, all cows and calves except on fair sized bull. Some were in the water and others were in an open park. The distance was 300 yards and it was impossible to get a shot at the bull to kill. However we chanced it, and, taking care not to hit the cows and calves, we singled him out and fired together. Off they went like a flash under cover of the spruce, and we followed, finding blood on the trail. After following the trail half a mile we concluded it was a flesh wound and returned to camp – thinking we might have done better and feeling like shooting eight or ten deer we saw while coming back.

Next morning before sun up we were off in different directions. At this season of the year the elk are beginning to band together, the velvet has just shed from the antlers of the bulls, and the bark can frequently be seen off of spruce trees eight feet from the ground where they have been rubbing their antlers. I made a long trip and struck the fresh trail of a band of elk, mostly bulls as the tracks were large. I followed the trail a mile or more somewhat toward camp and saw they were headed for a large body of spruce timber. As it was about noon and being close to camp I concluded to go in, get something to eat and then ride my horse over to the location of the elk and take my evening hunt, for one hour at sun down is worth the balance of the day in elk hunting. On reaching camp I was joined by Mr. Brown who asked if I had moved the jacks from where he had picketed them out in the morning. I had not and went to the park where they should have been. Gone? Yes, gone! Our Rocky Mountain Mocking Birds had "broke" camp and struck out for home, their pace doubtless accelerated by the scent of a gray silver tip. Mr. Franck and myself, after lunch, saddled our horses and rode over in the direction I had tracked the elk. After going a mile we rode out of the spruce on a point to look over the country. The sun was half an hour high and the shadows of the spruce groves were stretching out over the parks – and this is the hour for the elk to come from the forests and feed in the parks. Sitting quietly in the saddle, our gaze roving over the beautiful landscape, we sighted a band of elk a mile away just emerging from the spruce. We counted eleven; all were large, one in particular, and we remarked that there was an "Old Towser." He stopped and looked square at us – then moved on. Now was our opportunity. Slipping away from our saddles and leaving the horses for a "blind," we started on a run through the spruce groves, open parks, up, then down the ravines, across another park and finally reached the last spruce grove that separated us from the game. Stealing quietly through this we reached the edge that fringed the park. Peeping out I saw a great bull elk lying down in the tall grass 140 yards away and looking right at us. I saw he was a monster, and we gave him a double shot. Over he went – then he was up and off into the spruce like a flash! The others fled to the top of the hill and were gone in a second. We followed their trail in a forest of spruce twenty miles wide, found no blood, and the sun went down. We stared blankly into each others faces and wondered if it was possible to miss such a monster. Finally we decided to return to camp and pick up the trail early the next morning. We kicked ourselves back to camp and declared that if we had really missed that elephant we would fold our blankets, go to Canon City and never say elk again.

The next morning we were up with the stars and rode over to where we had left the trail. Staking our horses we were soon tracking the "Monarch of the Glen." Although the dense spruce forest was tracked by elk, we could easily follow the right one as it was almost an inch deeper and much larger than the other tracks. After tracking 200 yards we saw that one of us had our brand on him for occasionally we found a drop of blood. He kept in the heaviest timber, and I knew that was a good sign for the Indians say, "Heap hurt when go through heap brush!" We tracked him a mile into the heart of the forest to where the ground and logs were covered with a rich, green, velvet-like moss, and where the sun never penetrates. Here we "jumped" him and away he went; we fired five shots after him, and then I ran to the left about forty yards and gained a higher spot of ground from where I got a broadside shot, the ball breaking his left shoulder and down he went! We rushed up to him; he still struggled, shook those massive antlers and eyed us with vengeance. A merciful shot through the heart ended his career. We then gazed in aston-ishment at his gigantic size. He measured 15 feet and 4 inches from the point of horn to the hind hoof, and girted 9 feet. His antlers are the largest I ever saw; the beams are six feet long and are five feet between the points, having nine perfect points on one beam and eight on the other – hence the name of our camp, "Big Horns." Old hunters came to see him and they say he is the biggest elk ever killed in this country. He dressed over 700 lbs. of meat. We found that one of us had hit him in the neck the evening before, and on cutting out the bullet, which was imbedded in the neck-bone, it proved to be a Winchester – and my comrade used a Sharps.

After dressing him we returned to camp, taking some of his meat with us for supper, and as we kindled our camp-fire that night we gave three cheers for the Monarch Bull Elk, Harrison and Morton, and the boys of Tippecanoe.

The next day Mr. Brown returned with our "mocking birds" and we packed in our elk and boned the meat. The next morning we started to move camp again; our animals were packed and we were in the saddle at daylight. We struck a trail and had only gone half a mile when I caught a glimpse of three silver tip bears on the opposite side of an open park we were just entering. Hastily notifying Mr. Brown, who was just behind me, we slipped out of our saddles and started for the game. I gained a bunch of willows between the bears and myself, and Mr. B. kept to the right along the trees. I opened fire and down went a bear. I advanced and continued firing to keep him down. Mr. B. got into position and began shooting, while the other two bears slowly retreated up the hill snarling and stopping occasionally to snap viciously at us. I expected them to come at us, for the one I had shot lay kicking on the ground and squalling terribly; and so I filled the magazine of my gun with cartridges as I ran, expecting a dozen more bears to appear at any moment (I am glad they did not for I was out in the open park with no trees handy.) Mr. Franck, who was some 300 yards behind us fixing his saddle when the rumpus started, came riding into the fight on the dead run, and the first shot from his old Sharps rifle hit a bear in the neck and silenced him forever. The other bear carried off our lead and escaped. I tell you there was music in the air for a few minutes, the constant bang! bang! bang! of our rifles, the snapping and squalling of the bears, the bray of our jacks as they rushed terror-stricken from the scene, and our shouts to each other to "stand your ground and give 'em h—l!" made up a scene at once exhilaratingly exciting. But it was over in half the time it takes to write it. We came out without a scratch and got two bears out of the three. Their robes are fine and we will have them made into rugs to keep as mementos of a most thrilling experience.

After a close search for an hour we found our jacks huddled together with a part of their packs off and frightened nearly to death. We were soon on the move again and came down to our first camp, satisfied with our day's sport.

In the early morning we were up early and rode six miles to another locality, and then swung around to a "salt lick" where we had seen a band of mountain sheep several days before. It was sundown when we reached the ridge in front of the "licks," and we dismounted and quietly crept to the top. Three hundred yards distant was a band of eleven elk standing around the lick. It was too dark to see the antlers, but we were satisfied several of the larger ones were bulls, and singling out our targets we fired. At the first round they rushed up the mountain which was very steep. This gave us an advantage, although we were firing a distance of over three hundred yards. We continued firing until each of us succeeded in killing an elk – Mr. Brown bringing down a fine bull. We dressed them and returned to camp, arriving at 11:30, where we prepared a meal from the fat of the land.

In the morning we decided that the swelling was out of our necks, broke camp and started for home. We reached the railroad on the 16th and sent eight pack animals and two packers back to camp to bring out the balance of our game. Reached home on the 17th ready for business and feeling that we have a new lease on life which could not be had only through an elk hunt in the Rocky Mountains.

Dall DeWeese
Canon City, Colorado 🦌

Photo from B&C Archives

Non-Typical American Elk, Scoring 444-4/8 Points,
Taken by Ronald N. Franklin in Coconino County, Arizona,
in 2003.

Cat and Mouse

By Ronald N. Franklin

25th Big Game Awards Program

I HAD JUST RECEIVED THE NEWS I HAD BEEN DRAWN FOR ONE OF THE TOUGHEST UNITS TO GET A TAG IN THE ARIZONA DRAW. I CALLED EVERYONE I KNEW TO PASS ON MY GOOD FORTUNE. EVERYONE WAS SO EXCITED AND READY TO HELP ON THE HUNT. THEN THE SLEEPLESS NIGHTS STARTED, DREAMING OF BIG BULLS SCREAMING AND RUTTING. A FEW WEEKS LATER, THOUGH, I FOUND OUT THAT I HAD DRAWN MY SECOND CHOICE AND NOT THE UNIT I ORIGINALLY THOUGHT.

I started scouting, going every weekend and any chance I had some time to slip up to my unit. My brother Charlie, who also had a tag, was getting information from co-workers since he worked in the area we would be hunting. That information really came back to pay off in the long run.

No really big bulls materialized during my scouting, but as the season approached they started to rut. Some really nice bulls started to show, and I could tell from the antler growth on even the young bulls that this was going to be a great year to have a tag.

The season started uneventfully. We saw nice bulls everyday, just nothing I thought was worth taking so early in the season. It's amazing how each year it seems the elk change. One year it's all about bugling for a response, the next year it seems that a cow call was the ticket, but this year it definitely was the cow call I had. That call seemed to be the only one to get a positive response without sending the elk out of the country.

About a week into the hunt, things got really interesting. My buddy, Travis Mast, was supposed to join us, but got held up at work for a couple of days. I was excited because the last time we hunted together we had an opportunity at a huge 375-class 6x7 bull. That year my shot didn't connect. Since I was hunting alone for a few days, I tried an area that Charlie and I had heard about. Supposedly, a really big bull had been shot at and missed earlier. I ran into another hunter who had heard of this bull, but said he hadn't seen it. He seemed to say it with a gleam in his eye. Ha! I thought to myself that he wasn't giving it to me straight. The bull had to be around. The stage was set to find the bull of a lifetime.

That night, Travis showed up around 3:30 a.m. after driving all night to get there. When my lantern kicked on at 4 a.m., he said he might skip the morning hunt and get some rest. Then he jumped up and said he didn't want to miss anything. Driving out, I told Travis about the encounter with the other hunter. I also told him that I knew this big bull was still around.

What unfolded over the next several hours took teamwork. We arrived at our area of choice about an hour before daylight. We sat in the predawn silence and heard only one faint bugle way off. We moved up the ridge, where I had patterned the elk and their crossing each morning. We decided to wait near a water hole until something stirred. As the dark turned gray, a bull sounded off a bugle in the distance. We both pointed about 90 degrees off from one another, so we split the difference and off we went!

As it started to get light, we heard the bull bugle several more times, which helped us to pin down the direction. We knew we had to get there before they started to feed off, so we ran to intercept it. Eventually, we stopped to catch our breath. Just then, Travis said, "Stop. Did you hear that?"

We crouched down just in time to let two satellite bulls walk right by us at a short distance. As we started to get closer we saw very fresh sign. This was getting really serious, really fast. Just then we caught movement. Another satellite bull walked within 15 yards of us. As we moved up, we saw a few cows and heard a big smash as two bulls were crashing and fighting. Then Travis whispered, "Oh, my gosh! It's huge! I'm counting 10 or 12 points!"

Just then another bull bugled behind us, which worked to our advantage. It brought the huge bull around to our side of the cows at 80 yards. The bull then started to rake some trees. Finally, I decided every time it put its head down to rake, I would move up. This cat and mouse game went fast when I finally realized I was within range.

Everything was perfect. The bull had its head down, and I drew and released. Time froze, everything stood still, and the bull just turned and looked the other way where the arrow had blown through and bounced into the trees behind it. The broadhead had done its job. It took like what seemed forever before anything happened. I had already removed another arrow from my quiver when the bull started to run. It was almost like a dream. The bull went 40 yards and then it was over.

Travis charged me and started hugging me as I just stood there in shock. It was like it was meant to be. I would like to thank all the people who made this hunt possible: Steve Sherwood of TNT Taxidermists who was a great help and went above and beyond; to my friends and brother who helped with the hunt and scouting; and most of all to my wife and son who understand my passion for hunting and allowed me to chase those dreams I had of a summer of big bulls screaming and rutting. 🦌

Photo from B&C Archives

Typical American Elk, Scoring 411-3/8 Points,
Taken by Chuck Adams in Rosebud County, Montana,
in 2000.

Montana Mega Bull

By Chuck Adams

25th Big Game Awards Program

THE HUGE ELK CAUGHT ME BY SURPRISE. I WAS HUNTING MULE DEER WITH MY GUIDE WHEN A BULL BUGLED 200 YARDS AWAY. I SAY "BUGLE," BUT THAT'S REALLY NOT THE WORD. "GROWL" WOULD BETTER DESCRIBE THE SOUND.

Seconds later, a line of cow elk streamed from the timber, fanned across a clearing, and dropped their heads to feed. I locked my binoculars to my eyes.

I'll never forget what happened next. A very large 6x6 galloped into view, scattering cows as it charged headlong through the herd. And right on its tail was the biggest, gnarliest bull elk my guide and I had ever seen.

There was a deer tag in my pocket, but I had bagged my Montana elk four days earlier. That bull was also a stunner, with massive 6x6 antlers. Incredibly, the bull in front of me dwarfed my 6x6 in every sort of way.

The monster had heavy, deeply arching beams and seven long points per side. The spread was impossibly wide, and every point was long. Even the seventh tines would easily measure a foot. The third points (normally shortest on an elk) looked to be 17 or 18 inches long. Brow tines stretched forward beyond the nose, a sure sign of exceptional length. Main beams dropped downward over the bull's rump, making the huge "whale tail" back forks look even bigger.

We watched that elk until nightfall, and during those two final hours, I inspected the bull from every possible angle. I carefully compared it with the elk I'd already taken, and reached an astonishing conclusion. With main beams pushing 60 inches, an inside spread at least 50 inches, and long points all around, I decided this elk would score at least 50 inches more than mine! That meant we were looking at a bull that would score well over 400 points!

I shot a decent mule deer a few days later, and headed home with the image of that huge elk permanently burned in my brain. I told a few friends about it, and thought about that bull every day and every night for the next 11-1/2 months.

September 14, 2000, found me hiking the same drainage where the giant bull had been the year before. My trusty guide, a good friend of mine, was across the canyon glassing and listening for the bull. My pal prefers not be mentioned by name because he's afraid people will zero in on his elk hot spots. I don't blame him a bit.

I knew from past experience that mature elk often rut in the same place year after year. "Please, God," I thought. "Let that theory be true!"

I felt my neck hairs prickle as a familiar, single-note bugle rolled down the draw. The gravel-voiced monarch was back, less than half a mile from where we'd seen it in 1999. There was no mistaking the sound.

Half an hour later, I caught the herd as they crossed the last opening below a dog-hair-thick bedding hillside. Weather was beastly hot — already 80 degrees — and animals were racing for shade.

My view was not a good one, but I instantly recognized the bull as it trudged between two trees. It looked a bit smaller than I remembered. It had the same wide and downward-curving beams, and the same very long points, but only six tines on the right and a shorter seventh on the left. Yet, it was still a huge elk.

I believe it's always a mistake to pressure elk in their bedding areas. If you do, you risk running them off for good. We called it a morning, and went back to camp for lemonade and a snooze.

Elk move around a lot and don't bugle consistently when weather is warm. It was very warm in mid-September 2000. My guide and I heard and saw nothing that evening. We located only ten cows and one small bull the following day. The country was steep, remote, and densely overgrown — just the place for a giant herd bull to feed and breed silently without being detected.

I was certain the bull was still nearby. I could feel it in my bones.

Pale pink arrows shot upward across the sky as we hiked uphill at dawn on the third morning. Hot yellow light soon oozed over the mountains, followed by a blazing sun. I could barely see to shoot, and it was already 75 degrees!

We split to look and listen from opposite ridgelines. A cow elk popped into view 300 yards ahead followed by another and another. Soon more than 30 cows and calves were feeding in front of me, slipping in and out of the trees like ghosts.

I saw only one antler at first, but I recognized the rack as the animal came into view. The colossal bull crossed an opening and nudged a cow with its rack. Its left seven-point side flashed clearly before the bull disappeared, showing the dramatic down-sweep of the beam.

My heart was doing handsprings as I trotted crosswind and closed in on the herd. I knew my guide had seen them too and would be close behind. We'd hunted together like a well-oiled machine. As always, I'd hunt and he'd hang back to watch.

The elk were moving rapidly toward the same hillside where they'd vanished two days before. I veered away and loped uphill in a huge half-circle, well hidden by trees. With luck, I just might get a shot.

The big bull pushed its herd up a densely wooded draw. Cows chirped now and then, and the bull growled once. From past experience, I knew the ravine took a 45-degree bend half a mile ahead. I eased around a hill, chugged up a draw, and hooked back over the top at the most likely ambush point.

Good Lord! Elk were streaming past as I peeked above the ridge. A split-instant later, the giant bull appeared 50 yards below, strutting along the same trail as its cows. I grabbed my range finder, swung the reticule on the nearest elk, and punched the distance button — 39 yards.

I ducked down, drew the bow, and eased back up to shoot. I had to crouch, twist, and lean to clear a low-growing branch.

The bull came broadside, and I let go a single cow chirp with the diaphragm call I always clench in my teeth during an elk stalk. The monster stopped and whipped its head to stare. My 40-yard pin found its heart. Thirty minutes later I wrapped both hands around the biggest elk antlers I had ever seen. The animal had gone less than 75 yards before dropping.

The giant 6x7 rack spread 60 inches, weighed 39-1/2 pounds, and scored 411-3/8 official B&C points, making it one of the largest typical American elk ever measured by that fine organization. My bull was also declared a new Pope and Young Club's World's Record. In 2001, I was presented the Ishi Award, Pope and Young Club's top honor and only the 14th given in the Club's 40-year history, for taking this extraordinary elk. This bull stands as the second largest typical elk taken by bow or gun in Montana. Taking this elk is a high point in my bowhunting life. 🏹

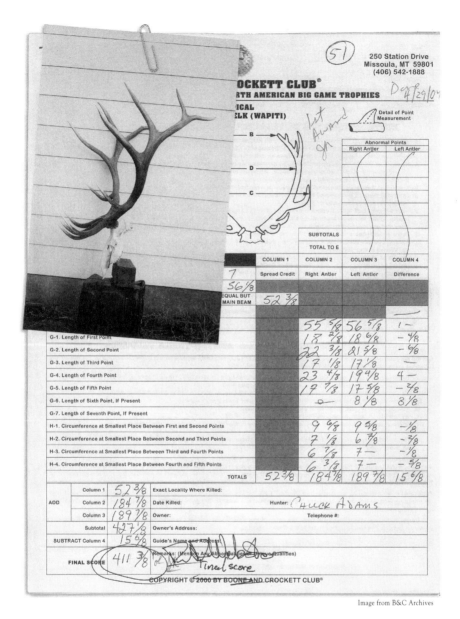

250 Station Drive
Missoula, MT 59801
(406) 542-1888

(51)

OCKETT CLUB®
RTH AMERICAN BIG GAME TROPHIES   D 4/29/04

ICAL
ELK (WAPITI)

1st
Award
9th

Detail of Point
Measurement

	Abnormal Points	
	Right Antler	Left Antler

	SUBTOTALS			
	TOTAL TO E			
	COLUMN 1	COLUMN 2	COLUMN 3	COLUMN 4
	Spread Credit	Right Antler	Left Antler	Difference
7				
56 1/8				
EQUAL BUT MAIN BEAM	52 3/8			
		55 5/8	56 5/8	1 —
G-1. Length of First Point		18 2/8	18 6/8	– 4/8
G-2. Length of Second Point		22 3/8	21 5/8	– 6/8
G-3. Length of Third Point		17 1/8	17 1/8	—
G-4. Length of Fourth Point		23 4/8	19 4/8	4 —
G-5. Length of Fifth Point		19 7/8	17 5/8	– 2/8
G-6. Length of Sixth Point, If Present		0	8 1/8	8 1/8
G-7. Length of Seventh Point, If Present				
H-1. Circumference at Smallest Place Between First and Second Points		9 4/8	9 5/8	– 1/8
H-2. Circumference at Smallest Place Between Second and Third Points		7 1/8	6 7/8	– 3/8
H-3. Circumference at Smallest Place Between Third and Fourth Points		6 7/8	7 —	– 1/8
H-4. Circumference at Smallest Place Between Fourth and Fifth Points		6 3/8	7 —	– 5/8
TOTALS	52 3/8	184 4/8	189 7/8	15 6/8

ADD	Column 1	52 3/8	Exact Locality Where Killed:	
	Column 2	184 7/8	Date Killed:	Hunter: CHUCK ADAMS
	Column 3	189 7/8	Owner:	Telephone #:
	Subtotal	427 1/8	Owner's Address:	
SUBTRACT Column 4		15 6/8	Guide's Name and Address:	
FINAL SCORE		411 3/8	Remarks: (Mention Any Abnormalities or Unique Qualities)	

final score

COPYRIGHT © 2000 BY BOONE AND CROCKETT CLUB®

Image from B&C Archives

Original score chart for Chuck Adams' typical American elk, which scores 411–3/8 points.

Photo from B&C Archives

Roosevelt's Elk, Scoring 353-4/8 Points,
Taken by Kenneth R. Adamson in Washington County, Oregon,
in 1985 (pictured with his wife, Theresa).

Tearing Up the Brush

By Kenneth R. Adamson

19th Big Game Awards Program

There were a thousand thoughts zipping through my mind as I crouched in my makeshift blind, straining to hear a hint of sound that would let me know that I was not all alone here in the woods. Thoughts such as, did I blow it? Did the wind spook the bull? Should I just pack up and leave quietly and return tomorrow? Should I have tried stalking the noises I had heard? Will I hit a branch if I get a shot? Is this hunt going to be one of those that end up as a good story, but no meat?

I felt the bull was still in the vicinity, and I wanted to be ready if I got a shot. So, I checked the pulley wheels of my compound bow for obstructions, checked the sight pins, drew a couple of times, and checked to make sure my broadheads were tight and aligned. By this time, I was as ready as I was going to get. I figured the elk, if it was an elk, should be settled down enough after a half hour to forget the sound and/or scent that had spooked it.

My previous bowhunting for elk hadn't produced anything in the way of meat or antlers. The Oregon bow season had opened the last weekend in August, and I had hunted for a full week with family and friends. We saw elk, but didn't manage to bring home any antlers. Since then, I had managed to hunt four evenings, with the same results.

Most of my hunting is done on private land, owned by the timber company that employs me as a forest engineer. So, I do have the advantage of being in good elk hunting areas several times throughout the year. My best friend and hunting partner, David Showerman and I have been hunting together for about 15 years. We have taken several elk and deer, but we were still waiting for the "Big One." Unfortunately, he was not along on this hunt.

I had spent many hours practicing with my Golden Eagle Hunter on a bale of cardboard in the barn, and I felt competent to put the 2219 Gamegetter arrows where they would do the most good. The day before this hunt, I had set my Hunter up from the 75 pound pull I had been shooting to 85 pounds, for a little extra "oomph."

Saturday morning, September 7, 1985, I left home before daylight and spent a couple of hours bowhunting with no success. I had promised my wife and her brother that I would attend the grand opening of the building where her brother works. That took up most of the midday, but if I hurried, I could still get in a couple of hours of late afternoon bowhunting. I wasn't about to pass up that opportunity.

I had seen several herds of elk on a 300-acre tract of land owned by our timber company earlier in the season, so I figured this would be a good place for the evening hunt. My wife, Theresa, and two kids, Jeramy and Leslie, hopped in our four-wheel drive pickup, and we all headed for the hunting area 50 miles west of Portland.

We arrived at 5:00 p.m., which would still give me three hours of good bowhunting daylight during the best part of the day. The sky was cloudy and completely overcast, with the feeling of rain in the air. For this country, rain is a pretty common occurrence, and I knew my wool hunting clothes would keep me warm even in a downpour. Theresa agreed to pick me up along a logging road (about a mile away) in three hours, so I headed for the woods.

My favorite method for hunting elk with a bow is still-hunting and stalking, as the cover is too dense for good glassing. There is plenty of feed for the elk in the logged-over areas, so they seldom venture into the more open meadows and parks. I spent lots of time practicing my bugling, using a Jones diaphragm call and grunt tube. But with all the bowhunting competition in the area, the bulls are cagey and seldom answered a bugle any more. Over the past couple of years, several bulls have responded silently to my calling, catching me completely by surprise. To date, I had not bugled-up a good bull to get a shot, but that didn't stop me from being ready.

I hadn't gone far down an old skid trail, when I began to see lots of fresh elk tracks in the trail. It had rained the day before, so I knew the sign was fresh, and that elk were in the area. I try to stay on good trails when hunting, because it is much quieter and easier to move through dense vegetation. I had traveled about a half-mile during the first hour, and I was seeing more and more fresh sign, when I heard brush breaking in front of me. About the time I heard the racket in the brush, I spotted a huge track in the muddy trail that I was sure had been made by a large bull. The huge track and breaking brush combined to get my adrenaline pumping, and I had to force myself to slow down.

I eased forward and could definitely hear what I took to be elk, moving through the heavy brush ahead of me. The wind had been in my face since I left the truck; but, as luck would have it, it was now swirling around in several directions. I tried to move off the trail and circle to see what was making the noise, but I couldn't because the underbrush was just too thick to get through. The only route open was a direct approach, which I didn't particularly care for. The decision was taken from me when a stray breeze blew down the back of my neck and I heard branches and limbs breaking, as whatever was ahead of me moved off.

In my experience with Roosevelt's elk, I have found that if they get a whiff of human scent, they will move off but usually not leave the area. They do stay on the alert, and movement or more scent will put them in high gear. However, if the hunter backs off and lets things calm down, the elk can usually be approached again, with caution. I moved back 100 yards up the trail, where I decided to build a blind to hide from what I was hoping was a bull elk. I draped bracken ferns from alder limbs until I had an almost solid blind facing the direction where I had heard the brush breaking.

After half-an-hour of planning and checking equipment, the time had come to do something. I bugled and grunted to the best of my ability. Almost immediately a bull came running into the small clearing on the trail that I had just vacated. My blind was too good, as I couldn't see much of his antlers through the hanging ferns. But, I could tell by his body size that he was not a small bull. He looked around for a minute, and then crossed the trail and went back into the heavy brush and timber, where he proceeded to tear up the brush with his antlers. I waited through another 10 to 15 agonizing minutes of silence, trying to figure what he was up to. I bugled again, and glimpsed the bull as he moved cautiously through the trees and up a small ridge, where he again started tearing up the brush.

I was beginning to wonder if I shouldn't just pack it up and go home. I didn't seem to be gaining anything, and I was sure I had spooked the bull to the point where he would never come close enough for a shot. My blind was no longer in the right position, so I slowly moved up the trail until I could get around a small bend and out of sight. I bugled once more, and once more the bull started tearing up the brush quite a distance above where I crouched. A few minutes later, I heard a sound in the opposite direction and more brush breaking. The bull had circled around and seemed to be stalking me from the opposite direction.

I figured I had only about 20 minutes of good shooting light left, and I knew I had to do something to get things off dead-center. I found a limb and started thrashing it through the brush, at the same time squealing for all I was worth with the diaphragm and tube. The bull went berserk as he headed my way, tearing and thrashing the brush and limbs. He was about 75 yards away and coming steadily, so I eased out onto the trail and came to full draw. He was moving through the brush, looking around, while I was concentrating on all the things a bow hunter should do at this point of the game. I argued with myself as to whether I would try a shot through the brush. I figured if I couldn't get a good shot, then I wouldn't take any.

The bull took a couple more steps, stopped, and then moved into a small clearing at about 40 feet and stopped again. He turned his head slightly, and as he did, he took one more step forward with the front leg on my side, giving a perfect "behind the shoulder" angle. I put the 20-yard pin half-way up his chest, and about 10 inches behind the shoulder, then lowered it about four inches to allow for the short distance, and released. The bull jerked, and then trotted about 30 yards, where he stopped and stood looking at me. I remember wondering, as he stood there 40 yards away with the arrow embedded up to the orange vanes, why I hadn't shot completely through him as I had supposed I would at that range.

I don't know how long we stared at one another before I thought to myself, "Man, get another arrow into him if he's just going to stand there." I got another arrow on the string just as he turned and started off. I let go with a bugle, hoping to stop him for the shot; but all that did was scare him into an all-out run for heavy timber. He disappeared in a second, leaving me standing there with a sinking feeling, wondering if I had really hit him as well as I thought, or if I would have to track him all night or maybe lose him in the rain that was just starting to come down.

The light was fading fast when I got to the spot where I last saw him, but there was still enough light to see the quantities of blood that seemed to be everywhere. Another 20 yards and I could make out his huge form lying on the forest floor. What an elk! His body was so big that I really didn't take a full look at the antlers before heading back to the truck to tell my wife and kids and to get all the help I could to get him home.

We were able to get the truck to within 150 yards of the bull and take him out whole. He measured 12 feet and four inches from hind feet to nose and would have stood 5½ feet tall at the shoulders. The meat weighed 580 pounds, which would have put his live weight at somewhere in the neighborhood of 1,200 pounds. His massive rack was six by six, with a couple of little extra points, and a score of 353-4/8 points. 🦌

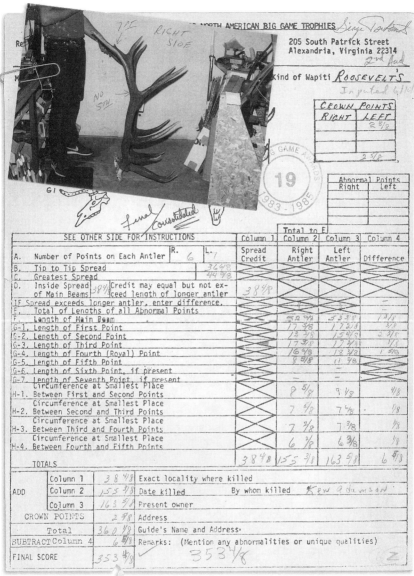

Original score chart for Ken Adamson's Roosevelt's elk, which scores 353-4/8 points.

Image from B&C Archives

Photo from B&C Archives

Non-typical Mule Deer, Scoring 265-1/8 Points,
Taken by Charles J. Hogeland in Hayes County, Nebraska,
in 1994.

A Hunting Tradition

By Charles J. Hogeland

23rd Big Game Awards Program

I AM ONLY A YOUNG MAN, BUT HUNTING IS A FAMILY TRADI-
TION THAT IS ALREADY DEAR TO MY HEART. I WENT ON
MY FIRST HUNTING TRIP WITH MY FATHER, MOTHER, AND
SIX-YEAR-OLD BROTHER WHEN I WAS THREE MONTHS OLD.
HUNTING IS BRED INTO ME, AS I COME FROM AT LEAST FIVE
GENERATIONS OF HUNTERS.

In 1994, I turned 16, which had its advantages. I now had
my driver's license and could go out driving to scout for deer on
my own. As a sophomore in high school, I participated in sports.
As soon as practice was over, I would head out into the surrounding country to scout for deer. I had received my hunting permit
for the Frenchman Unit of southwest Nebraska, so I knew that
I would be hunting deer that November. Many hours were spent
in the months preceding deer season looking through binoculars
and a spotting scope, glassing the countryside.

One particular evening will stay in my mind forever. It was just
prior to a huge red sunset. It had been very hot that day, and as the
sun dropped in the sky I caught a glimpse of a very large buck and
several does heading for a water hole. Through my spotting scope,
I realized that this deer was something special. I had never before

seen such a spectacular rack. I counted at least eight points on each side, and several smaller projections when the buck turned his head just right. I watched the deer until they walked down a draw and disappeared.

I was very excited and raced home to tell my parents. For awhile only Mom would believe that such a trophy could actually exist. Dad and grandpa had seen a large buck at the close of muzzleloader season the previous year, but I don't think Dad believed me about the size and the mass of this deer. Then one evening, a week or so later, my dad ran into the house with a big grin and exclaimed, "I saw him!" That meant he was real. However, my brother was still a nonbeliever.

Opening day was fast approaching, so we made our annual stops and phone calls to local landowners to get permission to hunt. Three days before the season, I had to attend the National FFA Convention in Kansas City. Several of us at the convention had licenses for deer, so it was my job to get the advisor to leave on Friday, early enough for us to get home. Our advisor was my dad, so I didn't have to work too hard to leave a few hours early.

Saturday, November 12, started out like a typical morning. We woke up early, got dressed, and had breakfast. The only thing different was that we were all more excited than usual, since we were loading the vehicles to go hunting. On this hunt, I was joined by my dad, who was our guide, my 62-year-old grandma, who was looking for any buck, and my brother, who was just going along, not really believing my story. As for me, I was only looking for "The Buck."

Finally, the time had come, and we were now off to find the monster buck. The weather that morning was overcast and chilly, with only a slight breeze blowing out of the south. We carefully checked each pocket in every draw we came to. As we approached each draw, tension mounted until the draw would prove empty. Occasionally, we would flush a few pheasants or have a covey of quail explode at our feet, momentarily stopping our hearts. At about 9 a.m., we saw a few does as we continued to check draws, but no bucks.

Dad was the first to spot a nice buck, but he was a long way out at 500 yards. Looking through the spotting scope we could see that he was at least a 6x7, with good width and some mass, but it wasn't my buck. Dad tried rattling the buck closer for grandma to shoot and got him to come within 150 yards, but it was still too far out for Gram. The buck did stop for a short time, looked toward the sound of the clanging antlers, then towards the two does he was leaving behind. This time the does won out, as the rut was in full swing. After the deer disappeared, my dad asked me if I would have shot that nice buck. I replied, "No, it is only the first day, and I am in no hurry. Besides, Grandma was in the best position for a good shot."

We moved to another set of draws and immediately started seeing more does. I also noticed that these deer appeared to be nervous. The next pocket produced the reason for the watchful deer. As we approached and were able to see more of the draw, I saw movement. My heart started pounding, only to see a woolly white coyote run over the hill. The time was now 11:30 a.m. and another two pockets were ruled out.

The next pocket started out the same. I didn't see anything at first. Then all of a sudden, I saw three deer. I quickly realized that one looked awfully big and awfully familiar. What probably took seconds seemed to take hours — like super slow-motion. I looked at the antlers and my mind went on autopilot. "Damn, it's him!" I said to myself. Range? 150 yards. I knew that my .270 was sighted in for 200 yards, so it was a dead-on hold. I felt this shot was a piece of cake, since I had taken hunter safety and practiced many hours for this shot. I flicked the safety off, took a deep breath, settled the crosshairs behind his front shoulder, and squeezed the trigger. I prayed that my shot would be accurate and the deer would not suffer. The majestic buck reared up on his back legs like a horse. I chambered another round as the deer came to the ground on all fours. He started to move, so I took aim and squeezed the trigger one final time. The big buck was down for good.

A new excitement now started as I approached the deer cautiously. My dad, brother, and grandma came up to me and my trophy; Dad let out a loud yell, and my brother shook his head and my hand at the same time. Grandma later said that by the time she reached the three of us, I was just sitting beside my buck stroking his soft coat and admiring his antlers. I guess I was in a state of shock, both happy and sad at the same time. I had great respect for that splendid animal.

Grandma had come prepared, pulling out her camera for some quick picture taking. By then, my smiles told it all. Dad asked if he could have the honor of field dressing my deer, and asked jokingly if I wanted this small thing mounted. Little did he know that I was shaking too much to handle the job myself.

We finally got the deer loaded, and headed first to the landowner's house to thank him and show him the buck that his land produced. He could not believe that a deer that size was taken a half mile from his house, and he had never seen it before.

We headed for home where mom and grandpa shared in the excitement as we relived the story. We then took the deer to the check-in station, where a few successful hunters congratulated me and admired the massive buck. On the way back home we had the buck weighed. My buck tipped the scales at 290 pounds, field dressed.

The following days were filled with many well wishes and handshakes. We estimated that close to 500 people stopped to see the buck the first week. Many people suggested we make sure to have the deer scored. I knew that the buck was an exceptional trophy, but little did I know how exceptional. A few days after the big hunt, Dad, Mom and I took my trophy to North Platte. Arrangements were made with Barry Johnson of Johnson's Taxidermy to do the mounting. He was impressed with the mass of the buck and suggested that we should make an appointment with George Nason. Mr. Nason is the District Manager of Programs Section with the Nebraska Game and Parks Commission and is an Official Measurer for Boone and Crockett Club.

On January 13, 1995, we watched patiently as Mr. Nason measured and re-measured the antlers. After what seemed like several hours, the totals were added. "It's official," Mr. Nason proclaimed. "Congratulations, Charlie, you are now the proud owner of the new Nebraska state record non-typical rifle mule deer. This head is the most perfect non-typical specimen I have ever seen," he continued.

From that moment on, the chain of events continued. My hunting idol, Ted Nugent, called and later mailed a letter to congratulate me on my deer. In August 1996, I had the pleasure of meeting him in person. Ted is a musician, an avid bowhunter, a strong supporter of family hunting, and an active member of numerous hunting organizations.

On April 30, 1995, my trophy was ready to be picked up from the taxidermist. Barry Johnson had a big surprise awaiting me. Art Thomsen, the previous record holder came to North Platte to meet me and see my deer. His state record had stood since 1960. We spent part of the day swapping hunting stories and getting to know each other. Before departing, Mr. Thomsen left me with these words, "Don't worry that your deer broke my record, records were made to be broken." 🦌

Photo from B&C Archives

Non-typical Mule Deer, Scoring 294-4/8 Points,
Taken by Robert H. Arledge in Elmore County, Idaho,
in 1997.

Ivory Tooth Buck

Written By Jerome E. Arledge

23rd Big Game Awards Program

My son, Robert Arledge, has been seriously hunting big bucks for four years. He routinely passes up several bucks per year, looking for a "big one." For one reason or another, three Boone and Crockett class bucks and one 37" four point had escaped all of our previous hunting efforts. Robert set a personal goal of harvesting a really big buck within four years, and 1997 was his fourth year. Another of his goals was to scout at least 30 days before this year's hunt. In 30 days of scouting, Robert had only located one good buck... but what a buck!

On the 29th day of scouting, we found a non-typical buck, which we were able to glass for an incredible seven hours. It was feeding with 12 smaller bucks and was twice the body size of his running mates. During these seven hours, he showed us something very interesting. The big boy changed beds four times and didn't move more than 75 yards all day. When any of the other bucks were changing beds or feeding, he would only feed or change positions when all of the other bucks were bedded... making sure that the other boys were maintaining a watchful eye.

On the last day of scouting, we didn't spot the non-typical, but felt confident he was still there, because we did see four of the other bucks that were with him.

After the opening day alarm and a quick breakfast, the decision was made to drive nine miles around to the top of the hunting area, in order to hunt down on the buck. We arrived on top an hour early, and to a strong, cold wind. As we began to see the brush and rocks in the dawning light, Robert led the trek downhill to find the exact draw where we had spotted the buck. As he cautiously peeked over the ridge, he saw three deer sneaking away from another hunter, down the mountain, right where the big buck should have been.

Robert remembers that he almost had a heart attack over his sudden bad luck, but composed himself by remembering we had heard no shots. He figured the buck would be using the escape route we watched him use before the season. Robert whispered back to me, "We've got to get into the next canyon, fast!"

We spotted a cow elk in the bottom of the next drainage, entering an aspen patch. Her mouth was open, and she obviously had been running hard, but was now walking, cautiously looking around. In a few seconds, the cow disappeared and our trotting resumed until Robert froze and turned back to me, pointing to a 15-foot-high cloud of dust lifting into the sunrise. Continuing another 25 feet, he immediately stopped and raised his rifle. He thought, "The heck with the non-typical, what about this huge typical." Quickly he realized that it was a four point bull elk running hard with another cow.

As Robert ran forward another 30 paces, I spotted a high racked, two point buck, with only one antler. I broke silence with a "Pssst!" Robert turned back to me, and I pointed to the bottom of the canyon and whispered, "Buck." He turned back on full alert, ran another 15 steps, and swung off his day pack looking for the sturdiest sagebrush. He threw his pack on a thick bush, took careful aim, and fired. I immediately grabbed my head with both hands, as in shock and thought, "Oh no... that was not the big buck." At the same time I saw movement above the aspen patch. I raised my binoculars and spotted two more bucks trotting to escape. The second buck stumbled, and I recognized the heavy webbing on the right antler. As the buck turned downhill toward the aspen cover, I saw the webbed left antler. It was then I realized that Robert had shot at the big buck after all.

Once in the cover, the two bucks stopped and stood broadside, looking in our direction. Robert fired two more shots. The buck then jumped out of the aspens, into the open, and stood broadside. Another shot rang out and the big buck went down. Even though he was down, we both thought he had the look of getting back up again. Robert reloaded, as I fed him cartridges out of his pack. As if on cue, the buck promptly stood up as I yelled, "You have to put him down again!" Another shot drew no reaction from the buck. The next shot put him down for good.

Robert fired a total of six times at a distance of 250 yards, and all of them were direct hits. Practicing shooting at gallon jugs filled with water at 300 and 400 yards all summer long had paid off handsomely! When I asked him about seeing the one-antlered buck, he commented that he had already spotted the other two bucks crossing in the shade, above the one-antlered buck. "Even after seeing his heavy horns and his huge body size compared to the other buck, I wasn't sure that he was our big non-typical. He had the big body size, and I was out of time. I had to take him now!" he continued.

The big boy also had an ivory tooth. We've only heard of two other bucks having ivory teeth and they were also non-typicals. The buck has 11 points on the left side, and 15 points on the right, with a main beam-like abnormal point near the base of the right antler and weighed an estimated 350 pounds. 🦌

Photo from B&C Archives

Non-typical Mule Deer, Scoring 264-1/8 Points,
Taken by Gilbert T. Adams, Jr., in Coconino County, Arizona,
in 1989 (from left to right: Kevin Harris, Adams, and Jeff Warren).

Kaibab North

By Gilbert T. Adams, Jr.

21st Big Game Awards Program

Fᴉʀsᴛ ᴛʜʀᴏᴜɢʜ ᴛʜᴇ ʙɪɴᴏᴄᴜʟᴀʀs, ᴛʜᴇɴ ᴀ sᴘᴏᴛᴛɪɴɢ sᴄᴏᴘᴇ. Yᴇs. Iᴛ ᴍᴜsᴛ ʙᴇ ʜɪᴍ — ᴛʜᴇ ᴍᴏɴsᴛᴇʀ ᴍᴜʟᴇ ᴅᴇᴇʀ ʙᴜᴄᴋ Jᴇꜰꜰ Wᴀʀʀᴇɴ ᴄᴀᴜɢʜᴛ ᴀ ɢʟɪᴍᴘsᴇ ᴏꜰ ᴛʜᴇ ᴇᴠᴇɴɪɴɢ ʙᴇꜰᴏʀᴇ.

When Kevin Harris and I came out of the mountains after dark, Jeff Warren met us at the designated rendezvous. Jeff was ecstatic. He said, "He's the biggest I've ever seen. It was almost dark, and he was moving. I don't know how many points. I didn't have time to count all of them. There are two huge drop tines coming off of each antler. There is a big bulb on the left drop. It's like dried velvet. He's in the mid-30s outside to outside."

For years Jeff, Kevin, Kim Bonnett, and I have hunted out of the same camp. We have hunted trophy mule deer throughout the West. Jeff was not exaggerating. It takes a heck of a mule deer to get Jeff that excited. In camp that night, Jeff dropped his head and said, as if talking to himself, "I've always wondered if I would see one that big on the hoof. Now I have." We knew it had to be one of the biggest mule deer bucks seen in Arizona' Kaibab for years.

After a hearty dinner, we carefully packed our daypacks. Intense planning and preparation for the next day's hunt kept the Coleman lanterns burning late in our tent. We reviewed the topographic maps as a precaution. We estimated it would take at least an hour to get to where we would need to be by the first light of day. We hoped we would be able to relocate the monster as he fed on sage before slipping into the dense pinion-juniper to bed for the day. We set the alarm for 4:15 a.m., but anticipation made our sleep restless.

The next morning, through binoculars, we strained our eyes, trying to push back the darkness. Gradually the sunbeams came over the Royal Arches of the Grand Canyon. It was another breathtaking daybreak, but this was not the time to watch the sunbeams light up the Vermilion Cliffs. Total concentration was needed to literally take apart each pinion and juniper.

Suddenly, there was a terrific-looking buck on the horizon. With increasing light, Kevin was able to use his 20x50 spotting scope. The heat waves had the giant rack dancing on the head of the distant buck. After a mere glimpse of the buck through the scope, Kevin said, "I believe that's him. It must be him. Let's go!"

Feeding on sagebrush, moving toward a dense sanctuary of pinion-juniper approximately one-quarter mile away, was our quarry. Was it possible to close the distance in time? The wind was in our faces. Fortunately, the rising sun was on our backs, because time did not allow a cautious stalk. Things were going according to plan so far.

Where was he? Had the gray ghost given us the slip? After all, they do not get big by being stupid. A draw and a ridge lay just ahead. Could he be in the draw? A two-pointer appeared. Had the giant buck in the scope been a mirage? We were about to head in a different direction when we heard the tinkling of rocks. Running out of the draw with their afterburners ablaze, heading for the top of the next ridge, were four does. In seconds, they disappeared into the pinion-juniper cover. Then, two bucks appeared, running in the same direction as the does. Was the buck with the six deer? Yes, there he was. Unmistakably, El Muy Grande.

The two bucks were running through the first trees of the cover. There were only seconds left; they were 200 yards away. There was no time to look through the binoculars to count points, measure a spread, or field-score the buck. It would be the shot of a lifetime. The moment of truth had come. Would I go home with a trophy or an alibi?

In moments like that, you draw on the refined hunting instincts you have developed through years of preparation and experience: the countless hunts for all sorts of game; the hours at the rifle range and at the computer with Bullet Simulator; the innumerable articles read; the fantasies and the physical training; and, of course, the many hunts when you came home with nothing, not because you did not see bucks, but because you did not find the buck that was a trophy in "your book."

I did not feel the recoil or hear the sound bursting from the muzzle of my Brent White Special .300 Weatherby Magnum, custom loaded to propel the 150-grain Hornady Spitzer at 3,315 feet per second. Through the 2.5-8x Leupold scope, I saw the mighty buck instantly untracked from a headlong run in the window-like opening between two junipers. Big bucks are famous for resurrecting from the dead. After watching through my rifle scope and waiting for what seemed like an eternity, I was certain that this buck was down for the count.

A total rush overcame us as we reached the side of the incredible monarch. At first, we stared and then reverently touched the magnificent horns. There were two huge drop tines and points everywhere. The rack was dark in color, like smoked metal. There were rough, gnarled bases and bladed tines. The left drop tine was covered in rawhide velvet. There was even rawhide velvet on the back side of one bladed tine that the buck had never been able to scrape off. It was immediately apparent that we were looking at a "book head." The moment had sanctity that words cannot adequately express. Kevin, Jeff, and I wanted to savor the moment for as long as possible. We knew that no matter how long we lived, no matter where we hunted, or how good we thought our skills were, there would not be another moment exactly like this one.

While the three of us reveled in the moment, we felt the presence of one whose physical absence was noteworthy. This person, a dear friend and hunting companion, was slowly recovering from a quirky, spontaneous tear in his lung, which had just weeks before brought him into the valley of death. That was the only reason he was not physically present. As we continued to study his rack, with its 14 points on the left, 15 on the right, and nearly 35 inches of outside spread, it seemed incredible that a buck could grow such magnificent antlers in a matter of six months. He would only have worn the regalia for another three months before returning it to nature. He was thin, without an ounce of fat. There was little hair on his knees or belly. It was obvious that he would have never made it through the winter. In 24 hours, he would weigh-in, field dressed, at 145 pounds. Later a careful examination of his molars would establish his age at 6-1/2 years.

Magnificent specimens such as this must always be carefully preserved and made available for general educational purposes, as well as for wildlife enthusiasts and admirers of mule deer to appreciate and study. With this object in mind, we were careful not to damage the hide or head while packing him out.

As soon as we could get to a phone, we placed a call to master taxidermist Ken Rowe, owner of The Arts of Wildlife studios in Phoenix, Arizona. He agreed to meet us at his shop. Ken's approach is that of a meticulous artisan. With detailed measurements, photographs and reference casting, Ken captured the qualities, features, and attitude that is unique to every animal. The result is a beautiful preservation for posterity to see and enjoy.

A significant part of the hunting experience is knowing the hunting grounds. What is called Kaibab North is isolated and remote country, above the Grand Canyon in north-central Arizona. After the Pleistocene, many life forms became isolated on the plateau when the Colorado River formed the Grand Canyon barrier on the south side, and an arid climate produced desert conditions on the other three sides. The Kaibab Plateau extends 60 miles, north and south and approximately 45 miles, east and west.

While most of us think of the area as mountainous, in reality, the area lives up to its Indian name, kaibab, or "mountain lying down." Flatness dominates the area, with numerous volcanic peaks and hills haphazardly sliced by eroded canyons and large winter-range valleys. All but 120 square miles are above 6,000 feet elevation. The highest point is 9,200 feet and the lowest is about 3,000 feet.

Before the state of Arizona began enforcing the law north of the Grand Canyon, this was an area where outlaws hid from the law and lay in ambush for anyone daring to follow them. There has never been a large settlement of either Indians or white men in Kaibab North.

Throughout the past century, there has been little change in the physical environment of the plateau, other than vegetative variations, due to drought, livestock, and deer population levels. There have, for instance, been no significant farms, orchards, dwellings or other obstructions to alter migration routes. Except for an occasional roadway or jeep trail, a person exploring Kaibab North will find it the way it was 100 years ago.

Even today, in an era of rapid transportation, the Kaibab is relatively isolated. A trip to the Kaibab North is a major undertaking for most hunters. However, more important than time is the requirement of winning the Arizona draw in order to obtain a hunt permit, the results of which are learned only weeks before the hunt begins.

There is a decided lack of available water in the area. If it were not for the man-made livestock and wildlife water catchments, much of the wildlife would not exist. Thus, biologists label Kaibab North as "fringe country" in regard to wildlife. Wildlife must be carefully surveyed on an annual basis; game and livestock populations, and their general health, must be evaluated along with the habitat.

North Kaibab is an area renowned for large bucks with many non-typical points. The habitat challenges, coupled with relatively sparse game populations, Arizona's restricted permit system, and dedicated management by the Arizona Fish and Game Department all combine to allow individual bucks to reach the maximum of their genetic potential. As a consequence, the Kaibab produces some of the largest racks on the North American continent.

There are two additional, significant factors that must have recognition. One is the proverbial hunter's luck. The other is the millions of hunters and wildlife conservationists, biologists, and public officials, all of whom help make moments like this possible today, and most importantly, to occur in the future. 🦌

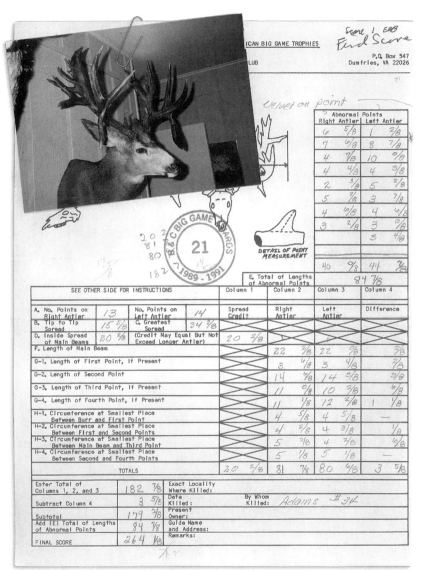

Image from B&C Archives

Original score chart for Gilbert Adams' non-typical mule deer, which scores 264-1/8 points.

Photo from B&C Archives

Typical Columbia Blacktail Deer, Scoring 182-2/8 Points,
Taken by Lester H. Miller in Lewis County, Washington,
in 1953. It is the Current World's Record.

The King

By Lester H. Miller

18th Big Game Awards Program

FROM THE VERY FIRST MOMENT THAT I SAW THIS BUCK, I KNEW I HAD TO HAVE HIM, NO MATTER THE COST IN TIME OR EFFORT.

He was standing at the back-end of an open hay field, near a patch of second-growth timber. His antlers glistened in the morning sun and he looked almost like an elk. I had been walking up an old railroad grade that was half obscured by willow and alder. It appeared that I might be able to get close enough for a clear shot at him, but that was not to be. I was carrying my Winchester, Model 94, .30-30 carbine, not capable of making clean kills at any great distance. My deer hunting had been limited to heavy brush shooting at ranges of 150 yards or less, and this big buck stood at least 300 yards away. I carefully moved to a small opening and peeked out. The buck either saw or heard me. He vanished into the second-growth in a flash.

For the greater part of every day of every legal hunting season in the years of 1950, 1951, and 1952, and until that all-important day in October 1953, I stalked, drove thickets, and took stands in the Upper Lincoln Creek Area of Lewis County, Washington.

On as many as a dozen different occasions during that period, we were able to see him in the vicinity of Lincoln Creek.

At Grange meetings, livestock auctions, and wherever people gathered in the nearby towns of Chehalis, Centralia, Fords Prairie, or Adna, it was not unusual to hear someone mention this majestic animal. Mostly, they would talk about his huge antlers, four points or bigger. Of course, the stories grew in the telling and soon he was almost a legend. Although I had twice jumped this deer out of his bed, and had seen him running down a runway on three or four different occasions, I still had never fired a shot at him, fearful that I might wound him and not make a clean kill.

And so it went. The sightings continued to be reported, with an occasional shot fired at the buck. He was seen often in the company of two other large bucks in late summer and early fall. He was seen in many different places (sometimes at the same time), from Doty Lookout to Adna, up Bunker Creek Road to Lincoln Creek. To hunt and to take this fine buck became an obsession with me. As the 1953 season approached, a gnawing kind of fear grew in me that a poacher might kill him or someone else would get him during the coming season.

I began to look for him on foot, cold-tracking him mostly, but many times hot on his trail. The purpose of this was for me to get familiar with his whereabouts and his habits, and hopefully to catch a glimpse of him and rid myself of a little of the "buck fever" I usually felt when I would see him. I covered a lot of ground during this period as I was not hampered by carrying a gun or being heavily dressed. This game came to an end two days before the general buck season opening in 1953. For the greater part of that day, I had been traveling along the creek bottoms and alder swamps, hoping to cut sign.

The day was rainy and the brush was wet. I was wearying of the game, when right in front of me in the muddy crossing, I saw the unmistakable tracks of several large deer and one smaller one.

My pace quickened as I began to follow the very fresh tracks. They led me up the side of a small hog-backed ridge, covered with thick hemlock. I worked my way through this wet brush and merged on the other side to look down into a large, open alder bottom. There, not 50 yards away, were two large bucks, one a fork-horn and one a very nice four-point. But the size and majesty of a third buck dwarfed the other two. Here was my prize buck! He was nuzzling the neck of a young doe, occasionally watching the other two deer as they sparred with each other.

As quietly as I could, I worked myself back into the heavy cover and made my way down to the creek bank where I sat down. I noticed that my hands were trembling, and they continued to do so for some time. Naturally, my mind was full of thoughts and plans for opening day of the buck season, 36 hours away.

My plan for the hunt was fairly simple. As I saw it, I would drive up the Forest Service road to a point where I could park. As soon as it was daylight, I would walk to the creek, which I felt certain would be an excellent place to start hunting. However, I reasoned that those deer could move some distance in any direction since sighting them two days before. Daylight found me parked on the road, preparing to enter the woods. My pack contained a hatchet, knife, whetstone, rope, first-aid kit, lunch, a water-proof tube of "kitchen" matches, a liver bag, and a handful of .30-30 shells.

Arriving at the crossing where I had picked up the tracks before, I discovered more tracks in the mud. They indicated that the deer had returned on their back-track to this creek bottom. It took me quite awhile to figure out the direction the deer had gone when they left the bottom. After several false starts, I finally found the right trail and proceeded to follow the tracks. The deer were obviously following a well established game trail to another locality.

Although it was raining once again so that any sounds I made were muted, it was difficult to travel this muddy runway without making considerable "sloshing" sounds. I had left the runway, walking on moss, grass, and rotting wood parallel to it, when I rounded a bend in the trail and found myself face-to-face with a huge four-point buck. He was no more than 25 feet from me! I don't know to this day what kept me from shooting that deer. He was a prize in any man's language. I guess instinctively I must have known that he wasn't the one. He whirled half-around and bounded 30 feet away to the creek, jumped it, and disappeared into the woods.

At the same time, a short way up the creek, I saw the ghostly figures of two other deer cross the creek and disappear. The relatively small clearing in which I was standing came to an abrupt end about 50 yards upstream. At that point, a fringe of sapling spruce made an almost solid wall. The runway went through this spruce thicket. As I moved up to peer through it, I saw the rump of a very large deer disappearing up the trail. I bent over and began to trot as best I could after the now running animal. My pursuit slowed, faltered, and came to a stop after a time, as I became winded and needed rest. I felt that unless the deer entered a clearing or an area of sparse timber, and stopped, I had lost him.

As I sat there, I could see a fairly high ridgetop over the alder trees and what appeared to be an opening on the side of the ridge. I got to my feet and began making my way toward that clearing. It was only about 150 yards through the bottom to the base of the ridge. When I arrived at the opening, I found that the clearing had been created by a massive debris torrent. Supersaturated dirt and debris had let go to slide down the ridge. In the middle of the clearing, 80 yards away, stood my buck! He was quartering away from me, looking downhill right at me. I raised my rifle and fired; the bullet struck him behind the shoulder. He went down in his tracks and never moved.

I have taken many elk in my lifetime. But, no animal has ever had the impact on me that this huge buck had when I looked down on him as he lay there on the side of that ridge.

The antlers were awesome to see with their spread, color, and symmetry. In addition, they were hanging heavy with moss and lichen that he had accumulated while feeding or "horning" the alders and willows along the creek.

I placed the game department seal on an antler and field-dressed him, putting the liver and heart in my liver bag. With my hatchet, I cut alder poles, turning the carcass belly-down on them to cool-out while protected from the rain.

With one last look at my magnificent buck, I hurried downstream to try and get help to get him out to the road. By my reckoning, the road was about three miles away.

Although this hunt began over 30 years ago, certain things are as clear now in my mind as they were then: the first time I saw him; the times he outsmarted me; and, of course, the day his luck ran out.

One of the things that keeps the hunt fresh in my mind is the never-ending stream of visitors that come to see and admire "The King," and the letters I have received from those who pursued him in vain. 🦌

Photo from B&C Archives

Typical Sitka Blacktail Deer, Scoring 125-7/8 Points,
Taken by Donald E. Thompson near Tenakee Inlet, Alaska,
in 1964.

The Fun is Over

By Donald E. Thompson

20th Big Game Awards Program

NOVEMBER IN SOUTHEAST ALASKA IS ORDINARILY A BLEAK MONTH. USUALLY, YOU CAN BE ASSURED THE WIND WILL HOWL. AS I WRITE THIS PIECE, I RECALL A BIT OF DOGGEREL THAT WAS PENNED LONG AGO THAT SUMS UP NOVEMBER PERFECTLY. IT SAYS, "FIRST IT RAINED, THEN IT BLEW, THEN IT FRIZ AND THEN IT SNEW."

The one redeeming feature of this month is the fact that the Sitka blacktail deer are in the peak of the annual rutting season. When they are about with amorous intent, the buck's behavior can border on the verge of stupidity.

The date was November 11, 1964, and I was employed by Island Logging Company of Sitka, Alaska. They were engaged in a massive clear-cutting operation involving acres of prime old-growth Sitka spruce and western hemlock in Tenakee Inlet, Alaska. They had a floating camp that was a compact affair, situated atop logs that were cabled together with support for a cook house, office, bunk house, and other buildings integral to the logging show needs.

I was employed as a back rigger, a very vital job. When I had completed the rigging, I often had several hours of free time to pursue my own interests. Much of this time was spent glassing the surrounding mountains for big game. Deer were abundant, and often the great coastal grizzly was spotted making his rounds. The area that I was hunting is located on a magnificent, scenic inlet that pierces the heart of Chichagof Island.

As I set out on the morning of the 11th, my chief concern was for the weather, as a brisk southeaster was whipping up the inlet. I was enroute by boat to an area that had always been generous in providing big bucks for the logger table. I fondly called the area "Valley of the Kings." Most logger-hunters were interested in the tasty steaks and tenderloins, and the antlers usually ended-up atop the gut piles, miles from camp. I have always remarked that you can barbecue, boil, bake, and make soup of these antlers, but I had never yet discovered the secret to making them a gourmet's delight. Consequently, many an antler ended-up supplying calcium to the mice.

In the incredible quiet that lies over a pristine wilderness, sound carries remarkably well in the still air. No sooner had I secured my boat in the lee of a sheltering point than I heard the sound of two bucks in battle. In my excitement I forgot what a miserable thing an Alaskan mountainside could be. As I tried to scurry upwards, I would often slide back two steps for every one I advanced. In my eagerness, it seemed hours before I came onto the scene of the conflict. There, the one level spot in the area was ripped and torn as the bucks had fought for the favors of the does.

The climb up the mountainside had taken its toll on me. At the time I was six foot one and weighed a solid 200 pounds. I had toiled over windfalls, plowed through thickets of the spiny devils club, and clung to the berry brush, to reach the battlefield. As I brushed the moisture from my streaming face, I wondered if it was all worth it.

As I surveyed the scene I was cradling my favorite firearm. It was an ancient center-fire Winchester, Model 1894, in .30 caliber, with an octagon barrel. Little chance of this piece running low on bullets; it held 10 rounds. In spite of the ever-present threat of bears, I had chosen the .30 caliber over a veritable arsenal in the bunkhouse. Those weapons included a .300 Magnum, a .308 Norma Magnum, a .338, and a .348 Winchester.

I had picked my favorite firearm that I fondly dubbed "Old Meat Getter". I have always had many uses for this old gun, as a walking stick, a paddle, and bringing home the bacon.

The sounds of combat had ceased, but I was nearly as excited as the combatants. Although I had killed countless deer in my long career, each hunt still contained the anxiety and anticipation of my first deer. As I paused for breath and peered intently up the wooded slope, I saw a blacktailed rump disappear behind a stand of spruce. Raising the old rifle to my shoulder, I waited. Just then a deer's muzzle poked tentatively from the cover. Like an anxious nimrod, I nearly squeezed off on a big doe. For a shaky second I mentally castigated myself for my tension and then settled back to watch.

As the doe cast coy glances behind her, the brush parted and the great stag with his massive rack gleaming in the pale light emerged. He appeared to be in a state resembling shell-shock. He was so intent on the doe that he was oblivious to anything but her.

I placed the sight on his swollen neck and squeezed the trigger. My brass was loaded with 190 grains of powder, and when the lead hit the buck's neck, he pitched forward and was dead when he struck the ground. Racing to my prize, I could scarcely believe the size of the animal lying before me.

The neck was enormous and the entire carcass gave off the sickening stench that only rutting bucks possess. I was quick to prepare the buck for field dressing. Alaskans say, "When you pull the trigger the fun is over." How true.

The massive animal emptied of his viscera was still more than I could hoist on my back and carry down the mountain. The only other way to transport the animal was to drag him by the antlers. Anyone familiar with the procedure of retrieving your prize from an Alaskan mountain knows that sooner or later (usually sooner), you will have problems. The very terrain is the enemy. With a giant body in tow down the steep grades, you will become entangled in brush and often the tow picks up speed and runs over you. After being run down several times with bruising consequences, I was able to fling myself sideways as the trophy once again plunged down at me. The deer went rocketing down the grade, unhindered, and when I caught up to it, it was piled up at the bottom of a deep draw.

By now being a weary hunter, I almost wished that buck was alive and well and back with his lady love. I was scratched, bruised, and sopping wet from my exertions. All for an old buck that I figured was so tough that you'd have a hard time sticking a fork in the gravy at dinner.

Now it was decision time. The options were to cut off the head and abandon it; butcher the animal and make several trips; or find another way. (You must remember daylight in Alaska's fall is brief and fleeting.) As I paused, a light flashed in my brain and I knew how the deer was going to remain intact (well not quite intact) as I reached down with my hunting knife and severed the lower jaw at the hinge. In some long ago jungle survival school when I was a Green Beret, I learned a trick that I had never before used, but now I put it to very good use.

Going in front of the huge beast, I put my foot on his nose and pressed the upper teeth firmly into the grade; then I grasped the antlers and leaned backwards and felt the animal move upward a few inches. It was working! Sometimes I gained a foot; at other times only inches, but the buck was moving upwards and out of the hole. Finally, a tremendous tug brought the buck over the top and I sank down atop the heavily haired carcass.

Few packs off the mountains of Chichagof are trouble-free, and the remainder of the trip was a continuation of the nightmare. Spiny brush, windfalls, brush, and muck underfoot made it interesting. The last 100 yards through the thinning timber to the beach seemed endless, and as I stumbled onto the graveled shore, I was numb with fatigue.

Even though I was at the skiff, there was still the problem of hoisting the big body on board. I wasn't a rigger for nothing. I gathered piles of rounded drift logs and, using a pole as a pry bar, I eased the head and shoulders aboard. Little by little, the rest of the deer finally settled onto the bottom of the boat. A world-class blacktail was headed for glory at last!

At the floating camp, I nosed the skiff up to the brow log and dumped the buck unceremoniously onto the deck. I then took a handsaw and removed the rack. I compared it to the buck I had taken earlier. I found that the earlier buck was larger, but it had an odd point protruding off the main beam that destroyed its symmetry, so I luckily decided to keep the prize of the day.

In 1965, I returned to the Juneau area and married. My new bride preferred the comforts of the Juneau-Douglas area, and I was soon enroute to camp to pick up my belongings and settle down to domestic bliss. Later, the rack was put on a plaque, but the years brought it close to disaster many times. As my house lacked a den, the rack had often brushed the garbage collection. Once when a teenage son was taking shop, it was in imminent danger of being converted into bone handles for hunting knives. But at long last, its true destiny has been found as a world-class trophy.

Photo from B&C Archives

Typical Whitetail Deer, Scoring 199-5/8 Points,
Taken by Don McGarvey near Edmonton, Alberta,
in 1991.

Deer Diary

By Don McGarvey

21st Big Game Awards Program

A s a lifelong resident of Edmonton, Alberta, I was aware of the trophy whitetail potential of the area surrounding my hometown, even prior to September 20, 1991. On that day, that trophy whitetail potential became trophy whitetail reality.

The area surrounding Edmonton, a city of 600,000 people, is a bowhunting-only zone and is comprised of farmland and woodlots. As a bowhunter for the past seven years, I was familiar with the area and had secured exclusive permission to hunt a certain parcel of land that I knew harbored a monster whitetail.

I had seen him twice during the 1990 season: once, in September, at 75 yards in a standing barley field; and another time in November, when I rattled him to within 12 yards. Unfortunately, the wily buck worked his way in behind the rattle to a position which afforded no shot. A brief change in wind direction allowed him to catch my scent, and he voiced his displeasure with my presence with an aggressive snort as he bolted away at top speed.

I have always bowhunted whitetails from treestands, usually placed at the edge of woodlots and along well-used transition routes between the bedding and feeding areas. My missed opportunity at 12 yards was the source of depression and frustration until the 1991 season began in September. Nothing was going to spoil another chance at the deer, or one of his brothers or cousins, which were undoubtedly in the area. I had seen many impressive whitetails in this area, but knew that I would have to play my cards right and be extremely lucky to harvest one of these tremendous bucks.

From the opening of the 1991 season, I had watched the whitetails intensely and used my detailed deer diary to determine which stand locations would afford the best opportunity of harvesting a nice trophy. Quite frankly, I had never expected to see the big buck again. No one deserves three sightings of such a magnificent animal, and I thought I had my last chance in November 1990.

With the use of the deer diary, I realized that the deer were favoring a route across a barley field and into an alfalfa field to feed. This forced the deer to cross through a narrow 15-yard opening in a treeline separating the two fields. The conditions would have to be perfect to avoid being detected, since I intended my treestand to face north, the direction from which the deer would be coming.

I waited for a steady northwest wind, and as I sat in my office on September 20, 1991, I realized that this could be the day. I was anxious at work and could not concentrate, so I left the office in the early afternoon, showered and went to speak with the landowner and solidify our relationship. After chatting briefly with the landowner, I made my way on foot to the stand location with small portable stand under my arm and a series of tree steps. I found a favorable tree, hastily put up the treestand, and left the area to allow the area to settle.

The north wind had a bone-chilling effect, and I silently cursed myself for not bringing my gloves. I had been in my stand for about 20 minutes when I had my first sighting — an impressive whitetail buck, approximately 100 yards to the north. The deer was almost directly in front of my stand. I had positioned it in the southeast corner of the barley field, along the opening in the tree line that ran from east to west. The buck was not the one I had seen the year before, but it was nevertheless an impressive buck. I hoped for an opportunity.

After two agonizing minutes, the deer came at a trot along the edge, toward my stand. He stopped only when he was within 15 yards of the stand. Unfortunately, the angle was all wrong. His vital organs were not properly exposed, and it would have been a risky shot. I decided to wait, especially due to the fact that the foliage was heavy, and I would have had to shoot through some leaves. I expected the deer to come directly in front of my stand through a patch of thistles and then through the tree line, but he had other ideas. He went into the brush to my right, through the tree line, and into the alfalfa field without offering me a shot.

Dejected, I turned to face northward, and the sight that awaited me was something I will never forget. A massive whitetail was working his way along the opposite edge of the barley field at approximately 200 yards. I entirely lost my composure. It is a wonder I did not drop my bow out of the tree, but somehow I managed to hang on. And thank God for safety belts! The time passed at an agonizing pace. As the buck worked eastward along the opposite edge, he came to the northeast corner of the barley field and then turned southward. He was on course to come along the same path as the previous deer.

Over the 15 minutes it took the deer to carefully and cautiously work his way toward my stand, I slowly gained a measure of control over myself. Concentration began to take over as the deer approached the corner of the field, coming within 15 yards of my stand. He stopped. He was looking intensely down the tree line toward the west, but I could not risk turning and looking to see what was attracting its attention. He must have stood there for a good three to four minutes before deciding to move. I silently prayed that he would come toward my stand and not evade me as the previous buck had done.

The measure of luck I had been dealt in seeing this deer three times was greater than I deserved. The deer began to walk slowly through the thistle patch. As he did so, the buck reached a point where I lost sight of him momentarily due to a heavily leaved, overhanging limb. I used that opportunity to carefully draw my bow. As the deer cleared the overhanging limb, my 10-yard pin sought its vital area. I released my arrow as the deer was 10 yards directly in front of me.

I cannot remember being excited at the time. Another opportunity at this deer had forced me to concentrate. Luckily, the last thing I saw, before the deer bolted northward into the barley field, was the yellow and green fletching of my arrow as it entered the deer behind the shoulder. The deer turned to the north and ran only 60 yards into the barley field before it stopped, turned, and went down.

Again, I was thankful for my safety belt; otherwise, I am sure I would have fallen out of the tree. As I had seen the deer expire, I couldn't wait the standard 20 to 30 minutes before going after the deer. I scrambled out of my treestand, raced out into the field, and admired my trophy.

I knew from the first time I saw the deer that it was an impressive animal. The magnitude of it all did not hit home until the next day, when I took it to Boone and Crockett and Pope and Young Official Measurer, Ryk Visscher. After green-scoring the buck, Ryk felt that it was quite possibly the Number 2 typical whitetail ever taken with a bow and in the top ten for Boone and Crockett.

The phrase "deer of a lifetime" is perhaps a cliché, but it is certainly an accurate description of this deer. I will continue hunting whitetails as long as I physically can, but having taken this deer, I can only look forward to the thrill and excitement of being outdoors in pursuit of one of the world's most beautiful animals. If I do not shoot another deer for the rest of my life, I will not be surprised. However, I will always have this deer to remind me of how lucky the average hunter can be in the great outdoors.

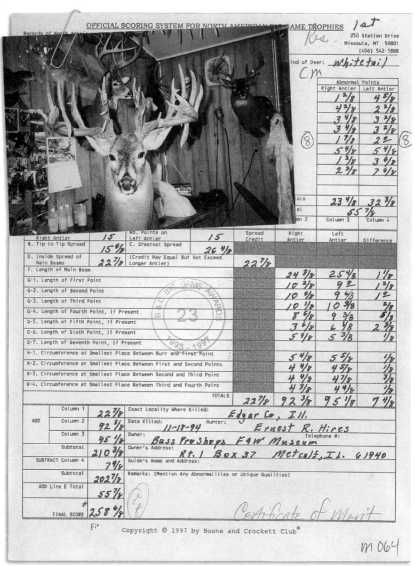

Records of North America

250 Station Drive
Missoula, MT 59801
(406) 542-1888

1st

Res.

Kind of Deer: _Whitetail_

CM

	Abnormal Points	
	Right Antler	Left Antler
	1 2/8	4 5/8
	4 3/8	2 3/8
	3 4/8	3 3/8
	3 4/8	3 2/8
	1 7/8	2 2/
	5 4/8	5 4/8
	1 2/8	3 6/8
	2 3/8	7 6/8

(8) (8)

Totals: 23 4/8 32 3/8

Total: 55 7/8

	Column 1		Column 2		Column 3	Column 4	
Right Antler	15	No. Points on Left Antler	15	Spread Credit	Right Antler	Left Antler	Difference
B. Tip to Tip Spread	15 6/8	C. Greatest Spread	26 4/8				
D. Inside Spread of Main Beams	22 7/8	(Credit May Equal But Not Exceed Longer Antler)	22 7/8				
F. Length of Main Beam					24 3/8	25 4/8	1 1/8
G-1. Length of First Point					10 2/8	9 2/	1 2/8
G-2. Length of Second Point					10 4/8	9 4/8	1 2/
G-3. Length of Third Point					10 1/8	10 3/8	2/8
G-4. Length of Fourth Point, If Present					8 6/8	9 3/8	5/8
G-5. Length of Fifth Point, If Present					3 6/8	6 4/8	2 6/8
G-6. Length of Sixth Point, If Present					5 4/8	5 3/8	1/8
G-7. Length of Seventh Point, If Present							
H-1. Circumference at Smallest Place Between Burr and First Point					5 4/8	5 5/8	1/8
H-2. Circumference at Smallest Place Between First and Second Points					4 4/8	4 5/8	1/8
H-3. Circumference at Smallest Place Between Second and Third Point					4 4/8	4 7/8	3/8
H-4. Circumference at Smallest Place Between Third and Fourth Point					4 3/8	4 4/8	1/8
			TOTALS	22 7/8	92 3/8	95 1/8	7 4/8

ADD	Column 1	22 7/8	Exact Locality Where Killed: Edgar Co., Ill.
	Column 2	92 3/8	Date Killed: 11-18-94 Hunter: Ernest R. Hires
	Column 3	95 1/8	Owner: Bass Pro Shops F&W Museum Telephone #:
	Subtotal	210 3/8	Owner's Address: Rt. 1 Box 37 Metcalf, IL. 61940
SUBTRACT	Column 4	7 4/8	Guide's Name and Address:
	Subtotal	202 1/8	Remarks: (Mention Any Abnormalities or Unique Qualities)
ADD Line E Total		55 7/8	
FINAL SCORE		258 6/8	Certificate of Merit

Fir

Copyright © 1997 by Boone and Crockett Club®

M 064

Image from B&C Archives

Non-Typical Whitetail Deer, Scoring 258-6/8 Points,
Taken by Ernest R. Hires in Edgar County, Illinois,
in 1994.

Lucky

Written By Les Davenport

23rd Big Game Awards Program

LADY LUCK OFTEN SEEMS FICKLE, BUT IN REALITY, SHE TENDS TO FAVOR THOSE WHO MOST DESERVE A SHOT OF GOOD FORTUNE. THIS TRUISM PROVES ITSELF REGULARLY IN THE WHITETAIL WORLD, WHERE HARD WORK RESULTS IN CONSISTENTLY GOOD RESULTS FOR CERTAIN HUNTERS. IF YOU NEED AN EXAMPLE, CONSIDER THIS THREE-YEAR EPISODE INVOLVING A PRACTICING TROPHY HUNTER FROM EDGAR COUNTY, ILLINOIS.

An antlered deer charged onto Route 1 during an early fall evening in 1992. Brakes locked, tires screeched and everything not affixed inside Ernie Hires' vehicle hit the floorboards. He barely avoided the whitetail, whose antler configuration was permanently etched in his memory. "Nice young buck," thought Ernie as he regained composure. "Thank God I didn't hit him." The buck had emerged from a 200-acre woodland where Ernie hunted.

The buck was spared a second time that year on opening day of the mid-November shotgun season. Ernie had been practicing trophy management over the past five years, and on that day, he elected to grant the young whitetail clemency at 10 yards. The suspected two-and-a-half year old needed more mass to be a true trophy in Ernie's eyes.

"That buck I almost hit on Route 1 escaped death a second time," Ernie reported to his wife, Kim, that evening. "He's a 9-pointer, and I've named him 'Lucky.'"

Lucky didn't seem to live up to his name the next day though, as he took a slug in the shoulder by an unidentified hunter. Ernie helped the man follow the blood trail, but the young buck eluded his pursuers. He was not seen again during the remainder of the '92 season.

Twice in 1993, Ernie had Lucky just out of range in the ebbing light of archery hunts. He noticed the deer's rack carried slightly more mass and width. Even though the overall symmetry still seemed good, the antlers appeared somewhat "different" from those he had seen the prior year.

Lucky was growing more nocturnal. It was suspected that he bedded on a large block of undeveloped acreage during daylight hours. Ernie still-hunted the waist-high cover on opening day of the '93 firearms season, and as expected, Lucky bounded from the tall grass and crossed Route 1. The big whitetail trod through a homeowner's front yard and into a small protected thicket. A running shot was possible, but Ernie, a respectful sportsman, refused the offering for fear of wounding the buck.

Ernie figured that if Lucky was pressured and crossed Route 1 again during the second slug season two weeks later, possibly he could be caught in transit. He repositioned his treestand in preparation for such an occurrence. Two hunters from another party foiled the scheme, however, by pushing Lucky in the opposite direction. One of the hunters fired a chancy shot and hit the buck.

Again Ernie assisted in following the blood trail, and Lucky stopped a second slug in a hind leg during that stalk. The seemingly invincible buck still refused to go down. Lucky was injured, but not mortally, and was seen later.

By legal quitting time that day, everyone but Ernie had long since given up the chase. The hunter unloaded his gun and stepped across a fence to head homeward - at which time Lucky popped out of a grass patch only 15 feet away and trotted out of sight! "Lucky was sure the perfect name for that darned deer," Ernie thought.

Ernie caught a glimpse of his quarry in late December, and the buck appeared to be in good health. Cleft hoof prints were found on Lucky's usual trails; apparently they were the result of the wounding incident. It surprised Ernie that Lucky had not permanently relocated to a less-pressured property.

The hoof print showed up again during Ernie's 1994 mushroom hunt. Lucky's rodent-chewed, left-side shed antler also was found by the hunter that spring. Harvesting this tough whitetail became even more of a priority, as he was now clearly a trophy-class buck.

The early part of the 1994 bow season turned out warm and uneventful. Ernie saw Lucky twice before the rut: once at sunrise, and once at sunset. His rack had grown considerable mass, with one drop tine off the left beam. Overall, the antlers had an odd look that couldn't be explained without closer inspection.

Ernie and his new hunting partner, Russ Lewsader, plotted their hunt for opening day of the firearm season. They'd perch in treestands; 100 yards apart, on opposite hillsides, overlooking a small creek. The adjacent ground had been mowed, eliminating one of Lucky's core bedding areas. Odds were fair that resident deer would now elude hunters by hanging in the rough creek bottom. Ernie and Russ hoped they each could fill either sex and antlerless permits by hunting this area from treestands.

They climbed aboard their stands shortly after 5 a.m. on opening day of gun season. It was a bluebird morning. Ernie hoped Lucky would show before another mature buck could tempt his trigger finger.

Deer began funneling back into the oak woods from fields about an hour after daybreak. Several does and three bucks meandered past Ernie at 8:15 a.m. Some of the deer walked across the creek toward Russ.

A doe and twin fawns rushed by Ernie, following the crack of Russ' slug gun. It had been decided that only a wounding would cause either hunter to leave his stand and request the other's help. There was no sign of Russ by 9 a.m., reasonably assuring Ernie that his friend had made a clean kill.

The doe and twins eventually bedded in knee-high grass about 75 yards away from Ernie, who watched them for an hour. Suddenly all three deer rose in unison and bounded for thicker cover. Something had spooked them. Ernie's attention focused beyond where the deer had been holding.

A doe and a wide-antlered buck were approaching at full speed. The doe veered, but her beau jumped a fence and came headlong toward the hunter, stopping behind a tree at 35 yards. The buck's rack carried a drop tine! Could it be Lucky?

The wary whitetail winded the air and peered from side to side for looming danger; his huge antlers swiveled like scanning radar. Ernie's Remington 20-gauge Wingmaster spoke once as the buck stepped into full view, but there was no apparent reaction from the buck, so the hunter fired twice more at the now fleeing trophy.

The final shot upended him. Innumerable tines buried themselves deep in the mud. It was an incredible sight to behold, Ernie remembers.

Russ knew something big had gone down when he heard his partner let out a holler and whistle. Soon afterward, the two friends met near the creek and congratulated each other. Russ had filled an anterless permit, and Ernie's dream had come true. They recapped the morning on the way to visit the elusive Route

1 buck's final resting place. Lucky was lucky no more!

Lucky's eye guards are his antler's most eye-catching antler features. The right and left G-1s measure 10-2/8 and 9 inches, respectively, and sport eight matching sticker points, tallying more than 25 inches total. Jetting straight forward like saw teeth, the G-1 stickers give Lucky a unique appearance.

It is likely that leg wounds on opposing sides caused the balanced growth of abnormal points on this strange rack. Why the typical frame grew symmetrically, unaffected by the injuries, remains a whitetail mystery. We can only wonder what Lucky's typical rack would have gained in inches had he not been wounded earlier in life. Could Lucky have been a World's Record typical in the making?

Photo from B&C Archives

Typical Coues' Whitetail Deer, Scoring 126-1/8 Points,
Taken by Robert G. McDonald in Pima County, Arizona,
in 1986.

End of an Era

By Robert G. McDonald

20th Big Game Awards Program

WANT TO KILL A RECORD COUES' DEER? BUCKLE ON YOUR BACKPACK, LIGHTEN YOUR RIFLE, AND HUNT THE WILDERNESS OF ARIZONA'S MOUNTAINS FOR 20 YEARS. I DID! IT WASN'T EASY, AND THERE WERE TIMES WHEN I WANTED TO GIVE UP, BUT THE REWARDS WERE MANY, MANY MORE THAN I ENVISIONED IN THE BEGINNING. LET ME BEGIN THIS STORY AT THE START OF MY LAST HUNT.

My muscles tensed, then recoiled upwards, propelling me to a standing position with the pack. The first steps were a bit awkward, then my strides began to flow rhythmically toward the mountain. I looked up, and it seemed to lie there, tantalizingly hiding my quarry in jumbled topography. "The climb will be tougher this year," I thought, "with food for 17 days in the pack. How many hunts have I made for these Coues' deer? It has to be close to 20. This is my 17th consecutive hunt since I killed the big mule deer in 1969, and I hunted them three other years, so this is the 20th one."

"Rrrrip," a catclaw grabs a thread from my wool pants. "Too bad I can't wear blue jeans," I thought, "but if it rains or snows, jeans are wet and cold compared to wool. And, it probably will rain; look at the clouds scudding across the desert to the southwest."

I pick up the fallen sprout of a flowering yucca and use it as a walking staff. Later, it will double as a support for my binoculars, so I can glass while standing. Now the mountain steepens, so that each step is labored. "Don't think about how far it is, just keep trudging up the mountain; it seems quicker that way," I tell myself.

Now, I am above the cholla and catclaw. But, I can never make the climb without a stab in the calf from a shindagger.

At the first live oak, I am heartened because I remember that the ridge is less steep, and it is not far to the campsite. As I set up camp, the clouds pile up against the mountain above and a drizzle begins. Hurriedly, I tie off the fly so I have shelter in front of the tent to cook and eat.

It rained all night and was still coming down in the morning. The canyons roar with runoff, and I'm glad the season doesn't open for five days. That will give me time to wait out the storm and then scout for my elusive buck. The tent hasn't leaked a drop, and it is warm and cozy inside. I put down the book I am reading and I begin thinking of my first hunt for Arizona whitetail.

I met my brother Fred in Springerville, Arizona. It took us an hour, driving south on the Coronado Trail, to get to the Rim road. We turned and bumped down that road for two miles to its end. From there, only a trail tracked the Rim for eight miles west to Rose Spring. And that is what fascinated us about the area, no roads. Neither of us had made a backpack hunt before and we were excited with senses of discovery and exploration. Three miles down the trail (and down 600 feet elevation to 8,500 feet), pine, fir, and aspen forested the top of the Rim. On its steep southern face (a 2,000 foot drop, slightly less steep than bluff), Gambel and live oak, juniper, and mountain mahogany were thick. During our three-day hunt, we saw does and bucks, a cougar, and elk, but not another hunter. We were disappointed after missing shots, but the experience was so satisfying that I knew wilderness hunting would become a way of life for me.

Two years later, I shot my first Coues' buck on the Rim. It was a mature buck, and for the moment, I was satisfied. While packing out, however, I thought, "Can I find a really big buck? One that will make the Boone and Crockett records book? Possibly, if I persist and don't shoot the little ones." Those thoughts spawned a change in my hunting ethic that led me down a difficult, yet rewarding, trail for the next 20 years.

I continued to hunt the Rim for several years. Every hunt there turned up a good buck, but I never saw one that met my standards. Then, I turned my focus to the mountains of southeastern Arizona. I scrutinized maps and records books. My Tucson hunting friends (and venerable Coues' deer hunters), John Doyle, and Jim Levy gave me advice. After digesting it all, mountain ranges with names of Indian and Spanish origin (like Chiricahua, Santa Catalina, San Cayetano, and Tumacacori, to name a few) beckoned to me because of their roadless areas and frequent listings in Boone and Crockett Club's records books.

I hunted these territories, with my oldest son, Jon, sharing my campfires for three hunts. Then, he moved from my home, and I lengthened my hunts to a full week, later to two weeks and more. Then Cosine, my Labrador retriever, became my only hunting companion, as my other friends couldn't spend that much time.

With Cosine's company I hunted the southern ranges for five years without finding a record buck. But I can't say the hunts were unsuccessful; discovering the mountains and their wildlife was my reward. On my 15th hunt I finally saw what I now think was a buck well above B&C minimum. But, he was walking at a steady pace and I couldn't be sure of his score, so I didn't shoot. From my backpack camp, I hunted for another eight days, but I couldn't relocate him.

Now the rain has stopped. The silence abruptly halts my reminiscing and, after lunch, this hunt begins. Taking only the camera until opening day, a routine is developed. After a freeze-dried dinner, I pack a lunch; go to bed; leave camp before dawn; and make a different circle each day, returning at dark. Deer are seen, but the mountain successfully hides the big one.

Opening day arrives and I take the .223 Ruger single-shot rifle. (I know its limitations: running or long-range shots must not be taken. However, it is worth the handicaps because the 5-1/2 pound weight, helped by a lightened barrel, is hardly noticed in the pack.) My routine continues for an additional five days, then I decide to move camp to new territory. Although the distance is not far as the crow flies, a labyrinth of a canyon intervenes and the hike takes three hours.

That afternoon, with the sun waning on the western horizon, a thunderstorm building in the foothills suddenly blossoms to full strength. It is as if a curtain is pulled across the sky, and twilight engulfs the area. The distant lightning and choruses of thunder mesmerize me; then, my trance is broken by the tinkle of a rock rolling to my left.

Looking in that direction for a minute or two, I see only empty landscape. My focus wavers, then wanders to a mesquite-dotted slope below. Again to my left, with startling suddenness, a buck is there. He stepped from behind an oak less than 20 yards away. Mutual recognition is almost instantaneous. Like a tyro, I am pinned with my rifle lying on the rock beside me.

His rack looks awesome as he stands silhouetted against burnt red clouds; for the second time ever, a sure record-book deer is in front of me. Saying a few silent epithets about the hopelessness of my situation, I s-l-o-w-l-y move my hand toward the rifle. The deer snorts, runs, and is swallowed by the boiling black clouds as the storm moves in.

That evening, while lightning bolts dance across the desert to the south, I note in my diary that the big buck's inside spread was about 16 inches, exceptionally wide for a Coues' deer and very likely of records-book dimensions. I stare into the flickering campfire and recall the probable record rack I saw on my 15th hunt. I hope that I will be luckier this year and relocate this big buck.

The next day, I hunt in the direction the big buck went, but I see only two does and a small buck. Time is running out. Tomorrow will be the 13th day of the hunt, and only three days supply of food remains.

The eastern sky is colored with pink pastel, but Venus still flickers visibly in the western horizon when I leave camp the following morning. I sit down on a knob east of my camp and glass a small buck meandering down a gently sloping ridge. I watch him for a while, then look elsewhere. I sweep the binoculars back to the buck, and I am unnerved to see a huge buck a few yards below the small one. A doe is with the big one.

They are a half-mile away, so I set up my spotting scope. Adjusting the focus to sharp, I gasp. The big buck is the one that pinned me on the rock two days earlier. My blood pressure ratchets up several notches, but years of acquired patience soon settles me down to watch until they bed. Soon they do, the small buck about 25 yards up the ridge from the doe and big buck.

The canyon runs to the desert floor to my left, and it rises to its source to my right. The opposite side of the canyon is a jumble of terrace steps punctuated with granite chimneys marching up the ridge to where the deer are. I reject a direct approach; the deer will immediately see me. I rule out a couple of other possibilities and elect to go to my right, down the ridge of the knob until I am able to drop into the canyon, out of sight of the deer.

I walk down the canyon to a sharp bend (a pre-planned spot) and climb to a lip of a terrace. I can see the deer, but I am not within range for the .223. The only way to get closer is to crawl, so I shed my pack. Then, with rifle on my belly, I slither down a rocky swale on my butt. Soon I am low enough so that a chimney rock conceals me from the deer. I climb the rock and peer over its top.

The obscure outline of the big buck is seen through a mesquite bush. The small buck is in plain view, higher up the ridge, so I can't get any closer. But, at 120 yards, I am within range of my rifle. I decide to wait for the big guy to stand and give me a clear shot.

Maybe 30 minutes pass, then the little buck gets up and strolls over the ridge, out of my sight. "Now's my chance," I think, and I stealthily advance to another chimney. I peek over it and suffer mixed emotions. The big buck is in plain view at a distance of about 60 yards but he is facing directly away from me. I don't want to risk a shot into his rear or head, so once again I restrain myself and hope the deer will soon stand. Carefully, I ease into a sitting position. The wait begins.

Time interminable passes. The rocks I sit on gouge and torture my motionless figure while I anxiously watch the buck nod his great head. Then, with the suddenness of a flash of lightning, the buck is up and out of sight. My confidence plummets into despair. However, a flicker of hope returns when the doe walks up the ridge. Then she looks directly my way. Sensing danger, she snorts and stomps the ground, bringing the small buck to his feet.

Exercising powers of will unknown to me, I sit, hardly twitching an eyelash. Finally the doe relaxes and ambles back down the ridge. A shadowy movement from behind a leafless mesquite alerts me that the big buck is still here. I recall leaving my extra cartridges in the pack; this must be a one-shot kill. The buck steps into a clearing, and I squeeze the trigger. He staggers two or three steps, then goes down. One would expect me to give a big "whoopee," but I didn't. It was 2:40 p.m., more than five hours since I saw the deer, and I had been sitting on the rocks for two or three hours. I stand up, and it feels so good that I don't get very excited.

I walk over to the deer, and I am overcome with contradictory emotions of elation and remorse that perhaps only a hunter can have after making a kill. I look at his rack and it is bigger than I thought. I also look at his teeth and guess his age as between six and eight years, an old-timer.

Some two months later, I took the skull and cape to John Doyle, a master taxidermist, for mounting and measuring. The rack was scored at 128 for the entry measurement. As I told the story of the hunt to this long-time friend, it was also with mixed emotions. I thought of the pride of accomplishment, yet I sensed the end of an era.

For 20 years, I had annually looked forward to these exciting and spiritually rewarding hunts. Now my enthusiasm is diminished by the loss of two friends: Cosine died a year later and I have learned of the passing of John Doyle. But when I walk back over the wilderness, feel the warm desert breeze on my back and watch the sunset in the west, I think of the memories, wonderful memories, of Cosine and John Doyle, who now do their hunting in the great beyond; of the camaraderie of my son Jon; and of the immeasurable pleasure of my association with the wilderness and its wildlife. ❦

Photo from B&C Archives

Typical Coues' Whitetail Deer, Scoring 133 Points,
Taken by Michael E. Duperret in Pima County, Arizona,
in 1990.

A Memory To Be Kept Forever

By Michael E. Duperret

21st Big Game Awards Program

IT ALL BEGAN AND ENDED WITH BOB KRAMME. I HAD KNOWN BOB LONG BEFORE I EVER MET HIM. TO ME, HE WAS MUCH MORE THAN A HARDWORKING, GENTLE, RUGGEDLY INDEPENDENT COWBOY. SIMPLY MENTIONING HIS NAME EVOKED THOUGHTS OF OLD-FASHIONED ROUND-UPS AND MESQUITE CORRALS, WILD CANYONS AND LOST MINES, RUGGED HUNTS AND HUGE COUES' WHITETAIL BUCKS. I FELT I HAD ALWAYS KNOWN BOB KRAMME, FOR HE FILLED A PLACE IN MY HEART FOR THE REAL OLD-TIME COWBOY, THE PRODUCT OF AN ERA THAT HAD COME AND GONE, NEVER TO BE SEEN AGAIN.

In fact, I was thinking of Bob when I placed my Leitz 10x40 binoculars on the tripod that precious morning of November 17, 1990. I did not realize that a magnificent Coues' whitetail would soon enter my field of view, the buck of a lifetime, a buck that would have made Bob proud, if he had been alive to see it.

My hunting partner, Jeff Volk, who had introduced me to Bob Kramme only six years before, and I were on the eighth day of our nine-day November Coues' whitetail hunt in southeastern Arizona. We were physically and mentally exhausted, our feet were stone-bruised from the rugged canyons, and we had enough scratches from catclaw, cactus, and shindaggers to last a lifetime. We openly cursed the unseasonably warm weather, yet knew in our hearts that the hunting had been excellent despite it.

We had begun our hunt in a different hunting unit of southeastern Arizona. Friday night after work, Jeff and I had left Tucson for something we dream about all year long: our annual Coues' whitetail hunt. We drove into our hunting area, slipped on our backpacks, which contained provisions for a potential nine-day backpack hunt, and began our journey. A half-moon cast its silvery glow on the rugged maze of canyons as we silently passed through, guided by familiar nighttime landmarks. Thrilled about our upcoming hunt, the three-hour hike was quickly over, and we pitched our tent under the brilliantly starry Arizona sky. Anticipation hung heavily in the air, so sleep did not come easily.

The next morning found us high on a vantage point, glassing with our binoculars, as the flame-red glow of the rising sun cast hues of coral and buff on the deeply cut, jagged canyon walls all around us. The stunning sunrise illuminated the tan grassy slopes where we searched for the elusive Coues' deer, turning the slopes into golden, shimmering seas of desert grasses, accented only by an occasional stately yucca. Red-tailed hawks soared high above in the lavender-blue sky, hunting for rabbits and Gambel's quail, like those that noisily cackled from their roost below us. The quail were silenced only momentarily by the lonely howl of a solitary coyote who, like us, seemed moved by the stark beauty of the Sonoran desert at dawn. But the mysterious desert hid its secrets well that first morning; we saw only a few deer.

Four days of warmer weather followed, with surprisingly excellent hunting. We saw countless deer, glassing up as many as 60 in a single morning. We never saw another hunter, and each day we moved into wilder, more remote areas. The right buck for Jeff did not emerge from the manzanita thickets, grassy slopes, and cedar trees that we glassed. We saw some very nice bucks, but we were in no hurry to end our adventure with a shot from the .243.

On the fifth morning of our hunt, we glassed up a very large buck with an unusual, non-typical rack, watching him the entire morning from a strategic peak a mile away. That evening we made a long, difficult stalk, but darkness closed in before we could locate him in the thick brush. We had to bushwhack around a huge mountain to get back to camp, arriving two hours later, tired and dejected.

We located the same buck at dawn the next morning, and Jeff led me on a long, grueling stalk. We ran, climbed, and crashed through brush, making a huge loop that brought us to a high ridge above the buck. An hour later we arrived at the ridge, sweating, gasping for breath; we waited, hidden, intently glassing the cedar-choked ravines below us.

A tense half-hour passed. Then, out into the open fed the non-typical buck and his two smaller companions. Jeff easily made the 300-yard shot using an 85-grain, boat-tail handload from the .243.

The enjoyment of picture taking and well-deserved con-gratulations were followed by the meticulous work of fielddressing and boning the meat. By midmorning we were finished, and for the next 11 hours, we hiked out, finally arriving at the truck at 9:30 p.m., tired and sore. Midnight found us at the nearest town, icing down Jeff's deer and eating a very late dinner.

I held a permit for Coues' whitetail in a separate hunting unit, so we drove to my area late that night, slept for two hours, and made the long hike in. That first day in my hunting unit, we were tired but we hunted hard, happy to be in new country.

The following morning, the eighth day of our hunt, we were downright exhausted. We arrived at our vantage point late, and quickly set up our tripods to begin glassing. It was then that I began to think about Bob Kramme. I thought about Bob often when the going became tough, because life had always been difficult and challenging for him.

Fond memories of Bob wandered through my mind as I glassed the slopes below me: the respect and love he felt for his wife Romaine; the joy in his eyes when he reminisced about adventures with his son Kolin; the excitement of guiding big game hunts near Jackson Hole, Wyoming, many years ago; the pride he felt after a hard day's work at their ranch in the rugged Galiuro Mountains.

My memory of first meeting Bob at their ranch was nostalgic, yet vivid: his work-hardened frame sitting beside the old wood-burning stove; his sparkling eyes and warm, handsome smile; his tales of wild, remote places; his respect for the land and creatures that inhabit it.

I shivered beneath my warm jacket as I recalled the harsh drought that had begun in 1988. The Kramme's ranch was hit hard. The grass shriveled up and blew away like dust, stock tanks went bone-dry, and the Krammes had to sell off many of their cattle. All of this weighed very heavily on Bob. I could see the worried look on his wrinkled brow. On March 28, 1990, Bob died in his sleep. It was a huge loss and a shock to all of us. I felt shaken and hollow inside. One of the most special people I had ever met had died, and an era passed with him, an era never to be seen again. The world has seemed like a smaller place since.

After Bob's death the drought quickly ended. A few weeks later, while at the Kramme's ranch, we sat in the old stone house once again with the wood stove burning. Bob was not with us, and our hearts were heavy and sad. He had made a deep, lasting impression on all of us, and we talked for hours about him, as a huge rainstorm raged on outside. In our hearts, we each felt that somehow Bob was responsible for bringing back the rains.

The spring rains came and went, followed by the summer monsoons. I am not superstitious, but I found myself thinking that Bob was watching over the desert, somehow bringing back the life-giving rains. The desert responded quickly to the long-awaited water and, by the time our hunt came around that November, the desert seemed almost lush by Arizona standards. The rocky, boulder-strewn saddle I was watching on the eighth morning of our hunt showed no signs of the drought. Long desert grasses and succulent green cacti poked up through the rocks. The desert canyon looked as it always had. Then, something happened that would change it in my mind forever.

Into my field of view stalked a huge, lone buck, carefully sneaking down the saddle with his head held low to the ground, as if avoiding some danger. I barely had time to glance at his dark body and magnificent rack before he disappeared into a manzanita forest. He was gone before I had time to share him with Jeff, put up the spotting scope, or fully evaluate his extraordinary rack.

What I did notice in those few short seconds from half a mile away was that his rack was extremely large and wide. How large I did not know, but my feeling was that he was bigger than anything I had ever seen before. Jeff sensed my excitement. Something very special lay hidden in the manzanita below us.

For the next two hours, we studied the huge thicket. The buck never left, convincing us that he was bedded there. There were two possible strategies: sneak closer and wait for the buck to reveal himself; or attempt a drive using Jeff as the "bird dog" to flush the buck toward me.

The debate of a lifetime ensued, but eventually Jeff's logic won out; we would attempt to flush him out, because he had already been alarmed by a hunter or lion and, therefore, might never show himself again. The wind was in our favor and the terrain was perfect for a deer drive. There was only one natural escape route, and overlooking it was a large, rocky outcropping from which to shoot. The only potential problem was that we had never, in all our years of hunting Coues' whitetail, attempted a deer drive. We had long since learned that these super-intelligent deer had a logic that far surpassed ours.

Nevertheless, desperate chances and uncertain outcomes are the fiber of an exciting hunt, and win or lose, we were thrilled with the prospects. Jeff set out on a hidden, mile-long loop to get to the far side of the manzanita thicket, while I setup for the shot. I found a strategic, comfortable vantage point and placed a round into the chamber of the .243. I swung the bipod down, cleared some obstructing grass in front of me, and breathlessly waited.

After an eternity, Jeff topped out on the far ridge, half a mile away, and slowly descended toward the manzanita thicket which lay between us. I had hoped the buck would slink out of the thicket toward me, offering a walking or standing shot from 200 to 300 yards. No such luck.

As Jeff entered the far side of the thicket, the buck exploded from the opposite end, sprinting for the small canyon below me. He leaped over 5-foot high manzanitas, twisting and turning as he ran. I followed him with the scope, amazed. The only whitetails I had ever seen run so swiftly and desperately were two does being chased by a mountain lion.

I carefully led the buck and I squeezed off a shot. The sight-picture looked perfect as the report broke the tranquility of the huge canyon, but the buck ran even faster. Quickly, I reloaded the bolt action, carefully aimed, and fired again. The buck twisted just as I shot and the bullet puffed harmlessly where I had hoped he would be. The miss did not matter, though, because the first shot from the .243 had connected. The buck crashed into a ravine 200 yards below me, never to leave it.

Jeff arrived at the deer before I did and met me just below the ravine where the buck lay. A large smile crossed his tired face and he said, "Mike, no matter how big you thought your buck was, he's bigger than you imagined. Congratulations." He held out his hand.

When I saw the magnificent deer, I was stunned and unsure what to think. The buck was huge, and he had the most incredible rack I had ever seen on a Coues' deer. Jeff watched silently, as I carefully examined the beautiful deer. We both knew it would be one of the largest Coues' whitetail bucks ever taken. I glanced up toward the saddle above me and felt sad that he had only a couple hundred yards to go to reach safety.

Time seemed to stop until Jeff broke the silence of the warm November day. "I never told you this, but Kolin gave me Bob Kramme's old camo hunting jacket after he died," Jeff said slowly, his voice unsteady. "This is the eighth day of our nine-day hunt. I figured we needed a change of luck, so I wore Bob's jacket this morning. For the first time ever. I guess Bob was smiling on us today."

Then I knew what to think. A trophy is much more than a big rack. It is a memory to be kept forever. I suddenly realized that, when I looked at this trophy, I would always recall our adventurous hunt, the huge buck, but most of all Bob Kramme.

We dressed the deer, carefully keeping all of the meat, the great rack, and the hide for a shoulder mount and fly-tying. Then, we hiked out of the ruggedly beautiful canyon with Jeff in the lead, carrying the rack. I glanced frequently at the old, faded camo jacket he wore and the huge rack in his hand. The connection between Bob and the buck seemed to be no accident. We hiked slowly, quietly savoring the experience. As the sun set, we somehow knew that we were a part of something bigger than ourselves.

We were humbled to be a part of it. 🏹

Moose & Caribou

CANADA MOOSE

ALASKA-YUKON MOOSE

SHIRAS MOOSE

BARREN GROUND CARIBOU

*CENTRAL CANADA BARREN
GROUND CARIBOU*

Photo from B&C Archives

Canada Moose, Scoring 211 Points,
Taken by M. Nathan Sabo near Red Earth Creek, Alberta,
in 2000.

In the Land of Giants

By M. Nathan Sabo

24th Big Game Awards Program

"NATH," MY DAD'S VOICE CUT THE TENSION, "YOU BETTER PUT THE CAMERA DOWN AND GET READY TO SHOOT. YOU CAN VIDEO HIM ALL YOU WANT ONCE HE'S ON THE GROUND." MY FATHER WAS BEGINNING TO EXPRESS HIS CONCERN THAT THE BULL WOULD GET AWAY, WHEN BOOM, THE SHOT FROM MY RUGER .300 WINCHESTER ECHOED THROUGH THE WILDERNESS. AT THAT MOMENT THE FIRST FOUR DAYS OF THE HUNT DIDN'T MATTER ANYMORE.

Our annual moose hunting trip was planned for September 28, 2000. My hunting partners Lou Gajdos, Don Sabo, Fred Bullegas, my father Moses, and I planned to spend ten days calling moose in the area near Red Earth, Alberta. Due to unfortunate circumstances beyond our control, the trip was not starting out very well. With flat tires on the trailer and mechanical breakdowns with the ATVs, we were beginning to wonder why anyone would spend so much time and money to be so frustrated.

On the morning of October 3, we were finally ready to put in our first full day of hunting. We awoke to a frozen, windy morning. Our spirits were a little down because of the howling winds, but we were happy just to be able to finally hunt. Lou and Don wanted to spend the day at a lake where Don had shot a young bull the previous afternoon, while Fred, my dad, and I decided to try a lake about three hours south of camp.

We arrived at the lake by mid-afternoon and started to call. While I was calling, I noticed something black on the other side of the lake through a clearing and into the willows. I didn't know if it was a bull or a cow, but I knew its body was big. Between wind gusts and sardine sandwiches I continued calling when I faintly heard a grunt. I then noticed something that resembled a sheet of plywood on the far side of the lake. Through my 10x42 binoculars I realized that the sheet of plywood was actually the antlers of a massive bull looking over the willows in our direction. As I continued to call, the bull sauntered toward the ice-covered lake. With the strong crosswind blowing, I gave out another cow call and the bull was hooked. He stood on the shoreline and seemed to be debating which was the quickest route to the love-sick cow. The direction he chose was the closest, but a frozen creek about 40 feet wide lay in his path. Failing to find a way across the creek, he decided to try and cross on the ice. Putting his front legs on the ice, he broke through causing him to make a hasty retreat. I let out a grunt hoping to persuade him to try and cross again. This got the big bull's juices flowing, making him mad. He started thrashing his head from side to side and ended the life of the closest willow bush. He then forged back into the creek. Using his front legs he began to break through the ice. We watched in awe as he disappeared and reemerged with his legs coming up on the ice in front of him, busting his way through. About half way through the creek, our hearts sank as we watched the bull turn around and head back to the bank he came from. We were starting to doubt he would be able to cross at all. I figured I had nothing to lose, so I let out the loudest bull grunt I could possibly conjure up. Without hesitating, he turned around and plunged back into the ice-covered creek, sending an array of water and ice into the air. Occasionally we would catch a glimpse of his antlers as he lunged forward through the ice. It seemed like an eternity as we waited for him to appear on the other side. Finally, out of the creek he emerged, looking for stable ground as he stumbled from exhaustion. Finding his footing, the bull stood and shook his coat violently, ridding himself of the freezing water. I gave a cow call to set his bearings straight and get him moving.

We decided to cut the distance between us, so we quickly made our way to a position around the lake, which gave us the best view. After getting to within 340 yards of the beast, I decided to video this exciting event. It seemed like seconds later the wind shifted, putting our scent directly in line with the bull. That's when my dad gave me a friendly reminder to drop the camera and pick up my rifle. One shot dropped the massive bull in its tracks. We quickly grabbed our gear and made our way to where the fallen giant lay. We were shocked beyond belief to discover just how big this bull was. With palms measuring nearly 20 inches wide and a spread of over 63 inches, this boy surely was a king of his domain. 🦌

Photo from B&C Archives

Alaska-Yukon Moose, Scoring 249-3/8 Points,
Taken by John R. Johnson near Tikchik Lake, Alaska,
in 1995 (Johnson's son, Doug, shown here packing out the rack).

The Best Present

Written By Doug Johnson

23rd Big Game Awards Program

M Y DAD AND I BOARDED A PLANE IN PORTLAND, OREGON,
ON AUGUST 27, HEADED FOR DILLINGHAM, ALASKA.
THIS WAS THE BEGINNING OF A 10-DAY HUNTING TRIP FOR
MOOSE AND CARIBOU, IN THE WOOD-TIKCHIK STATE PARK.
I GRADUATED FROM EASTERN OREGON STATE COLLEGE IN
THE SPRING OF 1995. INSTEAD OF GIVING ME A GIFT WITH
ONLY MONETARY VALUE, MY DAD DECIDED TO GIVE ME A GIFT
THAT WOULD BE LOADED WITH MEMORIES. THIS GIFT WAS A
SELF-GUIDED HUNTING TRIP IN ALASKA. WE AGREED THAT I
WOULD HUNT FOR CARIBOU, AND HE WOULD HUNT FOR MOOSE.
THIS WOULD BE OUR FIRST, BUT NOT THE LAST, HUNTING TRIP
TO ALASKA.

In preparation for the trip, we had to buy a lot of reliable
gear. This gear included just about everything you could think
of that was waterproof, from the tent down to our apparel. Tom
Slago, our air taxi for this trip, told us to be prepared for rain,
and that we would need trustworthy equipment.

We arrived in Dillingham the evening of the 27th. The sun
was going to be up until 10 o'clock, so we were able to fly out to

camp that evening. Our air taxi was Bay Air, owned and operated by Mr. and Mrs. Tom Slago. Tom used his Beaver with floats to fly us in. After a short flight, he dropped us at a small lake, with only a number for a name. We set up our tent and did the other necessary things that needed done around camp. There was nothing but lichen, moss, little patches of alders, rolling hills, and caribou within sight of our tent. This looked to be the makings of a great hunt.

Moose season did not start until September 1, so I would be going after caribou first. After getting all the camp chores finished, we decided to go for a look around. We had walked only 100 yards when we ran into two young bears that bolted after catching our scent. This was the first time I had seen a grizzly bear, and after all the stories I heard and read, it was nice to see they headed in the other direction. After this encounter, we hiked up to one of the many rolling hills to get a better look at the surroundings. It was getting late in the evening, so there were a lot of caribou coming out of the brush. We saw close to a hundred caribou in a short amount of time, with many good bulls mixed in with cows. I could not shoot one until the next day because it is illegal to hunt game animals in Alaska on the same day you fly in.

We awoke the next morning to rainy and windy conditions, just right for caribou hunting. The wind blew away the pesky mosquitoes and gnats, allowing the caribou to stay out of the brush longer to feed. We left as the sun was coming up, and were only a couple hundred yards out of camp before we spotted the first band of caribou. There were a few bulls in the bunch, but nothing that impressed me. We continued hunting the rest of the morning, using our binoculars to find them, and a spotting scope to see if they were worth stalking. It was not until noon that I spotted the bull I wanted. There was only one problem; he was a mile away and standing on the other side of a brushy swamp.

We guessed where he was going, since caribou never seem to stop moving, and took off to intercept him.

When we dropped down into the swampy lake bottom, we quickly lost sight of the bull. It took us well over a half hour to cover one mile in the rough terrain, but we finally arrived at our destination. Dad and I could not locate the bull, so we started walking toward a little rise, thinking he had slipped behind it. We had taken no more than 10 steps, when he came crashing out of the brush, and through a creek, not 50 yards away. The bull came out on the far side of the creek bed, and made a fateful mistake by looking back. I shouldered my .300 Weatherby and sent a 180-grain bullet into his right shoulder. The hunt was over and the work began. There was not a tree to be found for miles to hang the meat, so we field dressed and skinned the animal. We left the meat on the hide until we could pack it out the next morning. I felt the bull, heavily beamed and tall, with nice tops, would score well. He would later score 380-5/8 points under the Boone and Crockett scoring system. This was not enough for an all-time listing, but was enough for the award listing in ***Boone and Crockett Club's 23rd Big Game Awards*** book. We spent the next day packing out meat and enjoying the scenery.

The following day, Tom came and picked us up for our short flight to moose camp. Non-residents can not hunt moose in the unit where we were, so we moved 20 miles toward Tikchik Lake. On our way over to the next camp we saw a lot of moose, including two nice bulls. We landed on another small lake with no name, and proceeded to set up camp. It was early in the day so we decided to go look for the bulls that we had seen from the air. From several hundred feet up, the terrain did not look to be very challenging, but when we started walking through the brush, we found it was very rough going. The alders were over 10 feet tall and laid over on their side. They then arched five feet up, toward the sun. This made a lot of areas impenetrable, causing many detours. Beaver dams also caused a lot of problems. Every stream flooded the surroundings because of those little critters. The beaver ponds were very deep and also caused detours and lost time. Fed up with trying to take the low road, we headed for the hills. We found that it was much easier going in the hilly country, than down in the swampy bottoms.

When we got to the hilltop, near where we had seen the moose, we sat down and started to glass. It was a very warm and calm day, causing the bugs to be out in full force, which pushed the moose back into the brush thickets. We searched the little valley below us and found the two moose we had seen from the air, and they were both legal to shoot when the season opened. At the time, non-residents had to shoot a moose with three brow tines on a side, or one that had an outside spread greater than 50 inches. For two hunters who had seen only a few moose before, we decided to look for one that had three or more brow tines per side. When you consider how big a moose is, it was hard for us to tell how wide 50 inches really was.

On August 31, we awoke to a downpour and decided to stay inside the tent for the morning. The rain let up a little in the afternoon, so we took an excursion to the north side of the lake and saw lots of caribou and moose tracks, but no animals. Most of the area to the north of camp was low country with no way of getting up high to look for moose. The area, easily accessed by connecting meadows, was not our lucky place to find a moose. We had heard that bulls would come down into these lower areas as breeding season progressed. This was only the very beginning of the rut, with the biggest bulls just beginning to rub their velvet, and the bulls had not yet moved to the low country.

That night, back at camp, I convinced my dad we needed to go back to where we had seen the moose the first day. He liked the easy walking country northeast of camp, but we did not see any animals there. My dad and I have experienced a lot of hunting and packing into the wilderness in the Minam country of eastern Oregon. I knew that if he shot anything three to four miles from camp, we would have no problem retrieving it.

We awoke the following morning to partly sunny skies, and a quick breakfast of instant oatmeal and hot cider. With our fanny packs filled with the usual supplies of food, bug dope, and a first-aid kit, we set out with high hopes of finding a bull moose. Halfway into the valley, I spooked a bull with my noisy rain gear. It was not raining, but the dew on the grass and limbs was enough to soak you to the bone. We chased this little guy around for a couple of hours, but we never did get a good look at him. We proceeded to the hilltop where we could look down on the valley. We arrived at the top around 11:30 a.m., and began glassing. We did not see the bulls where they had been previously, so we began searching elsewhere. We did spot an exceptional caribou, bigger than the one I had taken, and I wished I still had my tag.

I decided to start looking a little closer in, since we had only been looking far out into the valley. Down below us, on a little shelf 200 yards away, I spotted a bull. He was hard to see because the brush was so tall. His antlers looked huge. Neither of us had taken a moose before and we did not know if the bull was legal. Dad readied his rifle, while I looked for brow tines. I could not tell through my binoculars, so we retrieved the spotting scope from my fanny pack. The scope had fogged up due to the moisture and almost cost us Dad's bull. The bull did not know we were there, and kept nipping the tender new growth shoots off the alders. From our angle, I couldn't tell with my binoculars if he was legal. I needed a front view to be able to see his brow tines. About that time, he laid down in the big alder patch, and all I could see were the tops of his antlers. It was now a waiting game.

While we were waiting, my dad had grown tired of the gnats

that were biting at his skin and buzzing around his head, so he pulled out a stick of bug dope. He had just finished applying the repellent when the moose stood up and looked right at us. The air currents had carried the nasty smell of the bug dope right to him. This, however, gave me enough time to see that he had at least four brow tines on each side. As the bull turned to run, I told my dad to shoot. My dad's 7mm roared and the bull did not even flinch. He shot again and nothing happened. As he prepared to shoot a third time, the bull stopped and looked back at us, allowing for one good shot. After the third shot, he was off to the races again, acting as if nothing was wrong. After winding through the alders, he stopped in a group of trees, more than 300 yards away. The bull stopped and hung his head in a small patch of trees. With a final shot to the neck, the hunt was over.

I scaled down the hill to find his trophy, while Dad stayed behind just in case the moose got back on his feet. After crossing a little stream and climbing up the other side, I located the patch of trees where we thought the bull would be. I approached with caution, but there was no need. There before me was the biggest game animal I had ever seen. What a magnificent animal. Dad quickly came down from the knoll to claim his trophy. We both stood in awe and wondered how in the heck we were going to butcher this giant. After a big struggle to move the bull, it was time for pictures. Unfortunately, the camera jammed after the first photo. While setting up for the "one" picture, we realized how wide his antlers were. Stretching his rifle from the outside of one antler, to the opposite side, the gun only made it a little over half way. Using this as a gauge, we estimated that the bull had an outside spread of at least 72 inches. We thought this was big, but neither of us had any clue how big.

Having good backpacks was a real bonus when we realized that we would be packing 600 pounds of boned-out meat on our backs. It ended up taking us four days to get everything back to our camp. The most challenging part of the pack ended up being the antlers, and I got the job of hauling the monstrous rack back to camp. The easiest way would have been to split the skull between the antlers, but my dad did not want to risk voiding entry into the records book, if they scored well. All that water and brush got the last laugh. While covering the four miles back to camp, I bounced from one bush to the next, slipping and falling in frustration the whole way.

Tom picked us up on September 6th, one day earlier than planned. This is when we really started to wonder how big my dad's bull was. Everyone who saw the rack stopped and asked questions. Many of the people we talked to said that it was the biggest bull they had ever seen in all their years living in Alaska. We put a tape measure on the rack and found it to be close to 78-inches wide. We promised that we would have the antlers scored when we got back to Oregon.

When we arrived back home, I had the rack green scored. They scored 255-3/8 points. We still didn't know how big was big, so Dad had Buck Buckner score the rack after the necessary drying time. Buck taped the bull at 254-1/8 points. He called us the next day and said that it would rank approximately third in the world, if the score stood. Wow! What a moose for two guys who had only seen a few Alaska-Yukon moose before this trip. My dad has since moved to Kodiak, Alaska, and took the antlers with him. They are now on display in the lobby at Kodiak Inn in Kodiak.

More than anything I will always cherish the memories and companionship I had with my dad on this trip. It was the best present I could have ever received for graduation. I will not look at this trip for the quality of trophies (they were a bonus) we were able to take; rather, I will always remember the good time we had together. 🦌

Photo from B&C Archives

Shiras Moose, Scoring 182-6/8 Points,
Taken by Patricia A. Wood in Caribou County, Idaho,
in 1983.

You've Been Drawn!

By Patricia A. Wood

19th Big Game Awards Program

MY HUSBAND ROD HAS NEVER BEEN PATIENT WHEN IT COMES TO WAITING FOR THE RESULTS OF A BIG GAME DRAWING. SO, I WASN'T SURPRISED WHEN I CAME HOME ONE DAY TO FIND HIM WAITING FOR ME WITH A BIG GRIN, "YOU'VE BEEN DRAWN ON THE MOOSE HUNT!" AFTER TELLING ME THIS, HE LOST HIS SMILE. MAINLY, BECAUSE I WASN'T SMILING.

All I could think of was the hunting season the fall before. I had been drawn on an elk permit. The hunt was only 12 days, but it was an extremely hard hunt for me. Our children were quite young that year. I would spend my precious time at home doing a day's worth of work in two or three hours. Then, I would hunt with Rod and his friends almost every daylight hour. I didn't even get an elk. I had a chance for cows and calves. But, I wanted a large bull that would make a nice mount. Of course I took a lot of ribbing from people about how picky I was.

I wasn't always picky. I was raised in Grace, Idaho, about 12 miles away from my present home in Soda Springs. My dad, James Parkhouse, started my hunting career when I was 14 years old. Being raised with three brothers, and no sisters, brought on the responsibility of hunting for game meat as a family. Opening day of my first hunt, I got the only buck shot that morning. I shot him in the lower spine. Dad always bragged about what a good shot I was.

Rod brought me back to the present by saying, "I thought you would be happy." Well, I was happy. I just couldn't imagine keeping up the pace that I had on my last hunt for the 30 days.

The afternoon before the opening of the hunt, Rod took me to practice with the Remington .270 I was going to use. For over a month, all Rod could tell me was that a .270 just would not put down a moose with one shot. I was only able to take three practice shots. I had hurt my right shoulder previously, and I didn't want it to get too sore to shoot during the hunt.

I was still concerned about our children. Our son, Larry, was only ten and our daughter, Suzie, was eight. At the time, though, we had a 17-year-old exchange student from Sweden, so I left them in her care.

Opening morning was October 5, 1983. My area was 376-1, which runs next to the east side of Soda Springs. We decided not to camp out, it would be just as easy to load our horses and drive to the hunting spot each day. Opening day, our friends, Jerry and Candy Young, were going to hunt with us. Another friend, Terry Sanderson, had an elk permit in the same area.

Terry started from a different canyon, saying that he would meet us later in the day. The Youngs, Rod, and I saddled our horses and headed over the mountains. Later that morning, Rod and Jerry were in front of us a little way. I told Candy that moose hunting was a little more fun than elk hunting, because Rod didn't think that I needed to be as quiet as we had to be when elk hunting. As I turned to talk to Candy, I saw a moose. It was a long way off. As I got off the horse, Rod was looking with binoculars to see if it was a good-sized bull.

Just as I got the moose in my sights, it ran. I hurried back on the horse, and we took off after the moose. Jerry and Candy rode along the bottom of the hill to push it back if it came into the open. Rod and I rode as far as we could on the horses, then started walking through the trees, hoping the moose would stop. He was much better at running through the dense forest than we were. After earnestly searching for him to no avail, we decided he had given us the slip.

After a long hunt that day, we rode back to the horse trailers. We unsaddled our horses, then sat in the grass for a while to rest. Terry Sanderson drove up. He didn't have any luck finding an elk, either.

He did say, however, that he had seen a moose in the trees on the mountain next to our horse trailers! After a long, hard day this was very ironic. Pretty soon, as we sat talking, the moose came out of the trees and started to wander across a clearing. We looked through scopes and determined that he had a small rack. Rod asked me if I wanted to try to shoot him. I said that I hated to shoot such a small moose on opening day. Candy then told me that she had heard how picky I was, but hadn't believed it until now. So, we calmly sat and watched the moose cross back and forth in the open.

The next day, Rod, Terry, and I took our horses onto a friend's land. It was a quiet hunt, and we didn't even see any game that day.

The third day of the hunt was Friday, October 7. I was so saddle sore that I begged to walk. Rod, Terry, and I drove into Angus Creek area, about 15 miles northeast of Soda Springs. We saw a nice moose early, but the silly thing had a beautiful antler on one side, and only a spike on the other. Rod asked me if I would want to shoot him. I said that I only wanted a nice mount. Then, I joked that maybe our taxidermist, the local Fish and Game officer, could add a plaster antler on the other side so that we could hang the moose in our family room.

As we went on, we spotted another bull moose walking across a clearing. It was the same size as the one we saw opening day by our horse trailer. Then, Rod and Terry spotted something moving in the quaking aspen below the small moose. They saw two moose, one with what seemed to be a nice rack. The moose were down at the edge of a large triangle, thinning to a small patch at the right of the moose. Other than that, it was open mountain side. Rod and I left to find a position where we could better see the moose.

Terry went to the place where the quakies thinned. If I only wounded the moose, he would try to drive it into the open. If it went any other direction, I would have a second shot. Rod and I had to cross a very large beaver pond, with narrow footing. I'm not at all fond of water, so this was not exactly a thrilling experience for me. All I could think was that if I fell into the water and couldn't shoot my .270, I would have to use Rod's 7mm. I didn't want to shoot his rifle. Well, I thought, once we cross, it will be easy from there on. Hah! Have you ever walked on a steep slope covered by deer brush? It was impossible to be quiet.

I knew when we finally got into position that the moose must have heard us and would be miles away. We went around the hill, and I took a look through my scope. The early morning sun was glaring in the scope. We decided to walk back behind the hill and then go lower. It wasn't the best idea. When we got into position, the glare was worse. I wanted a clear shot. The other moose lying by the bull was a cow, so I really needed a better vantage point. Rod suggested that we climb the north face of the hill and look down on the moose. We climbed another 200 yards through deer brush. Finally, we came out in the open.

Bad news. From the bottom of the hill, the hill looked flat; it wasn't! Now we could not see the moose because of a slight ridge between our position and that of the moose. Rod said, "Let's crawl on our hands and knees to the juniper tree in the middle of the sagebrush on the rise." We crawled out to the tree, holding our rifles up with one arm. It must have been another 100 yards.

You should have seen the juniper tree. It might have been six inches taller than the sagebrush!

Rod told me to steady myself and raise up and shoot. I told him that I hadn't really had a clear look at the pair of moose yet. I didn't want to shoot before I was sure that the cow was out of my line of fire. He told me to raise up a little, take a look, then stand and shoot. I raised up and whispered, "He's got his back to me." At that point, I forgot my sore shoulder. I stood up, took steady aim at the middle of his back, and fired. What happened next, I never expected. He started to raise up on his front legs, then toppled over. We found out later that the bullet severed his spine right behind his hump.

I'm not a very mature hunter, based upon what I did at that point. I glanced at Rod who was standing, staring at the moose, completely stunned that he was down. I don't remember traveling the 150 yards to the moose, but I do remember crying and yelling, "I got him," the whole way. The moose was still alive, so a final bullet through the neck killed him almost instantly.

The action was all over by 9:30 a.m. I was so excited. All I could think of was what a nice, even mount he would make. Terry had brought a camera, by chance, and he took our only pictures in the field. The first clue that this moose was very large was when I tried to place my rifle across the rack. It fell through!

Rod and Terry then told me that it was time for me to clean my kill. The hide was so thick, I couldn't get the knife through. After laughing at my predicament, they pitched in and did all the work. It took them until midnight to finish, and also deliver the meat to the store to be butchered.

I have to admit that my husband is the best hunter I know. If it wasn't for his skill in locating the game we hunt, I surely would never have gotten my beautiful trophy. It was one of the most exciting days of my life. 🦌

Photo from B&C Archives

Shiras Moose, Scoring 185-5/8 Points,
Taken by Mary A. Isbell in Bonneville County, Idaho,
in 2000.

Quest for the Giant Moose

By Mary A. Isbell

24th Big Game Awards Program

HUNTING HAS ALWAYS BEEN A VERY IMPORTANT ACTIVITY FOR OUR FAMILY. MY GRANDPA ISBELL TAUGHT MY DAD HOW TO HUNT AND THE TRADITION HAS CONTINUED THROUGH THE GENERATIONS. OUR FAMILY CONSISTS OF MY MOM, DAD, AND FOUR DAUGHTERS. I'M THE YOUNGEST OF THE GIRLS. DAD STARTED EACH OF US SHOOTING WHEN WE WERE ABOUT FIVE YEARS OLD WITH .22S AND USED VARIOUS FIREARMS WORKING UP TO A BOLT ACTION, SCOPED .22 LONG RIFLE. WE'VE ALL SPENT COUNTLESS HOURS PRACTICING SHOOTING. ONCE WE REACHED TEN YEARS OF AGE, WE STARTED WITH HUNTING RIFLES. WE ALL STARTED WITH THE SAME .243 AND THEN PROGRESSED ON TO OUR .270 AND .30-06 RIFLES. SHOOTING ISN'T ALL; WE JUST LOVE THE OUTDOORS AND THE WILDLIFE. WE RIDE OUR HORSES, HIKE, STUDY ANIMALS, AND THEN WHEN WE'RE HOME, WE POUR OVER BOOKS AND VIDEOS.

The hunt for my moose took place when I was 12 years old. Even though this was the first trip I was the hunter, I'd been going for years when my sisters and dad were hunting. I've hiked with them over some of the most difficult country in southeastern Idaho that you could imagine. My dad loves the steepest, roughest, and rockiest mountains he can find. My sisters and I have given them names like "Death Mountain," "Heart Attack Hill," or "Heart-stroke Mountain." I actually shouldn't complain, though, because we've been very successful in finding our game.

In Idaho each hunter can apply for special controlled permits for hunting. If you apply for moose, sheep, or goat then you can't apply for special deer, antelope, or elk permits. Each year seems to be a ritual in deciding what each of us wants to apply for. My quest for moose actually began in late summer 1999. On a late August morning, my dad and one of my sisters had gone on an early morning hike while the rest of us stayed at our cabin. When they returned, my dad was almost speechless. He claimed that he had seen a moose bedded about a mile away that appeared to be a top-end B&C class animal. They had hiked down reasonably close to the animal and studied it through the binoculars. As I listened to the excitement in their voices, I could tell that this one must be very special. Dad's very objective and knowledgeable about evaluating trophy game and doesn't usually get as easily excited as he was this time. Right then and there it was decided that all of us would apply for moose, hoping that someone could draw a permit while this special animal was still alive. None of us had drawn in 1999, but one of our close friends did. She took a gorgeous bull, but it wasn't the one that Dad had seen.

As 2000 approached, we did the traditional application scheme. We'd check on the Internet each evening until the results were posted. When the results were out, we couldn't believe it. Even though drawing odds are low, my older sister Becky and I, along with our close friend Craig Heiner, had drawn! The quest for the giant moose began.

It was traditional in our family that I would use my grandpa Isbell's .30-06 for the hunt. It is a Model 70 Winchester that he bought in 1945. My dad had a custom stock made for it in 1982 and had developed some handloads with 165-grain Nosler Partition bullets. It shoots very well and my older sisters had taken great game with it including trophy Shiras moose. Dad had me practice all summer with the rifle in anticipation of the hunt. My sister, Becky, would also use the rifle since it wouldn't be likely to have us both see two great bulls together at the same time.

Summer is a hard time to find trophy bull moose. They are in the thick timber bedded during most of the day, and we didn't see very many large bulls on our scouting trips. We did spend a lot of time scouting by hiking, by horseback, and by riding in the pickup. About two weeks before the hunt, our close friend, Bob Hudman called. He could hardly speak. When he started telling us about the moose, I could tell it was the one we had hoped to find again. I could get a good impression of the size of the animal by listening to my dad and his friends. When they seem uncontrollably nervous, then I know it's special. As he described this great animal and its location, we decided that we'd all try to keep an eye on him until opening day in August 2000. We tried to keep track of the animal, but he seemed to disappear a few days before the hunt. We were afraid that something had happened to him or that he'd just left the country. Even though we hadn't seen the moose for four or five days, opening day was a must. After some discussion, it was decided that I'd have the opportunity on opening day and my parents arranged for me to miss school. I must thank our dear friend Craig Heiner. He was present and helped on the hunt, and didn't even bring his rifle so that it would be my day.

We all met at Hudman's cabin near the Tex Creek Wildlife Management Area on opening morning. Our group included my mom and dad, Bob, Sandy, and Charity Hudman, and Craig and Debbie Heiner. This was one big moose expedition. We traveled by ATVs to a place where we could glass. It wasn't 30 minutes until the monster was spotted. He was back in the exact spot where Bob had seen him two weeks earlier. We immediately maneuvered in front of him, but couldn't get a shot. We watched him through binoculars as he went into the next canyon and into an aspen stand. Then we crept over the ridge above him and I prepared for the shot. The wind was howling, blowing a light drizzle of rain and the range was about 250 yards. All in all, it was a perfect moose day. My dad got me set up on a large rock. Bob and Craig were using separate video cameras so we'd be sure to record the event. The rifle seemed to jump around uncontrollably with the wind and the pounding of my heart. It seemed like a long time, but my dad told me to wait until there was a break in the wind and then take the shot. When the wind slowed, I carefully pulled the trigger. Immediately after the shot, Bob exclaimed, "You got him! You don't realize how big of a moose you just shot! He's going high in the records book!"

This really got me shaking. All of a sudden the moose stood up again, Dad and Bob both told me to hit him again. As I squeezed the trigger for the second shot the bull went down for good just as the shot went off. The next few minutes were pure chaos. My dad, Bob, Craig, and Sandy were all acting almost crazy with the excitement of this great animal. They hiked down to the moose first, leaving Dad and me on the ridge in case the moose got up.

As my dad and I hiked down to him, I can still hear Craig almost screaming what a monster he was. He was everything we'd imagined and more. Bob and Sandy went to get the remainder of the crowd. Dad, Craig, and I simply marveled at the size of the animal. Not only were his antlers huge, but his body was immense. We all discussed this, and later when the carcass was weighed at the meat processor, they confirmed how big he was.

The photo session went on for a long time. There was video with both cameras and several rolls of film from three different 35mm cameras. After the photo session, I really learned how big a large moose is. With all eight of us helping, it was a real chore to take care of and pack out a large animal like that. When we checked my moose in at Fish and Game the excitement rose again. It was a continuous emotional high.

Our moose hunting didn't end that day. For the next two months we hunted every Saturday, several weekdays, and after school for my sister Becky's and Craig's moose. We spent those days hiking, riding, and checking out several trophy bull moose. There are many unique stories about those two other great bulls like the day my sister got hypothermia, but that's another story. They both did get their trophy animals near the end of the season.

After getting this bull, we took him to one of the premier taxidermists in the west, Jay Ogden, in Richfield, Utah. Even though he's mounted some amazing trophy animals, he was excited about the opportunity to mount this magnificent specimen and will create a mount that compliments my trophy. We have already chosen a spot in our home for him.

I'll probably never take another animal as large for its species as my first bull moose. This day will be with me forever; the memory of the hunt, the family and friends, and the privilege to be in the great outdoors hunting. 🦌

Photo from B&C Archives

Barren Ground Caribou, Scoring 465-1/8 Points,
Taken by Roger Hedgecock near Mosquito Creek, Alaska.
in 1987.

If You Have to Look Twice

By Roger Hedgecock

20th Big Game Awards Program

On one hand, I can say Boone and Crockett has never really been the objective of any of my hunting trips. But on the other hand, I can never remember sitting on a cold deer stand, rifle in hand, that thoughts of a record whitetail didn't cross my mind. In fact, on my second elk hunt, I felt the rush of adrenalin on a Wyoming mountain. But that big bull, the largest one in the whole world to me at the time, measured 320 unofficially and it takes 360 to make the Awards book.

That elk hunt was back in 1986, and I figured that was the biggest of big game for me. There's an old adage about not knowing what the future holds. I believe in it.

At the time of the elk hunt, I had never seen a barren ground caribou. I had never seen a caribou of any kind. To be perfectly clear on the matter, I had never seen a caribou until September 25, 1987, the day we flew into a base camp that was located about 80 miles north of Nondalton, Alaska.

The next day, about two miles from camp, I squeezed the trigger on my .300 Weatherby. It was nearly one o'clock, an hour-and-a-half after the guide, Bob Tracy, had spotted the animal and said we were going after it. I could detect some excitement in his voice as he pointed it out in a herd of about 20. As we slowly worked our way from Mosquito Creek across barren tundra, using ridges as shields, trying to reach the highest point nearest the herd, I kept remembering what Bob had said, "If you have to look twice at the size of the rack, it ain't worth going after."

We were going and going hard. We crawled the last 200 yards. The cows, apparently sensing something was wrong, got up and started moving from left to right. Flat on my-stomach, I was watching through my 3x9 Nikon scope. My eyes were watering, my vision was blurred, and I raised my head to wipe my eyes. At this point, I got my first really good look at the rack. Rack was all I could see. Quickly I put my binoculars before my eyes to take another look. I saw the rack, the head, and then the body. He was walking slowly behind the cows.

As I eased the rifle into a shooting position, Bob was whispering, "Wait. Wait. Give him just a little more time, and you, take your time. Make the first shot a good one."

Finally, after what seemed longer than the trip from North Carolina to Alaska, the big bull showed me his right shoulder. I fired! The animal spun completely around and just stood there. I fired again, and he spun completely around once again. Each time I could hear the impact of the 220-grain bullet. The novice of my caribou hunting came out. I asked Bob, "Did I hit him?"

He nodded his head and added, "He'll die standing. Just wait, you have placed two bullets right on target."

The cows ran and the bull didn't, and I began feeling comfortable. Finally, the huge body crumbled to the tundra. At such a time I guess most hunters find something to worry about. I knew the hip boots were lighter as we walked the 200 yards, but I was worried about a broken tine, or just simply broken antlers. You allow a lot of things to pass through your mind. Bob's first words were comforting.

"It's a really big one," he said. "And it may make the book."

Of course we took a lot of pictures before caping the animal out and quartering the meat and packing it out, but my real excitement didn't come until we were back at camp. We did not score it at camp, but Bob talked seriously with my wife Molly and me about the possibility of a records-book caribou.

Bob packed the meat and antlers and sent them back to Nondalton. I knew it was a super way to begin a hunt. For the next nine days, we hunted moose and brown bear. It was the kind of hunt you dream about. I was able to fill both tags, a moose that rough scored 218 and a bear measuring 9-1/2 feet. Molly bagged a moose, caribou, and brown bear.

After the hunt, we returned to Nondalton and began rough scoring the caribou. Three people scored it from 470 to 477. Bob told me that after the 60-day drying period, he felt sure the animal would score close to the current World's Record. This makes you get a lot more excited about records than you have ever been.

After the drying period, an official measurer for the Boone and Crockett Club scored the antlers at 465-1/8. Then, we shipped the cape to Cody Taxidermy in Wyoming, where the trophy was mounted and then shipped to North Carolina.

It was a long year-and-a-half, waiting to know if this trophy will go in the records book, and how it will rank. It's like Christmas morning for a 45-year-old farm boy from the foothills of the Blue Ridge Mountains in North Carolina, who until recently seldom dreamed of a records book trophy, especially a records book caribou. 🦌

NOTE: Shortly after the 20th Awards Banquet, Roger Hedgecock agreed to a continuing loan of his trophy to the Boone and Crockett Club's National Collection, where it can be enjoyed by the vast throngs of hunters who visit the Buffalo Bill Historical Center in Cody, Wyoming.

Photo from B&C Archives

Central Canada Barren Ground Caribou, Scoring 407-6/8 Points, Taken by Kendall J. Bauer near Repulse Bay, Northwest Territories, in 1996.

Inuit Culture

By Kendall J. Bauer

23rd Big Game Awards Program

BOARDING A PLANE IN WINNIPEG, MANITOBA, MY HUNT-ING PARTNER, CURT WELLS, AND I, ALONG WITH EIGHT OTHER HUNTERS, STARTED ON A NINE-HOUR FLIGHT TO RE-PULSE BAY IN NORTHWEST TERRITORIES. ONCE THE PLANE LANDED WE MET UP WITH OUR OUTFITTER, JACK SMITH OF SWAN RIVER, MANITOBA, WHO HELPED US GET OUR CARIBOU TAGS. AFTER LOADING OUR GEAR INTO THE BOATS DRIVEN BY OUR INUIT GUIDES, WE STARTED OUR 30-MILE BOAT RIDE TO BASE CAMP.

As we headed to the base camp we passed icebergs floating freely in Hudson Bay, and seals looked like bobbers floating in the big water. Leaving the 90° heat of North Dakota for the 30° weather of Northwest Territories, I was glad I packed my good wool clothes.

Once we arrived at our base camp our guides set up the canvas tents we would call home for the next week, and we carried our gear from the boats in preparation for our first day of hunting. Joe was to be our guide, while his helpers Richard and Steve, would use a 42-foot whaling boat and a 14-foot aluminum boat to cruise between the mainland and the islands.

Since we could take two caribou, Curt and I had decided that we wanted to fill both tags with a bow, but we did bring a rifle along since we had hunted caribou before in Quebec and were unsuccessful. The first two days we did spot and stalk a few caribou bulls, but it was early in the hunt and they were not quite the size bulls we were looking for. After the second day, Steve said, "You want big bulls? We go to Qikitaluk Island." The sea was rough and the island was 20 miles across Hudson Bay, so while we waited for calm seas, we continued hunting the mainland.

Finally, on the third day, I had an opportunity to take my first caribou with a bow. Cutting the bull off as he worked his way up a hill, I narrowed the gap to 40 yards and made the shot. After the photo session the guides went to work on the caribou, skinning and preparing the meat. As we watched, Steve cut the heart into pieces and began eating it raw, like you would an apple. He said, "I like the heart when it is fresh and warm like this," as he wiped the blood from his chin. This was our first dose of Inuit culture. When we got back to the boat, Steve said, "The wind is good. If you want to go to the island we must go now." In the blink of an eye, we were on our way.

Once we got to the island we followed an inland waterway and beached the boat. Escorted by Joe with his .223 Ruger, which he carried for polar bear protection, we went after two good bulls. The island was comprised of rough, rolling hills of rock and valleys covered with lichen. Curt made a stalk on a nice bull and got a long shot, but missed. It was nearing low tide, so we had to go or risk being stranded by the 25-foot tides. Once back on the big boat, the guides treated us to a supper of Arctic char and fried potatoes.

The next day, September 1, we began skirting the island. To our surprise, a polar bear was cruising the shoreline as we came around a point. We captured the moment on film as the bear began swimming out to an island, 12 miles away. At one point, he snapped his teeth at the 42-foot boat in defiance, just before swimming off into the morning sunrise.

It didn't take long before we spotted a white-maned caribou bull on a hillside, grazing by himself. It was Curt's turn for a shot, so he grabbed his bow and I carried the rifle. Closing the gap to 200 yards, the bull somehow spotted us and started to take off. Curt decided to take the bull with the rifle and placed two good shots behind his shoulder, dropping him. Joe, Steve, and Richard were there in a flash to take care of the bull. This time they cut a huge slab of fat, or tallow, into bite-sized chunks and ate it raw. It was their favorite part of the caribou. Maybe that is why we were wearing heavy winter clothes and they stayed warm wearing just sweatpants and sweatshirts.

After Joe and Richard had the bull packed, Curt grabbed the antlers and we all made our way back to the boat. Steve had gone up on a large hill and was soon waving his arms after spotting three large bulls. We left the rifle behind and began slipping around rocks, stalking the bulls. While feeding 300 yards away, the bulls caught wind of the guides and took off running. They eventually bedded down and Curt put an outstanding stalk on the biggest bull. His bull ended up scoring 369-2/8 points with 54-inch main beams and a huge shovel, ranking him in Pope and Young Club's top 10.

By the time we arrived back at the boat the wind was gusting and we had to anchor in a narrow bay for the next day and a half. With the temperature dropping and the sudden snow squalls, it made for tough hunting conditions. I had a chance to stalk a huge bull with double bez tines, but couldn't put it all together. On September 3, the wind finally let up. Steve said we had to go back to base camp, and that meant our hunt was over. On our way back we would first stop at a small island where I would have one last chance to fill my second tag. Up until now, the bulls had been getting bigger and bigger, but I had my chance and passed, so I was happy. I told the guides I would take the next caribou we saw. Joe laughed, "A big fat cow maybe?" I replied, "No, a big bull!"

We pulled up on the shore of a tiny island and immediately found fresh sign. The guides told us that bigger bulls like to go to the small islands to get away from the other caribou until rutting season. With my bow in hand, Curt and I went in one direction and Joe went in another. Soon Joe was signaling us to get back to the boat. He had spotted three caribou on the windward side of the island. We hopped back into the small boat, went around a rocky point, and beached on the nearby shore. Joe told us approximately where the caribou were headed and I took off with my bow, still hoping to fill my second tag with an arrow. Curt followed carrying the rifle and video camera.

As we closed in, I finally spotted a bull's antlers and identified three bulls bedded in a small draw. The wind was blowing nearly 40 miles per hour now and it looked like a stalk with a bow was going to be extremely difficult. Curt peeked over the ridge and saw a bull I did not see at first, and said, "Kendall, he's a monster, a World's Record! Don't even try to get closer, use the rifle!"

I thought, "Boy, the bull I saw wasn't that big!" But when he showed me the bull he was watching, I couldn't believe my eyes. The bull was bedded facing away and my jaw dropped as I saw a beautiful, white-maned caribou with an enormous rack that almost touched his back. I decided this bull was North Dakota-bound and took the rifle from Curt. I slipped up to a rock 75 yards away and looked at him through my riflescope. That's when I saw a loose chip of glass floating around inside the scope. The rifle had been passed around so many times on the hunt it must have been dropped somewhere along the line. I prayed as I put the crosshairs on the caribou and pulled the trigger. The bull struggled to his feet and I anchored him with a second shot.

I was speechless. The two other bulls, both good bulls, just stood and watched the whole episode. As I approached the bull I started to shake and couldn't believe what I'd just accomplished. Curt said, "Kendall, you just shot yourself a world-class caribou."

I was still stunned. The rest of the crew came running like wolves to a kill and Joe said, "Nice cow, Kendall," as he shook my hand and laughed.

The bull scored 407-6/8 points and was absolutely gorgeous. We quickly took photos, caped the bull and packed it back to the boat. The wind was getting worse and we ended up spending most of the night working our way back to the mainland in rough seas. Steve's GPS unit helped keep us on course.

After reaching base camp the next morning, we met up with the other eight hunters who all had taken bulls. We even took time to catch a few lake trout on an inland lake before heading back to Repulse Bay, and our plane ride home.

The impact of this hunt really didn't hit me until we were in the air, on our way back to Winnipeg. It was then that I felt I had just had the experience of a lifetime. A hunting trip that will never be equaled or forgotten. 🦌

Horned Game

PRONGHORN

BISON

ROCKY MOUNTAIN GOAT

MUSK OX

BIGHORN SHEEP

DESERT SHEEP

STONE'S SHEEP

Photo from B&C Archives

Pronghorn, Scoring 93–4/8 Points,
Taken by Michael J. O'Haco, Jr., in Coconino County, Arizona,
in 1985.

The Longest Night

By Michael J. O'Haco, Jr.

19th Big Game Awards Program

IT WAS THE FIRST WEEKEND IN AUGUST 1985, AND I WAS OUT OF TOWN. I CALLED HOME BECAUSE I KNEW THE ARIZONA HUNTING PERMITS SHOULD BE IN THE MAIL. MY WIFE LINDA SAID THERE WAS GOOD NEWS AND BAD NEWS: I SAID I WANTED THE BAD NEWS FIRST. SHE SAID THAT I HAD NOT RECEIVED AN ELK PERMIT. HOWEVER, THE GOOD NEWS WAS THAT I HAD RECEIVED A DEER AND PRONGHORN PERMIT. ALREADY HAVING A MULE DEER IN THE ARIZONA STATE RECORDS BOOK, I WAS PLEASED AT HAVING DRAWN A DEER PERMIT, BUT NOT HALF AS PLEASED AS I WAS WITH THE PRONGHORN PERMIT. THIS WAS THE TWENTIETH TIME I HAD APPLIED FOR AN PRONGHORN PERMIT; THE 19 PREVIOUS TIMES I HAD BEEN REJECTED. THE COMPUTER FINALLY CAME THROUGH.

After getting home, I called my hunting partner Phil Donnelly. We got together to plan how we were going to scout the unit for which we had been drawn. Being a rancher in that same area, I would scout the top half of the unit, while Phil would scout the lower half. The top half was closer to where I was working cattle, and the lower half was closer to Winslow, where Phil lives. We got together after a couple of weeks and discussed what we had seen. He seemed to think that he had two records-book bucks in the lower half of the unit, and I thought I had three records-book bucks in the top half, but one buck was exceptional.

I tried to get a look at the bucks Phil had spotted, but I was unable to find them. I kept track of two of the bucks I had spotted, but I couldn't find the big buck. I almost panicked! After a little research on pronghorn, I found that during early September in Arizona, a buck will be looking for his harem, but will return to his own territory after putting them together. The big buck did, and I found him again the week before the hunt. I explained to Phil where I had seen the buck the day before, and asked him to take a look. Phil came by the ranch that night and told me this definitely was the biggest buck he had ever seen. We agreed the buck would go high in the Boone and Crockett records book, but we didn't realize how high.

The afternoon and evening before the hunt, we decided to watch the big buck until he bedded down for the night. Phil watched until he couldn't see him in the spotting scope anymore, then he returned to the ranch. After supper, he explained to me exactly where the buck had bedded down. My family has ranched in this area for years, so I knew exactly where the buck was. We talked about using horses, or going in on foot, and if we should come in from the north or from the northeast. We decided that hiking would be better, and that the northeast route would be the best. This way, we would have everything working for us, with the wind and the most cover, and also the sun at our backs.

Since this was my first pronghorn permit, I would get the first shot. If I missed, it was anybody's ball game. I had worked up a super accurate load of a Sierra 85-grain, hollow-point bullet, a Remington case and primer, and 41.5 grains of IMR 4350 powder. This load would be used in a Sako .243 rifle, with a 2-7x Leupold scope. I didn't intend to miss!

That night was one of the longest of my life, as my mind was filled with thoughts of the day's hunt on my mind. Would the buck be there in the morning? Would we spook them before I could get a shot? Would I miss? Finally, about 3:00 a.m., I couldn't take it any longer. I got up and put the coffee on. Phil got up and asked how I felt. I said that as many times as I had shot that pronghorn in my dreams, we should be able to drive out there and load him up.

We drove to within a mile of where the buck and his does had bedded down for the night. It was still an hour before daylight. We discussed how we would make our stalk, and tried to visualize all aspects of the stalk so there would be no mistakes.

Finally, it was light enough to make a move. We had to crawl over a fence and then use the scattered cedar trees for cover. We moved slowly. When we were about 300 yards from where we had seen them the night before, I spotted the does, but couldn't see the buck. We continued crawling slowly and easily. When we were about 200 yards from the pronghorn, something caught my eye to the left. It was a buck. Phil was about 20 yards to my left. The buck was looking straight at me, with a slight right turn, and I could see just part of a shoulder. Not being able to tell if it was the big one, I whispered to Phil, "Is that him?" I knew the buck was big, but I couldn't see the prong from my angle.

Phil said, "That's him." I shot. The buck broke and ran. I thought I had missed.

I jammed another shell into my rifle. I hollered at Phil to shoot. He said, "No, he's hit hard." The buck slowed down, then stopped and looked back. I shot again, nothing. The adrenalin was really pumping through my body and I couldn't hold the crosshairs steady. Phil said to use his shoulder for a rest, but he was shaking worse than I was. I took a deep breath, got my composure, and squeezed. The buck finally went down and didn't get up.

When we got to the buck, we were awed his size. Two days later, I had Jerry Walters, an official Arizona state measurer, measure the buck and he came up with a 95-2/8 green score. After the 60-day drying period, the buck was officially scored by Mike Cuppell, a Boone and Crockett measurer, at 94-6/8 for entry into the records program. 🦌

NOTE: This trophy, and the fine, fair chase hunt for it, received special recognition at the 19th Awards with the Sagamore Hill Award, the highest trophy award made by the Club. This was the first time ever that the Sagamore Hill Award was given to a pronghorn trophy. It was only the 13th time this award was given, and it was the first time the award had been handed out since 1976.

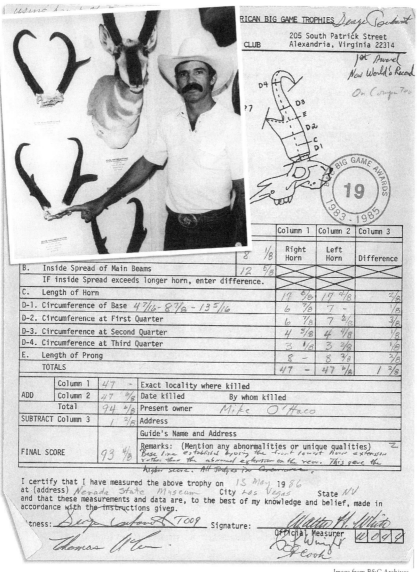

RICAN BIG GAME TROPHIES *Serge Coutant*

205 South Patrick Street
Alexandria, Virginia 22314

CLUB

1st Award
New World's Record
On Computer

			Column 1	Column 2	Column 3
			Right Horn	Left Horn	Difference
B.	Inside Spread of Main Beams	12 5/8			
	IF inside Spread exceeds longer horn, enter difference.				
C.	Length of Horn		17 5/8	17 4/8	2/8
D-1.	Circumference of Base 4 7/16 - 8 7/8 - 13 5/16		6 7/8	7 -	1/8
D-2.	Circumference at First Quarter		6 7/8	7 2/8	3/8
D-3.	Circumference at Second Quarter		4 3/8	4 4/8	1/8
D-4.	Circumference at Third Quarter		3 1/8	3 2/8	1/8
E.	Length of Prong		8 -	8 2/8	2/8
	TOTALS		47 -	47 6/8	1 3/8

(above row B:) 8 | 1/8

	Column 1	47 -	Exact locality where killed	
ADD	Column 2	47 6/8	Date killed	By whom killed
	Total	94 6/8	Present owner	Mike O'Haco
SUBTRACT	Column 3	1 3/8	Address	
			Guide's Name and Address	
FINAL SCORE	93 4/8		Remarks: (Mention any abnormalities or unique qualities) Base line established exposing the front lowest horn extension rather than the abnormal extension on the rear. This gave the higher score. All judges in concurrence.	Z

I certify that I have measured the above trophy on 13 May 1986
at (address) Nevada State Museum City Los Vegas State NV
and that these measurements and data are, to the best of my knowledge and belief, made in
accordance with the instructions given.

Witness: *Serge Coutant* T009 Signature: *Walter H. White* W009

Thomas W. Cox *G. Wright* *Cook*

Image from B&C Archives

*Original score chart for Michael O'Haco's pronghorn, which
scores 93-4/8 points.*

Photo from B&C Archives

Bison, Scoring 126-6/8 Points,
Taken by Holland D. Butler in Garfield County, Utah,
in 1990.

Big Bullets Do Big Work

By Holland D. Butler

21st Big Game Awards Program

A GREEN ISLAND IN THE MIDDLE OF ROCK AND SANDSTONE, THE HENRY MOUNTAINS OF UTAH ARE AS UNIQUE AS THE LAND SURROUNDING THEM. FOUND HALFWAY BETWEEN THE CANYONLANDS AND CAPITOL REEF NATIONAL PARKS, THE HENRY'S MOUNT ELLEN REACHES ALMOST 11,500 FEET INTO THE SKY JUST NORTH OF LAKE POWELL.

Once the haunt of Butch Cassidy's outlaw gang, the Henrys were rumored to hide an old Spanish gold mine. Today, the Henry Mountains are famous for one of the last free-roaming bison herds in America.

The bison were never native to this area, and by 1835 the last of the species were gone from what is now Utah. During the 1950s, Utah's Division of Wildlife Resources transplanted a small group of bison from Yellowstone into the Henry Mountains area. As a result of careful management and loving care, the population was estimated to be 400 animals by 1990.

At the age of 51, luck was with me in 1990. I drew one of Utah's coveted once-in-a-lifetime bison permits for the Henry Mountains. Reared in a hunting family in Oregon, a love for the outdoors and respect for its creatures were lessons my brother and I were taught by our father. Since our move to Utah in 1975, I have been fortunate to draw both moose and desert sheep permits. Because I retired in 1985, I was able to concentrate completely on preparations for the bison hunt. The three weeks prior to the November 3 opening were spent scouting. This familiarized me with the country and its bison; it also served as a conditioning exercise.

Being a firearms enthusiast and a fan of pistols in particular, I naturally picked a handgun for the hunt, but only after extensive deliberation. A C. Sharps rifle in .50 caliber was my first pre-hunt choice. However, delivery would have taken 90-plus days. To stay with the traditional single-shot, falling-block action, a Ruger No.1 in .458 Winchester Magnum was selected as my "buffalo rifle." For several years, I have hunted with a .45-70 single-shot pistol from M.O.A. Corporation. It is big, heavy, and very accurate, so I included this one as well. My real love, though, is a Ruger single-action Bisley, skillfully and beautifully converted to .475 Linebaugh by John Linebaugh, the Cody, Wyoming, gunsmith. This revolver is fitted with a special 5-1/2-inch barrel and matching five-shot cylinder. The cartridge is based on the .45-70 case, trimmed and loaded with a cast LBT bullet weighing 430 grains. The muzzle velocity is 1,300 fps.

Millions of bison were killed on the plains of the West with rifles less powerful than this revolver. Practicing three times weekly. I had a sore hand and a keen eye.

Skookum is my partner. A wonderful Keeshond, she is always ready to go and never complains about the cook.

On our first scouting trip to the Henrys, Skookum and I started low on Stevens Mesa. Our first sighting of bison was memorable. A cloud of dust in the distance turned into a small herd of the shaggy beasts. We soon discovered that by using cover and being careful, approaching a group was not too difficult. We drifted along parallel to the feeding animals, down wind and using junipers to break our silhouette. Watching these animals, with the sun low behind them and hazy dust diffusing the soft evening light, I imagined myself in the company of Sioux or Blackfoot hunters as they stalked their traditional prey.

After three weeks of pre-hunt practice, we had a pretty good handle on what it would take to be successful during the November hunt. Although these Henry Mountains bison are wild, they certainly are not as spooky as elk. They can be approached within pistol range if the hunter is careful, quiet, and deliberate.

There are two types of bulls. The magnificent, shiny-black 5- to 8-year-old bulls generally stay together in groups. The old loners, out by themselves, join other animals only occasionally or during the mating season. It is among the older, blonde-humped individuals that the largest animals are found, and of course these bulls are the most difficult to locate.

The week previous to the November 3 hunt, we were comfortably camped near McClellan and Willow Springs. Our scouting had identified four different herd groups, one of which had several nice bulls. On Thursday before the Saturday opener, Skookum and I discovered an absolutely perfect specimen — completely coal black very large, and impressive, shiny black horns. He was the one. The bull was feeding around a hidden water hole and the situation seemed perfect. We would simply return on Friday, follow the great animal until dark, and he would surely be ours opening morning. Oh, yeah. Sure. You bet. We never saw a hair on Friday.

Saturday morning and dawn found me and Skookum in a cool canyon with a water hole at its upper end. We had found it and a small bunch of large bison about a week earlier. After a long, hard hike, we surprised 11 nice animals bedded around a seep. For me, it was adrenalin time, because to exit from this very narrow cut they had to pass within 20 feet of my position.

Following the bigger ones with the muzzle of the .475, I decided not to shoot. Later that evening, we crawled up into a bunch of about 20 head, but we were so close and it was so dark that all we could do was crawl back out and wait for the next morning.

Sunday broke windy and cold, and we soon discovered other hunters were sharing that part of the mountain. After hearing shots, we departed.

Back at camp we packed enough food for a couple of days and a tarp in the Land Cruiser and started for Bull Creek Pass and Table Mountain. As we climbed higher, the snow got deeper. Deer were browsing the abundant plants, standing in belly-high grasses. This contrasted sharply with the lower elevations, where heavy grazing had left little feed.

It was soon apparent that the road was almost closed by drifted snow, and no one had driven the pass lately. I was surprised, because in almost a month I had never seen anyone on foot.

Near the top on the east face, we found a single set of large hoof prints. They meandered down the road, sometimes off into the brush, then across to another tidbit. Half a mile farther, the tracks stopped at a bed, right in the middle of the road. Well, big bulls are loners, and up there on Bull Creek Pass I was alone too, except for the wind and my dog.

I parked the Cruiser at a wide spot, buckled on the .475, shouldered a small pack, and went up the trail. We were in pine and aspen patches, with the south ridges bare. Thick low brush grew in the gullies. It was fairly steep, and the tracks we had followed down turned to go up again. There were some snow patches in the shade so tracking the bull was not really difficult if I went slowly, watching carefully. By 3:00 p.m., we were in about 3 inches of snow, and from the tracks it appeared the bison had some place to go. I wondered if he had sighted us as we were driving down, because he was sure headed for the top.

It was 5:00 p.m., the sun was below the ridge in front of us, and the wind was really beginning to rise as the temperature rapidly fell. We broke out of the quaking aspens along the lower edge of a large hill, and there he was. All I could see was the top of a woolly hump. With only one small pine between the bull and us, Skookum and I started one-stepping it, hunched over and moving slowly toward the single patch of cover. The bison was feeding directly away from us. The range was about 150 yards. When we closed the distance to 100 yards, I realized I had nothing to judge this bull by, no points to count, nothing with which to compare him. So I added up what I knew: solitary bull, big tracks, horns curved, shaggy head and blonde hump equaled old bull. This was it.

Behind me, Skookum lay down in the snow while I pulled the .475 Linebaugh and tried to shrink into the sagebrush. I had only gone about 10 yards when the bull turned to his right, feeding directly broadside. The revolver came up. Too late. I was dead still as he fed directly toward the upraised muzzle. At about 60 yards, I knew it was time to do it. The plan was to slip a 430-grain bullet between shoulder and ribs, on a line with the heart. Careful. Careful. Sight picture, trigger, BOOM! I was watching the target so intently that I actually saw the hair part and dust rise from the exact spot the front sight had occupied. There was absolutely no reaction.

Second later, the bull wheeled around and started away at full speed. At 75 yards he turned slightly. I shot again. He never broke stride. The bull was going downhill, perhaps 100 yards away and nearing a grove of old pines and aspens, when he turned broadside. I was chanting, "Front sight, front sight." At the shot, the old bull pitched full-length and slid 20 feet on his left side.

I was running then, pushing out cases, and groping for ammunition. By the time I covered half the distance, he was back on his feet, but badly hurt.

I had just accomplished the goal of the hunt and was feeling elation and pride, but I also felt sadness, sympathy, and admiration for that truly grand animal. A quick shot and it was finished for the old bison.

It was far from finished for this old hunter. What an animal! He was simply huge. It was almost dark, my feet were soaking wet, the temperature was in the 20s, and a hard, cold wind was blowing. Skokie and I ran about three miles down to the Land Cruiser. By dark, we had returned to the bison. I luckily found a dead pine stump and coffee and dinner were soon heating. By lantern and firelight, the cleaning and skinning chores started.

At midnight, the temperature was down to 10 degrees and one weary old man was done. Almost.

The first slug from the Linebaugh had penetrated between the shoulder and ribs as intended. When the first rib was hit, the big lead bullet didn't cut through. It was deflected slightly and caught the second rib edgewise, cutting it completely. Then, the bullet punched through half of a third rib and angled up and across, exiting after busting another rib on the far side.

The second, raking shot was too far forward, I guess my concentration was focused on the shoulder, because that's exactly where it hit. The angle was so acute that the bullet cut a six-inch furrow in the hide before entering behind the right ear. It was later found by taxidermist Sam Raby, just under the nose-pad skin.

My third shot broke the right femur, cut straight through a rib, ripped arteries from the heart and lungs, broke another rib, penetrated the shoulder bones, and disappeared into the woods. Big bullets do big work.

The bull's final score is 126-6/8 points. It presently ranks first among bison taken in Utah. It was also the first with a pistol. 🦌

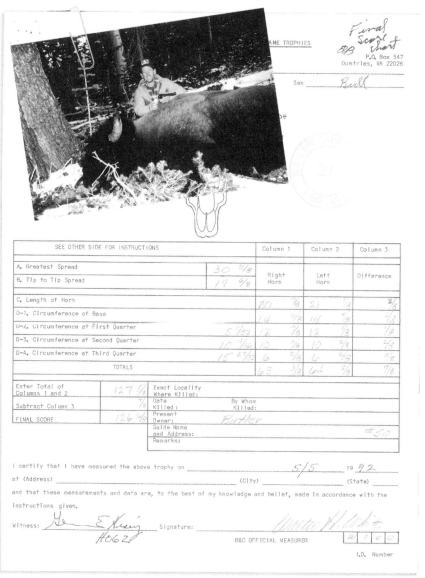

SEE OTHER SIDE FOR INSTRUCTIONS			Column 1	Column 2	Column 3
A. Greatest Spread		30 2/8	Right Horn	Left Horn	Difference
B. Tip to Tip Spread		19 4/8			
C. Length of Horn			20 7/8	21 1/8	2/8
D-1. Circumference of Base			14 4/8	14 4/8	4/8
D-2. Circumference at First Quarter	5 9/32		12 7/8	12 1/8	1/8
D-3. Circumference at Second Quarter	10 9/16		10 7/8	10 5/8	2/8
D-4. Circumference at Third Quarter	15 27/32		6 3/8	6 4/8	3/8
TOTALS			63 3/8	64 7/8	7/8

Enter Total of Columns 1 and 2	127 5/8	Exact Locality Where Killed:	
Subtract Column 3	7/8	Date Killed:	By Whom Killed:
FINAL SCORE	126 6/8	Present Owner:	Butler
		Guide Name and Address:	#50
		Remarks:	

I certify that I have measured the above trophy on _____ 5/5 _____ 19 92

at (Address) _____ (City) _____ (State) _____

and that these measurements and data are, to the best of my knowledge and belief, made in accordance with the instructions given.

Witness: _G. E. Keavy_ H062 Signature: _Walter H. White_

B&C OFFICIAL MEASURER

I.D. Number

Image from B&C Archives

Original score chart for Holland Butler's bison, which scores 126-6/8 points.

Photo from B&C Archives

Bison, Scoring 131-6/8 Points,
Taken by Duane R. Richardson in Coconino County, Arizona,
in 2002.

My Last Bull

By Duane R. Richardson

25th Big Game Awards Program

I WOKE UP MY SON, RUSS, THE MORNING AFTER HE HAD JUST PLAYED AND COME UP SHORT FOR THE ARIZONA STATE CHAMPIONSHIPS IN FOOTBALL. I TOLD HIM I HAD SOME GOOD NEWS AND NEEDED HIM TO VERIFY WHAT I WAS LOOKING AT. HE WANDERED IN AND LOOKED AT THE COMPUTER SCREEN IN MY OFFICE AND CONFIRMED MY FINDINGS OF HAVING THE NUMBER ONE OF FOUR BISON TAGS FOR THE HOUSE ROCK RANCH HUNT IN NORTHERN ARIZONA. MY EXCITEMENT WAS SHARED BY HIM AND EVERYONE ELSE I COULD CALL AT THAT EARLY HOUR WHO MIGHT BE INTERESTED IN MY GLORY.

My son wanted me to do the hunt with my bow. The tag allows you to hunt with any legal weapon, but I agreed with my son. My choice would be that of the stick and string.

Scouting started in January before the season to get the lay of the land, and possibly find a few big bulls in some out of the way places. The ranch manager stated that he had not seen nor heard of any bison since the first part of September. He also said that we would really have our work cut out for us. That sentiment went right along with the videotape that the Game and Fish sends successful applicants. It basically says, "Congratulations, but get ready for the hardest hunt in the world."

I was never one to forego a challenge, so I put together a team of people who had expertise in each area needed. We were able to execute a wonderful game plan. I am blessed to have a family and group of friends who are without a doubt some of the best hunters in the entire west.

I would start my hunt in a very remote spot separated from the other hunters by many miles and an entire mountain range. I had the pleasure of meeting two of the other hunters on previous scouting trips, and they were really nice people who were going to be fun to hunt with. I told them of my plans to pursue with stick and string, and they thought I was either crazy or just not really fond of bison steaks.

Orientation day was now here. Two weeks earlier, I had located four bulls I believed would push the state record. After orientation, I drove back to camp in a blinding snowstorm that stopped around 3 a.m. "Perfect," I thought to myself.

We really needed to cover some ground and look for tracks in the area where I last saw the four bulls. At the end of day one, my dad, George, and Bill Bolt were able to come up with some signs we determined were three days old. Phil Dalrymple and I decided to track around and see what we could come up with on the next day. My uncle Bob and Craig Thornton would try to eliminate other areas where we might have missed the bulls from the day before.

Day two panned out nothing but cold, wet feet, and sore leg muscles. Day three was pretty much the same thing. We would leave camp well before sunrise and return with headlights, covering literally hundreds of miles between us and not so much as a track found.

On day four, our excitement level soared to a new high. Phil had found some huge tracks leading east toward the plateau. I had already had visions of two huge bulls traveling together and just hanging out away from the rest of the herd. The further we tracked, the deeper the snow got, to the point where we guessed it to be 36-inches deep. We finally reached the time of day where we were running out of light and the tracks were still heading up the plateau. We decided to back off and come back the next morning.

While en route to where we had cut tracks the day before, we cut one single set of tracks headed out of the deep snow to the west. We tracked them over 10 miles, taking up most of the day, only to find they belonged to the biggest bull I had ever seen! The problem was the bull was a stray cow from a cattle herd. The tracks of a cow and a bison are identical, and cannot be told apart by even the most seasoned hunter or rancher; however after day five it was pretty depressing to say the least.

We determined that we needed to change location, and day six was spent moving the camp a hundred miles away, closer to the House Rock Ranch. Arriving at the ranch, we learned that two of the four hunters were finished. One hunter remained and had taken his horses back to Phoenix for some fresh stock.

Several years ago, the first archery bison hunt on the North Kaibab was undertaken by my father. He was able to connect on a bull the first day of a 30-day hunt. Dad's experiences on the Kaibab for those many years were invaluable when it came to planning the rest of our hunt. There was an area above the ranch that we knew would hold some big bulls. We spent the afternoon of the seventh day trying to figure out a way to access that area. Phil had some commitments he needed to get back on the seventh day, so he left around noon.

While looking for an access point across a huge canyon, we came across two very large sets of tracks. Dad was elated at the freshness and size of the tracks. He told me, "Corky, this is a huge bison."

I remember telling him (after spending day five tracking down a cow), "No, Dad, those are just rogue cattle."

He answered back, "If these are rogue cattle, then they are carrying around bison hair and fur with 'em because I found enough to stuff a volleyball with."

He was right! After seven days, we finally had a track that was under two days old. I grabbed my pack, bow, and quiver and began tracking. The bison seemed to be spending most of their time in an open field that provided good feed. I cut some tracks that had very sharp edges on them. They had to have been made that morning. The bison chips were extremely fresh. The tracks headed down a pinion-juniper point that is half a mile long and half a mile wide — a good bedding area, heavy with shade.

A light snow had fallen, and I decided to check around the bedding area to see if I could find tracks leading out. I made a circle around the point without finding any tracks leading out. It was around 4 p.m., so I decided to start at the end of the point and work my way back to the feeding fields to the west. Four hundred yards into the point, I found two fresh beds still warm. What really got me excited and had me nock an arrow on my string was when I found foamy urine with the bubbles popping on a flat rock.

The wind was perfect, blowing from west to east as I entered the feeding area. All of a sudden, the ground began to shake as two bulls came running from the south and headed toward a small draw. What went wrong? The wind was perfect, and I knew they had not heard me. Something or someone had spooked them.

After spending seven days looking for the quarry, I was just thankful and praising God that I had seen bison — running or not. I hurried over to the edge of the draw where they had disappeared, only to find the biggest one had stopped across a small draw. I remembered thinking to myself, "If that bull would just turn and come back to the feeding grounds I will be in good shape."

As if on cue, the bull (not knowing what had spooked it) turned and headed back uphill to the west of me. I hurriedly took off my boots to do the shoeless dance one more time. I ran 200 yards while quartering towards the bull in order to get a lane where I could get a good shot.

The bull stopped in an opening 35 yards away, with only its head entering the opening. I could see its right side and knew it was something special. If it would only stop for a minute to give me a good shot. I was already at full draw for about 15 seconds, waiting for it to move. The bull finally stepped forward and I released the arrow. The arrow got there faster than I anticipated. I hit it square in the front shoulder, just up from the leg, with my first shot.

I immediately grabbed another arrow and ran up the hill to cut the bull off in order to get another shot at it. I was uncertain how much penetration I had made from my first arrow. To my amazement, the bull had already begun to weave and was having a hard time standing up. The arrow had penetrated to the opposite shoulder and only my fletching remained visible.

I followed it about 150 yards before it stopped for the first time. This time the arrow penetrated dead middle and dead center. The bull walked away, and I pursued it, grabbing for arrow number three.

While in pursuit I was locked in and focused on getting shot three away. Then I heard a sound, "Psst."

"Psst." I think I heard something again.

"Corky," I hear, in a loud whisper. Standing on a small rim, above where the bull had just stopped, stood Dad and Craig. They went on to tell me how they had found these two bulls in the feeding area that they had spooked after catching sight of them. They felt about as high as a wart on a snake's belly after running off the only two bulls we had seen in a seven-day period, especially without being able to find me They explained that they were just following the tracks where the buffalo had spooked, when all of a sudden, they saw the largest of the two coming toward them. Unbeknownst to me, the bull had stopped no further than 10 yards below them. My dad was wondering where I was, when all of the sudden he heard the sound of an arrow. The next thing he saw was an arrow sticking out of the bull in the ten-zone. He kept telling me that I needed to slow down on my pursuit, but the view he had of the bison was of its left side, and he didn't know that I had a well-placed arrow on the right side. The bull went down no more than 75 yards from our conversation.

Kaibab is laced with wilderness area from one end to the other, but this bison chose to die on a two-track logging road; Packing would not be a problem. Once we approached the bison, my dad knew right away that he had never seen a picture nor heard of one with this size of horns. The bull expired with one side of the horn down in the dirt, and it took all three of us to turn its head around and see if we had two sides that matched; indeed we did!

I was able to contact Phil before he had made his trip back to Tucson. He had traveled halfway when he heard part of a broken-up cell phone message from me. He determined that one of two things had happened: either I needed help, or I had gotten a bison. Either way, he headed back. He found us around midnight.

I drove down to the game manager's house to get him to confirm a bow kill before any fielddressing took place. He couldn't believe that I had actually killed one with a bow on one of Arizona's most difficult hunts. When he saw the bison, he said that to his knowledge, he had not seen that particular bull. He aged the bull according to the jaw age charts at over 16 years.

God had blessed me way beyond my wildest dreams with an exceptional animal and extraordinary friends and family that will remain with me for a lifetime and an eternity. Did I mention that he died on an old road? If you have ever skinned and quartered a 2,000-pound animal then you know how truly blessed I was. 🦌

Photo from B&C Archives

Rocky Mountain Goat, Scoring 55 Points,
Taken by David K. Mueller on Cleveland Peninsula, Alaska,
in 1997.

Goat-Hunting Bug

By David K. Mueller

23rd Big Game Awards Program

AFTER MOVING TO SOUTHEAST ALASKA ALMOST 10 YEARS AGO, IT DIDN'T TAKE ME LONG TO LEARN I WAS LIVING IN SOME OF THE BEST TROPHY MOUNTAIN GOAT TERRITORY IN NORTH AMERICA. I KNEW SOMEDAY I WOULD HUNT FOR A TROPHY GOAT, BUT AT THE TIME, I WAS HUNTING DALL'S SHEEP EACH YEAR, AND THAT WAS USING UP MOST OF MY HUNTING TIME AND MONEY.

I am a trophy hunter and have been for many years. To take just any billy, just to have one, didn't really interest me. If I were to go after a goat, I wanted to find an area with no hunting pressure, where a billy could grow to trophy size. So for years I kept my ears open and talked to everyone I knew who had hunted goats gathering tips on where I could find a trophy.

I also spent many hours reading Boone and Crockett Club's *Records of North American Big Game* to see where the big goats had been taken in southeast Alaska. I was in Ketchikan, Alaska, in the late fall of 1996 when I stopped by the Alaska Fish and Game office and talked to the goat biologist. I asked him about an area on the Cleveland Peninsula I had heard about. The biologist said the Cleveland Peninsula has produced some of the biggest goats from Alaska, but they were few and far between. He also said the area was not hunted because of very difficult terrain and this also accounted for the area having some large billies. That was all I needed to hear. Now I had the area to hunt I had been waiting for. Big goats and no hunting pressure!

I live in Craig, Alaska, which is a small town on Prince of Wales Island. To get to the Cleveland Peninsula, I would travel by boat across Clarence Strait, which is about 10 miles wide.

August 1, 1997, was the opening day of goat season. The weather was raining and windy, but by the 4th the weather was starting to clear. On the morning of the 5th, I pulled my boat 30 miles on a dirt road to Thorne Bay, on the east side of Prince of Wales Island. There I launched the boat and started across the strait to Cleveland Peninsula. It was a calm morning and the water in Clarence Strait was as smooth as glass, making for an easy trip. In less than two hours I was in a small protected bay. I anchored the boat out in the bay so the out-going tide would not leave the boat high and dry. After making sure the anchor would hold, I started up the mountain to where I thought some billies might be.

It wasn't going to be an easy hike. The mountain has an elevation of 2,800 feet and I was starting from sea level. It was definitely going to be a tough test! As I left the boat, the sky was clear, but three hours later I could see a storm brewing in the distance. One thing about Alaska weather, it can change in a heartbeat! Within another hour it was pouring rain, but I wasn't going to turn back. I learned a long time ago if the weather upsets you, Alaska wasn't the state to live in, so I just kept plodding up the mountainside. After an hour, the rain stopped and fog moved in, limiting my visibility to 50 yards. I was thinking I would get to the top where I would set up my tent and hunker down to wait for the fog to lift. After eight hours of hiking, I knew I had to be close to the top. I could see the sun trying to break through the fog. I hiked up another 200 yards and the rays of the sun came shining through the fog, as if our Creator sent them from heaven, just for me. I could see the top only 100 yards above me.

Once on top, I sat down and dropped my pack. I was burned out from the long, steep hike through the rain, fog, brush, and broken-up terrain. But after a sandwich and candy bar I was ready to look for a trophy goat. The first impression I had when I looked around was this was not goat habitat. I hiked north and soon started getting into an area with cliffs and rocky ravines. This was more of what I had in mind. I put down my pack and starting hunting along the edge of a cliff. I slowly worked my way along the edge, glassing down the rock ravines and cliffs below me. I didn't get too far before I spotted a bed in the grass a few yards from the edge of the cliff. It was too big for a deer and after a closer look I found tracks that were definitely made by a goat, and they were huge! They also looked to have been made that morning, so I carefully eased up to the edge and looked below. Instantly I saw a goat 200 yards away, feeding on a grassy bench at the end of a rocky ravine. I pulled up my 10x40 Zeiss binoculars and could tell by the yellow, off-white color it was a billy and his horns looked big!

The wind was blowing up the ravine right into my face so the billy didn't have a clue I was watching him. I slowly started down a ridge to the right from the ravine in which the billy was feeding. I stalked to within 50 yards of him and laid my .300 Weatherby across a large rock. I took one more look through the binoculars even though I was so close I could hear him eating grass. He was definitely a trophy mountain goat. His horns were very long with heavy bases, and with the sun shining down on him, he was a beautiful sight. I maneuvered my shoulder behind my .300 Magnum, put the crosshairs on his shoulder and squeezed the trigger. After the recoil, I looked up and was shocked to see the billy running up the grassy slope to the base of the rock cliff!

I knew goats were tough, but I was shooting a .300 Weatherby with 180-grain Barnes X bullets. He should have at least acted like he was hit. I knew I couldn't have missed at 50 yards! I quickly chambered another round and threw the rifle up to my shoulder, putting the crosshairs on his shoulders. Just as I was beginning to squeeze the trigger, through the scope I saw the goat's hind legs bend and start to shake. It was now obvious that he was hit hard. The billy then fell over backwards and rolled down the grassy slope to his final resting place. I carefully made my way down to him and could not believe how big his body was and his horns looked very impressive. I knew I had a trophy goat and one that would qualify for the records book.

He was magnificent, and for a long time I just sat there beside him on that mountain thinking how lucky and thankful I was to get such a beautiful animal. There were more storm clouds coming, so I quickly took some pictures. In two hours I had the billy caped, the meat boned out and in my pack. I made it halfway down the mountain that night before it was too dark to go on. I stayed right there on the mountainside, and the next morning headed down the rest of the way to the boat. After an hour and half boat ride, I was back at Thorne Bay. I couldn't wait to show the trophy to my wife, Rhonda, and my three kids, Ashley, Kyle, and Wyatt. I knew they would be excited too!

Once I got home, I green-scored my billy at 55-7/8 points. After the 60-day drying period, he was officially scored at 55 points. I knew some day I would hunt for a trophy mountain goat, but I never dreamed I would get a trophy billy that would rank that high in the records book. I have had the sheep-hunting bug for years. Is there such a thing as a goat-hunting bug? I know I've got one! 🐐

...M FOR NORTH AMERICAN BIG GAME TROPHIES

250 Station Drive
Missoula, MT 59801
(406)542-1888

...C AND CROCKETT CLUB®

...CKY MOUNTAIN GOAT

RECEIVED

DEC 08 1997

1 OF 5
12-2-97   WN

BOONE & CROCKETT CLUB

1st Award

	Column 1	Column 2	Column 3
	Right Horn	Left Horn	Difference
C. L...	11 4/8	11 2/8	2/8
D-1.	6 2/8	6 2/8	0
D-2. ...ence at First Quarter	4 7/8	4 6/8	1/8
D-3. Circumference at Second Quarter	3 2/8	3 2/8	0
D-4. Circumference at Third Quarter	2 0/8	2 0/8	0
TOTALS	27 7/8	27 4/8	3/8

Cleveland Pen. Alaska (02)

ADD	Column 1	27 7/8	Exact Locality Where Killed: *Cleveland Peninsula, AK*
	Column 2	27 4/8	Date Killed: *AUG. 5, 1997* Hunter: *DAVID K. MUELLER*
	Subtotal	55 3/8	Owner: *DAVID K. MUELLER* Telephone #:
SUBTRACT	Column 3	3/8	Owner's Address:

Guide's Name and Address: *UNGUIDED*

Remarks: (Mention Any Abnormalities or Unique Qualities)

FINAL SCORE	55 0/8	*Male goat, age 7 1/2 years.*

I certify that I have measured this trophy on *14 OCTOBER* 19 *97*
at (address) *2030 SEA LEVEL DR. KETCHIKAN* State *AK*
and that these measurements and data are, to the best of my knowledge and belief, made in
accordance with the instructions given.

Witness: *Lila Chatham*   Signature:

B&C Official Measurer

I.D. Number   L 0 4 3

Copyright © 1997 by Boone and Crockett Club®

Image from B&C Archives

*Original score chart for David K. Mueller's Rocky Mountain goat,
which scores 55 points.*

Photo from B&C Archives

Rocky Mountain Goat, Scoring 55-6/8 Points,
Taken by Gernot Wober in Bella Coola, British Columbia,
in 1999 – Current World's Record (tie).

Just Shoot It!

By Gernot Wober

24th Big Game Awards Program

IT ALL STARTED ON SEPTEMBER 4, 1999, WHEN LAWRENCE MICHALCHUK NEEDED TO FIND A NEW GOAT HUNTING PARTNER AFTER HIS WIFE ANNOUNCED SHE COULD NOT ACCOMPANY HIM ON IIIS NEXT HUNT. LAWRENCE AND I HAVE KNOWN EACH OTHER FOR EIGHT YEARS AND HAVE SPENT MANY HOURS HUNTING AND FISHING TOGETHER. I WAS NOT SURPRISED TO HEAR HIS VOICE ON THE OTHER END OF THE PHONE. "CAN YOU LEAVE TOMORROW?" HE ASKED.

Work was not a problem — I had been unable to find work as a mining exploration geologist for almost six months. But how was my relatively new girlfriend going to take the news that I was leaving that afternoon to go goat hunting? I put on my most loving attitude, drove to her shop at the ski resort, and mentioned my plans. Within the hour I phoned Lawrence to tell him I would arrive on Sunday at noon.

I drove nearly 500 miles from my home near Kamloops to reach Lawrence's home in Bella Coola, British Columbia. Not entirely prepared on such short notice, I borrowed longjohns, a backpack, Thermarest, rain gear, and fleece pants to round out my skinny supplies. We packed homemade granola bars, trail mix, and Mr. Noodles packages for food, as well as a tent, small stove, and our bowhunting gear. Dividing the load between us, we each had approximately 60 pounds of gear to haul up the trail for a planned seven-day hunt.

From the trailhead, we slogged our way uphill for eight wet hours, climbing approximately 5,000 feet over five miles of trail. In retrospect, the only pleasant fact about the hike was that it was overcast and cool, and the view as we climbed out of the Bella Coola valley was spectacular. Low clouds draped themselves along the steep walls of the green valley and fog moved up and down the slopes as the wind changed.

The main Bella Coola valley, which is tucked into the Coast Mountains about 250 miles west of Williams Lake, boasts some of the most magnificent views in British Columbia. Lush green valley bottoms host great salmon rivers such as the Atnarko and Talchako, where grizzly bears roam freely. Rows of large mountainpeaks line the main valley, rising from sea level to over 8,000 snow-capped feet. Blacktail deer and mule deer follow trails along valleys and steep mountain slopes. Recently, the cougar population has been increasing and wolves seem to be thriving as well.

Canadian heritage abounds as one hikes along the nearby Alexander Mackenzie Trail. Native petroglyphs can be visited along Thorsen Creek, and the rock where Alexander Mackenzie carved his name in granite in 1793 can be reached by boat on the Bentick Arm from Bella Coola harbor.

We pitched our tent in what seemed to be the only dry 10 square feet for miles around. Fall rains had saturated the ground, and small lakes and ponds were everywhere. We were centrally located in an area that held Rocky Mountain goats, with only a few miles between the locations Lawrence wanted to check out. Lawrence had been up in this area hunting for goats numerous times and knew the terrain very well.

We had a few hours before dark, so we pushed our weary legs a little farther, walked to the closest spot overlooking the Bella Coola valley, and started glassing for goats. Along the edge of this east-west trending valley, it is very precipitous, well-vegetated, and perfect habitat for goats. We eventually spotted what looked to be a lone goat and probably a billie. We walked a small ridge parallel to the one the goat was on until we were 150 yards away from him. Lawrence put the spotting scope on the goat and said that it looked fairly large and was probably worth pursuing.

We both backed away slowly, walked around to the top of the ridge and started down to get closer. As we crept down small ledges without much cover, the goat spotted us and was staring directly at us from approximately 60 yards. Lawrence motioned that he was going to climb back up the ledges with the hope the goat would watch him and allow me to get within bow range. The ruse seemed to work as I got to within 40 yards. I was directly above him with a steep downhill shot. As I made the shot, I saw the arrow sail directly for the goat and then deflect off a small tree just in front of him. I missed! The goat bounded down the rock walls into the steep gully.

Tuesday morning we debated whether we should go back after the same goat we had seen or try somewhere else. We decided to head north to a cirque in which Lawrence had seen lots of goat activity before. Two hours of fast walking found us along the edge of a very steep walled cirque from which we could glass a large valley. We spotted eight goats in pairs and singles on a number of different ridges and ledges well over a mile away. Several seemed quite large, although we were still too far away to be certain they were billies.

Unless we could get a lot closer, determining whether these animals were billies would be impossible. Both sexes have black, well-polished horns; the nanny's horns are generally longer with narrow bases and a wide spread, while the billy's have larger bases and heavier overall circumference measurements. On average, body size is not a reliable indicator. Later that day, Lawrence made a stalk on a goat that appeared to be a billy until the very last instant. I watched him creep toward the goat carefully trying to see over rises and rocks until he was within 10 yards of the animal. He took an arrow from his quiver, readied for the shot, and suddenly froze. I took a step forward and realized, as Lawrence had, that this was a very large nanny.

By afternoon, we were quite a distance from camp so we thought it best to head back the way we came. We stopped to see if some of the goats we had spotted earlier had moved into a more favorable position. Looking over the steep edge on our side of the valley, Lawrence noticed a goat standing in thick brush approximately 50 feet up from the base of a cliff. As he looked through the scope, Lawrence said, "the bases of those horns are the biggest I've ever seen. Too bad we can't get to him from here." We watched the big goat for a while and then headed back toward camp. At the time, neither of us knew we had spotted a potential World's Record.

For the next two days we spotted and stalked numerous animals. I managed to deflect my arrows off more twigs and miss two shots on decent billies. At night as we cooked our meager dinners, all we could talk about was the large goat we had seen and the problems of accessing the area he was in. Lawrence was convinced that the goat was the largest he had ever seen in 16 years of hunting and I realized that thoughts of stalking it were consuming him. We discussed moving camp closer to the valley the goat was in but knew we couldn't climb down the cliffs at the headwall.

Friday morning brought a thick frost, but also the promise of sun for the first time in four days. After we had dried out and were comfortable again, we started hiking back to the truck. Lawrence and I had discussed things the evening before and reached a consensus that we should go after the big goat. The only way to get to him was to head home, get rid of most of our gear to lighten our loads, and start the grueling hike up the valley from the bottom. We headed to Lawrence's place looking forward to a change of socks, a hot shower, and to eating something other than sweet granola bars and Mr. Noodles.

The next day, we thrashed up a sidehill full of slide alder and devil's club for five hours to get up the new valley. Slide alder is nasty business. It grows sideways and upward 10 to 15 feet, and there is never a clearing through it—you simply climb on it or under it, often at the same time. Devil's club is aptly named for its toxic barbed needles that work their way into your skin until sufficient festering pops them out. As we had passed through a mature timber stand in the lower part of the valley, we noticed grizzly bear claw marks high up on the trees and clumps of hair stuck in the sap. It made us a little nervous, and we hoped the bear was in the lower valley looking for fish.

We almost turned back twice when the terrain and vegetation had us asking each other just what the heck we were doing here (whose brilliant idea was this anyway?). I pushed on, encouraging Lawrence to follow, but I was soon at wit's end and very frustrated with the thick brush. Next, it was Lawrence's turn to encourage me, pushing me to reach the next ridge. Finally, it appeared that the vegetation was giving way to rocky slide chutes, and we knew we were closer to our goal.

By noon, we were across the valley about a mile from the spot we had seen Mr. Big. At first we didn't see any activity, but as we were eating our lunch, Lawrence whispered, "He's there!" We watched him in the spotting scope and were amazed once again at how obviously big the billy seemed. Another billy was about 500 yards up the valley from him and we noticed that both goats had been watching our progress up the south slope for quite some time. The large billy was in exactly the same spot where we had seen him days before.

Lawrence had his bow and I carried his .270; I had given up on bowhunting. We agreed that Lawrence would get the first shot with his bow and if he couldn't get a shot, I could try with his bow one more time or just shoot with the rifle. We dropped down to the valley creek where we cached our large packs next to some huge boulders, which served as a good landmark. After crossing the creek, we climbed up the slide, staying hidden in the slide alder, then proceeded on our hands and knees for about an hour through tall wet grass and stinging nettles. About 100 yards from where we last saw the goat, we noticed numerous trails and tunnels through the grass where he had been feeding. The billy had a veritable grocery store to feed from with very little competition. As luck would have it, he had come down off his perch and was feeding at the base of a cliff.

Lawrence took the lead with his bow, and we continued forward even slower, keeping a willow bush between the goat and us. We arrived at the base of the cliff and there was no sign of the billie! We stared at each other for a second, not wanting to admit that we had spooked him, then continued our stalk. Lawrence climbed up the cliff a little ways and then moved right, following some small ledges. I moved sideways and to the right, staying in the grassy talus so I could keep a larger area of the cliff in view.

Lawrence crossed above me to the right and started gesturing emphatically that the goat was right there in the thick bushes on the cliff. I couldn't see the billy yet so I scrambled up to where Lawrence was frantically pointing. I put the scope of the .270 up and sure enough I could make out the goat's vague outline at 70 yards. I told Lawrence I had a shot, though it was chancy through a bush. Lawrence told me to keep the scope on the billy, and he was going to try and sneak around the other side and get a bow shot at him. I watched Lawrence stalk around to the other side and then he went out of sight. Both the goat and I heard the muffled scrapes and rockfall that Lawrence couldn't help but make on the steep terrain.

After about 25 minutes of trying not to pull the trigger, I heard Lawrence yell, "Just shoot him." Microseconds later the echo of the rifle shot was ringing through the valley, and the goat dropped out of sight. All was silent.

"Did you get him?" Lawrence shouted.

"I think so," I replied, as I waited a minute longer to see if the goat was going to reappear for another shot.

As Lawrence climbed down from his perch, I crawled up on all fours to where I last saw the goat. The bed created by the goat was huge. We could have pitched a tent on the platform created in the bushes. The billy had obviously made this home for quite some time. He had an unrestricted view of most of the valley. I glanced over the edge of the bed and spotted the white fur of the goat in the bushes 10 feet below. I carefully scrambled down to him and poked him with the rifle to make sure he was dead.

I had not expected the body to be so large; the billy appeared to weigh between 350 and 400 pounds. The horns were bigger than anything I had seen in my short goat hunting career.

"Is it a small one?" Lawrence yelled from the base of the cliff. I knew he was being facetious—he knew it was a large billy, but just how big was the question.

All I could reply was, "Nope!"

Lawrence yelled back that he had just fallen 30 feet and didn't really feel like climbing up to where I was. "We've got to take the cape off up here so come on up," I shouted. By the time Lawrence scrambled his way up the cliff to where I was, I had tied a rope from a stunted spruce to the goat's head just to make sure we didn't lose it over the edge.

"Holy goat," was all that Lawrence could say over and over again. "You don't know what you just shot!" was all the variation to the first theme that he could muster.

We took photos as best we could where the goat lay, as dragging the goat back up to his bed was impossible. We took the cape and head off and let the body slip over the cliff. We clambered down the cliff to the goat's body and continued to roll the carcass all the way down to the creek in the valley bottom. We quickly deboned the hindquarters and took out the back straps, packing as much as we could carry. The blowflies found us right away and we had to fight to keep the eggs out of the meat. We carried the meat to our packs by the boulders and made camp under the overhang of the largest one. We started a fire and walked back to the goat carcass to pull off a rack of ribs and cut some steaks from the front end. Two hours later, our socks were dry, and we were feasting on what we knew was a very large goat.

Sunday morning we were well rested and ready for the long thrash back through the slide alder to get home. Five hours later, we made it to the truck and were on our way to Lawrence's home. After unpacking, I skinned out the goat's head and we green-scored the horns. Knowing that the horns would shrink a little with drying, we conservatively measured the horns rounding some of the measurements downward. After we added all the totals and took off the deductions we ended up with a score of 58-2/8 points. The size of the billy we had just shot started sinking in after we realized that the goat might be in contention for the World's Record.

After the compulsory 60-day drying period, an official measurer for the Boone and Crockett Club measured the horns. With an official score of 56-6/8 points, the goat ties the current World's Record Rocky Mountain goat taken in 1949 in the Babine Mountains of British Columbia. What is intriguing is that the left horn had 1-1/8 inches broken off from the tip and could have scored even higher. 🦌

NOTE: This trophy, the excellent adventure, and fair chase hunt for it were all contributing factors that led the 24th Awards Final Judges Panel to bestow the coveted Sagamore Hill Award to the hunter, Gernot Wober.

Photo from B&C Archives

Musk Ox, Scoring 126-2/8 Points,
Taken by M.R. James near Kugaryuak River, Nunavut,
in 2000.

Our Way or No Way

By M.R. James

24th Big Game Awards Program

"NO CLOSER!" CAUTIONED MY INUIT GUIDE CHARLIE BOLT, RAISING HIS RIFLE JUST IN CASE. "SHOOT NOW. SHOOT THE WHITE-HORNED BULL."

"Easier said than done," I mumbled to myself. Over 50 yards of frozen, windswept tundra still stretched between us and the two huge musk ox that stood facing us, pawing at the snow menacingly while lowering their heavy-horned heads as if contemplating an imminent charge. What would have been a simple shot for any rifleman was next to impossible for a savvy bowhunter. Even if the buffeting crosswind miraculously failed to affect my arrow's flight and accuracy, I knew from four decades of bowhunting experience that a frontal shot on such a large animal would be pure folly. Too much thick hair and hide, tough muscle, and dense bone stood between my shaving-sharp broadhead and the bull's vitals. Somehow I had to cut the remaining distance by nearly half and work myself into position for a broadside shot — preferably without further provoking my obviously worried guide or the two agitated bulls. Fair chase bowhunting for musk ox, I was quickly discovering, can be an exercise in frustration. My hunting partner, Bob Ehle of Pennsylvania, and I had lost a full day of hunting to the fickle Arctic weather gods. Then, after locating two good bachelor bulls just after dawn on our first clear day afield, we parked the snow machines and began our stalk only to watch in stunned disbelief as the twin bulls instantly whirled and galloped away upon catching sight of us. Time after frustrating time throughout the long day, stalk after fruitless stalk, we tried and failed to move within good bow range. Fifty to 60 yards was as close as we could get. That's tempting yardage, but impractical in bitter cold, wind-whipped shooting conditions. The last we saw of "our" two trophy bulls they were disappearing over a ridgeline a couple of miles away — still running!

Leg weary, wind-burned, and emotionally drained, Bob and I returned to our comfy tent camp that night with a much better appreciation of the daunting task facing us. However, despite our disappointment, we agreed it hadn't been worth the risk of wounding and losing one of those great shaggy beasts — or forcing our guides to finish off a poorly hit bull with a bullet. We'd do it our way or no way.

The next morning we climbed into our enclosed sleds that were roped behind the guides' snow machines and headed out across a great flat that resembled a snow-covered moonscape. Soon we cut the meandering trail of two big nomadic bulls made sometime the previous night. After a hurried and animated conference, our excited guides turned their snowmobiles to follow the tracks. One hour passed. Two. Three. The sunny but frigid morning slipped slowly away as we paralleled the bulls' trail, our hopes soaring each time we approached a promising ridge, but falling each time we topped the rise only to see more empty tundra stretching endlessly ahead of us. It seemed as if we were following tundra phantoms, not flesh and blood creatures whose ancestors have tracked across these same icy wastelands since prehistoric times.

Riding in a bouncing wooden sled across miles of frozen tundra is a bone-jarring, tooth-rattling experience. Our base camp was perhaps 90 to 100 miles from the small village of Kugluktuk on the shores of the Arctic Ocean — and how far we ranged from camp in our daily search for *oomingmak*, the bearded one, is anyone's guess. All I knew was it would be a long hike back to civilization in the event of any mechanical breakdowns. But there was obvious comfort in hunting in pairs and in knowing a radio was our link to the outside world.

It was late March. Already several days had passed since I winged north from my Montana home, overnighted in Yellow-knife, and met my hunting companion and two other musk ox hunters who had also booked a hunt with veteran north country outfitter Fred Webb. Together we caught a morning flight to Coppermine to embark on what was an unforgettable adventure. I was discovering, just as every musk ox hunter I knew had told me, the appeal of this hunt lies in the overall experience. In this stark, frozen land. In the native guides whose knowledge of the Arctic and its wildlife is amazing. In testing oneself in an unfriendly environment where wind and bitter cold are constant companions. In finding a unique creature that is a true survivor in an inhospitable world, a special animal largely unchanged since Stone Age hunters pursued the forebears of these same beasts armed only with flint–tipped spears.

Back to the present, our whining snowmobiles crested yet another ridge — and there they were! The two bulls, dark dots against a sea of frozen white, were plodding on perhaps a mile ahead. The Inuits quickly braked their machines and held a brief conference while Bob and I studied the distant bulls through our binoculars.

Then we were off again, Bob and his guide veering to the left while Charlie steered his snowmobile in a looping arc to the right. Moments later we eased to a stop just below a ridgeline. As Charlie shouldered his pack and rifle, I stretched ride-stiffened muscles and pulled my bow once to make certain the rough ride or sub-zero cold hadn't rendered it useless. And then we were moving to the top of the ridge and beyond, dropping into a shallow bowl where the bulls should appear.

And suddenly the bulls were there. But this time there was no turning and running. This time when these two old bulls spotted us moving slowly down the frozen rise they simply stopped and turned to face us, waiting and watching without apparent concern. It wasn't until we'd closed the distance to perhaps half a hundred yards that they began to paw the snow and shake their woolly heads. That's precisely when Charlie readied his rifle and warned we'd moved close enough for me to shoot the white-horned bull.

Turning, I shook my head. "Closer," I said. "Can't shoot. Too far." And with each word I took another cautious step closer to the waiting bulls.

Shaking his hooded head, Charlie moved after me. "Close enough," he insisted. "Shoot now."

"Can't," I said again. "Too far."

At 40 yards I raised my tinted goggles and slipped the mitten off my shooting hand, slowly easing to my knees to study the musk ox, with my worried guide crouching just behind me. The bulls still offered only an impossible head-on shot. Cautiously, I inched closer still, not taking my eyes from the shaggy apparitions looming before me, wispy guard hairs fluttering in the whipping crosswind.

Although I would have preferred to close the distance by another 5 to 10 yards, I sensed this was as near as I could get without inviting real trouble. Staring at two agitated musk ox occasionally pawing the snow — with only some 100 feet of empty air between us — I couldn't help but recall Fred Webb's story of one rifle-toting client who had been charged, trampled, and injured when he violated a bull's perceived "safety zone." I certainly didn't want to have to explain how I came to get hoofprints all over my snow parka.

Speaking softly, I asked Charlie to move slowly to my left. If the bulls concentrated on my guide and turned to face him as he eased sideways, maybe I could get the broadside shot I needed. And the tactic worked perfectly, except when the bulls turned my white-horned bull was perfectly screened by his traveling companion. And even when Charlie moved behind me and edged to my right, the bigger bull wouldn't turn far enough to present me with the shot I needed for a quick, clean kill. Talk about a frustrating standoff!

As my mind raced for some solution, I spotted Bob and his guide watching the unfolding drama from a ridgeline maybe 150 yards away. A new idea struck me and I motioned Bob to circle around and approach from behind us. Within 10 minutes he was kneeling beside me, listening as I quickly explained what I had in mind while Charlie and Bob's Inuit guide warily eyed the increasingly nervous bulls, rifles ready for instant action in case the bulls charged.

Wishing Bob good luck, I carefully got to my feet and began sidling to my left. On cue, the two bulls turned as I moved and moments later I saw Bob draw, hold, and release. His arrow caught the second bull mid-body, angling forward. Immediately the mortally hit bull spun and lunged away in a spray of hoofchurned snow. My white-horned bull trailed close behind.

Bob's arrow quickly weakened the lumbering bull. He labored to the nearest ridgetop before pausing to bed down while his companion paced close beside him. Trailing quickly after them, Charlie and I ducked out of sight and crept closer. When I finally rose to peer over the ridge, Bob's bull lay only 20 short yards away. My bull was standing just behind him, stubbornly refusing to leave. And when he turned and strode into the clear, he was perfectly broadside. My arrow struck him just behind the right foreleg, its 3-blade broadhead burying deep in the off shoulder.

The huge white-horned bull spun in a tight circle and mere seconds later collapsed beside Bob's bull. Our frustrating, memorable, once-in-a-lifetime Arctic adventure was over. Not only had we collected two great big game trophies, we'd done it our way — a very special way. 🏹

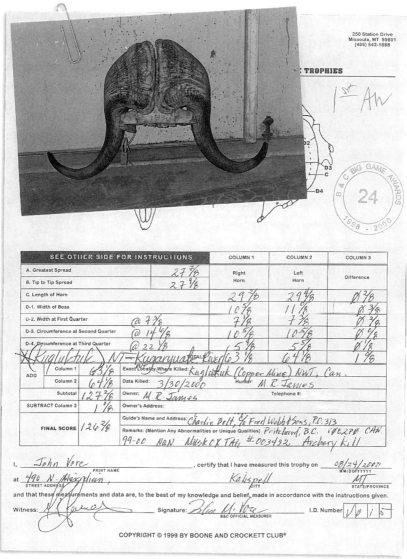

Image from B&C Archives

*Original score chart for M.R. James' musk ox, which
scores 126-2/8 points.*

Photo from B&C Archives

Bighorn Sheep, Scoring 204-7/8 points,
Taken by James R. Weatherly in Granite County, Montana,
in 1993.

Twenty-Two Years Later

By James R. Weatherly

22nd Big Game Awards Program

I MOVED TO MONTANA IN 1971 TO TAKE ADVANTAGE OF GREAT HUNTING AND FISHING OPPORTUNITIES. EACH YEAR, I APPLIED FOR EVERY TAG AVAILABLE, INCLUDING BIGHORN SHEEP, MOOSE, AND ROCKY MOUNTAIN GOAT. IMAGINE MY SURPRISE WHEN IN AUGUST 1993 I RETURNED HOME TO FIND AN ENVELOPE FROM THE DEPARTMENT OF FISH, WILDLIFE AND PARKS WITH A PICTURE OF A BIGHORN SHEEP ON IT; 22 YEARS OF APPLICATIONS FINALLY PRODUCED A PERMIT.

I knew the tag I drew was in an area with exceptionally large rams. I realized how little I knew about sheep hunting, so I prepared for the season by getting in physical shape, learning the territory and studying hunting techniques. I started an exercise program, watched sheep hunting videos and read numerous sheep hunting books. Five scouting trips were made prior to the season to learn about the hunting area and location of sheep. My friend Mike Moore volunteered to show me several areas where he observed sheep.

Seven scouting trips later I was comfortable with my ability to find the rams. I located several record-book rams for which the Rock Creek drainage is famous. The season in this area ran from September 15 to October 31 which allowed ample time to find a trophy ram. I set a goal to spend the first month searching for a super ram that scored more than 190 points. Since the hunting area was within 50 miles of my home, I decided to hunt three days per week for the first three weeks and full time for the remaining three weeks of the season.

The hike to the hunting area from the main Rock Creek Road required a three-mile trek up 2,400 feet each morning. Opening day brought pouring rain as I left my vehicle at 4:30 a.m. I neared the top of the ridge as the rain stopped. Occasional snow squalls made glassing for sheep difficult. I met a band of small rams at the edge of the timber and let them pass as I continued deeper into ram country. I sighted three more bands of sheep, including one herd that included a promising looking ram. Snow and poor light conditions made it impossible to properly judge the ram's size.

I made six additional trips to various parts of the mountain. On another hot afternoon, I was hunting alone and moving very slowly through the timber, scouting a new area. While watching a deer move through the trees below me, I noticed three rams staring in my direction. I rested my rifle against a tree and glassed the rams. A very large ram forced its way to the head of the band. Judging the left horn, I knew it was more than 190 points, and I instantly reached for my rifle. I was in very heavy timber with numerous limbs. I needed a solid rest to shoot through the small opening if the ram turned its head to allow me to verify the right horn. As I moved to the side for a rest, I was momentarily out of sight. The herd bolted.

As the herd turned from me, I saw both sides of the big ram and it was well over 190 points. A dozen rams were suddenly around the big ram as they bolted through the timber. I never had a clear shot and followed the herd through three drainages but could not catch up to them again. As I passed the area where I first saw these rams I noticed they were bedded on the top of a rock cliff. I would have had serious problems retrieving the big ram by myself.

I began to hear stories of sheep being taken by other hunters in Western Montana and began to wonder if I should lower my goals starting the second week of October. On October 9 I decided to visit the area where the big ram was last seen to determine if it had returned. I left Missoula about 3:30 a.m. to make sure I was on top of the mountain well before daylight to catch the big rams moving into the timber. Cold temperatures and three inches of snow were the conditions.

As I reached the bottom of the first large clearing near the top of the ridge, I could barely see two animals through my binoculars near the top in the clearing. I saw several ewes and immature rams in the clearing on previous occasions and walked through the band in the dark one morning. I figured the two animals I saw were this band. Since I needed to climb in their direction to get to the big ram, I proceeded up the ridge towards the sheep. Light was coming, but the dark, overcast skies limited visibility.

I eased up to the ridge and knew I was looking at two rams feeding in tall grass. I noticed three single trees on the ridge at even intervals, which would allow me to crawl out to the ridge to glass the sheep. From the first tree I could tell the lower ram was small but the upper ram would not lift its head from the grass.

At the second tree I had a few quick views of the upper ram as it fed uphill, arriving at tree line about sunrise. The ram appeared to be very respectable, but I needed to get closer since I left my spotting scope in the truck to reduce my weight. As I reached the upper-most tree, I was at the same elevation as the sheep and 175 yards downwind. The upper ram finally raised its head and the size of its horns were startling.

The ram turned around to look at the smaller ram and I verified its right horn was equal to the left. I did not attempt to score this ram as one look told me it was as good or better than any of the other rams I viewed to date. I suddenly began to shake violently as I decided this was the sheep for which I waited 22 years.

I realized I was freezing. The brisk wind blew through the light shirt I wore to climb the mountain. I put on my jacket and realized it was too cumbersome for shooting and took it off again. I removed my day pack and my fanny pack to get comfortable for my shot. I propped the rifle in the fork of the tree and found it impossible to get comfortable for a shot. If this sheep had been on a dead run, I'm sure I would have shot it without a second thought, but since I was given time to think, I was a nervous wreck. I settled myself, took careful aim, and squeezed off a round.

The ram hunched up and turned straight away from me. All I could see was its rump and the back of its massive set of horns. I readied myself for a running shot if it bolted. The ram spun 180 degrees and faced me, shaking its head and attempting to rid itself of the effects of the bullet. The ram spun 180 degrees away from me and fell dead.

I stood frozen in my shooting position for several moments, trying to comprehend that 60 days of apprehension had just come to an end with a viable trophy. I gathered my gear that was scattered around the tree and walked over to the ram. I stood in total awe at the size of this magnificent animal, knowing I would never experience anything like this again. A local outfitter helped me pack the ram off the mountain where we green scored it at more than 205 points.

The taking of this ram was a great hunting experience and it allowed me to meet and associate with some of the finest sports-men and sheep fanatics of our time. These sheep lovers donate countless hours and dollars to insure the viability of sheep hunting for future generations. The taking of this trophy caused me to read dozens of books on sheep hunting along with spending many hours on the mountain watching and filming sheep.

Photo from B&C Archives

Bighorn Sheep, Scoring 200-1/8 points,
Taken by Mavis M. Lorenz in Granite County, Montana,
in 1993.

Lady's Day in the High Country

By Mavis M. Lorenz

22nd Big Game Awards Program

"DAMN, DAMN, DAMN. I SHOULD HAVE TAKEN THAT LEAD RAM OF THE FIVE I SAW OPENING DAY," I THOUGHT AS I PLANNED MY NEXT THREE DAYS OF HUNTING.

I saw 25 or so rams, with at least 12 of them presenting good shots, but they all appeared too young. I was warned by sheep-wise hunters, outfitters, and game experts not to take the first ram I saw because they always look big to the novice hunter.

I was a novice hunter but I spent considerable time learning about bighorn sheep. I studied videos about sheep behavior and learned all I could about field judging of trophy bighorn rams. I read masters' theses from the University of Montana that reported the studies of bighorn sheep in my hunting permit district in Granite County, Montana. I picked the brains of as many knowledgeable people as would answer my questions. Still, I felt there was so much to learn in such a short time.

Would I find the ram I hoped to find? What if I didn't?

After 18 years of unsuccessful attempts to draw a permit, this was my one and only chance. I would not be eligible to apply for another permit for seven years. By that time, I would be well over 70 years old and no longer able to climb mountains.

My plan for the next three days of hunting was to climb to

my spike camp (a tiny mountain tent with backpacking equipment), hunt the benches on the northwest side of the mountain, drop into the next drainage, hunt out the pockets on a south-facing drainage, on the third day, hunt down a long ridge back to the bottom.

I left the pickup in the dark and started climbing the 3,000 feet to the top of the mountain where I hoped to find sheep. I moved slowly and did a lot of looking and listening. I reached a point on the ridge at 9 a.m., set up my spotting scope and examined the edges of the openings above me.

I picked up four sheep in the scope. They were feeding away from me towards some benches near the top of the mountain. One ram looked like it deserved closer scrutiny. I decided to work my way up the mountain and position myself in order to locate the rams on the benches later in the day. I backed off the point and climbed up along a fringe of timber to a fallen fir free. The sun was starting to feel good, so I sat with my back against the downhill side of the log when I heard a rattle of balsam root leaves behind me.

"Nuts, here comes another hunter," I thought

Out of the corner of my eye I saw a ewe walking. It went around to the end of the log behind a Christmas tree-sized fir and stood 40 feet from me. It bleated softly and repeated it insistently. I heard the balsam leaves again. Mother ewe appeared and joined the first one. This was repeated and the pair became a trio. All this took place in a space of three or four minutes. The ewes nonchalantly moved across and down into some timber. They had no idea I was there.

I gave the ewes a half-hour to get out of the vicinity so I wouldn't spook them and started to put on my pack to move up the mountain. Just then, the five young rams trotted across the open hillside 150 yards above me. I waited for them to feed out of sight. Before they were gone, three more young rams appeared in the far corner of the hillside. I was surrounded by sheep. Every sheep in Rock Creek, Montana, seemed to feed between 10 a.m. and 1 p.m.

I waited another half-hour and worked my way up through a line of trees to the timber A storm came in from the west so I hunkered down in a patch of young firs while the thunder grumbled. The rain didn't amount to much, so I decided to explore a few grassy benches toward the top of the mountain. As I worked my way through the benches, another storm cell came across the mountain. I decided to move to my spike camp before the storm hit.

I moved along too fast, not paying attention to my surroundings. Three magnificent rams stood up and stared at me from 40 to 50 yards. I had my hat in my left hand because I was hot and sweaty. My rifle was in my right hand. I remember thinking I didn't want to drop my hat for fear the sudden movement would spook the rams. The hat was still in my left band as I brought my rifle up slowly and grasped the forearm. Which of the rams was the biggest? I couldn't tell. They weren't going to stand there much longer.

"Come on, Mavis. Put your research and experience to work Make up your mind," I thought.

The middle ram turned and gave me a profile. That was it The ram's horns matched the criteria I studied on videos. The size of the hole in the curl, the drop of the bottom of the curl below the jaw line, and the way it carried the mass of its base out to the fourth quarter told me this was a keeper. I didn't dare move into a kneeling position so I took an offhand shot. I was close and didn't want to shoot over the ram, so I held on its shoulder. I hardly remember squeezing the trigger.

KAPOW! Down went the ram. I jacked in another cartridge, hit the safety, and climbed up to the ram. I hardly believed my eyes. The size of the ram looked huge with all those horns and large head.

"Yahoo! I did it! I did it!" I yelled. I was shaking as I cut out the month and date on my permit. I must have figured it three ways to confirm the date was October 6, 1993.

About the time I marked my permit all hell broke loose. The storm that had moved my way hit with thunder, lightning, snow, sleet, and rain. The wind howled and the three snags overhead groaned. It was too dark to take pictures. I had to work quickly since it was almost 3 p.m. A taxidermist had shown me how to properly skin out the animal for a full mount, so as the storm howled around me, I set to work I had the ram skinned with the heads and horns draped over a stump and the meat quartered in three hours.

Darkness was falling at 6 p.m. when I started down the mountain. I alerted a local outfitter that I had taken a ram and would need help in the morning hauling everything off the mountain. Rain poured all night and I didn't sleep much, worrying about the meat and cape. The ram wasn't disturbed when we returned the next morning. Four inches of fresh snow had fallen in my spike camp and rain and sleet made the day miserable, but I was so happy I hardly noticed. My feet were barely touching the ground.

After the 60-day drying period, my ram was scored by an Official Measurer of the Boone and Crockett Club at 200-1/8 points. Not bad for a woman who will never see 65 years of age again. 🦌

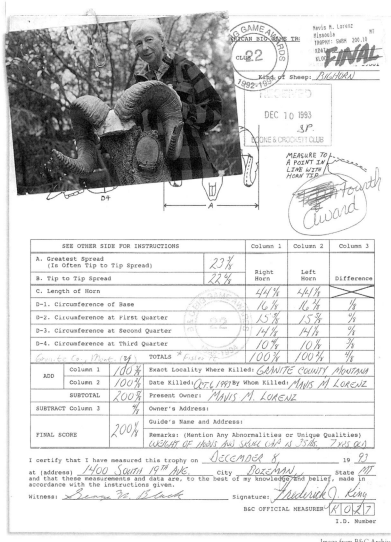

SEE OTHER SIDE FOR INSTRUCTIONS		Column 1	Column 2	Column 3
A. Greatest Spread (Is Often Tip to Tip Spread)	23 7/8			
B. Tip to Tip Spread	22 4/8	Right Horn	Left Horn	Difference
C. Length of Horn		44 4/8	44 1/8	
D-1. Circumference of Base		16 1/8	16 2/8	1/8
D-2. Circumference at First Quarter		15 5/8	15 5/8	0/8
D-3. Circumference at Second Quarter		14 1/8	14 1/8	0/8
D-4. Circumference at Third Quarter		10 4/8	10 1/8	3/8
TOTALS		100 1/8	100 2/8	4/8

ADD	Column 1	100 1/8	Exact Locality Where Killed: GRANITE COUNTY MONTANA
	Column 2	100 2/8	Date Killed: OCT. 6 1993 By Whom Killed: MAVIS M. LORENZ
SUBTOTAL		200 3/8	Present Owner: MAVIS M. LORENZ
SUBTRACT Column 3		4/8	Owner's Address:
			Guide's Name and Address:
FINAL SCORE		200 1/8	Remarks: (Mention Any Abnormalities or Unique Qualities) WEIGHT OF HORNS AND SKULL CAP IS 35 LBS. 7 YRS OLD

I certify that I have measured this trophy on DECEMBER 8, 19 93
at (address) 1400 SOUTH 19TH AVE. city BOZEMAN, State MT
and that these measurements and data are, to the best of my knowledge and belief, made in accordance with the instructions given.

Witness: George M. Black   Signature: Frederick J. King
B&C OFFICIAL MEASURER K O 2 7
I.D. Number

Image from B&C Archives

Original score chart for Mavis M. Lorenz's bighorn sheep, which scores 200-1/8 points.

Photo from B&C Archives

Bighorn Sheep, Scoring 197-1/8 points,
Taken by Armand H. Johnson in Sanders County, Montana.
in 1979.

Bighorn Vacation

By Armand H. Johnson

18th Big Game Awards Program

I BEGAN APPLYING FOR A PERMIT TO HUNT BIGHORN SHEEP IN 1957. TWENTY-ONE YEARS LATER MY PERSISTENCE PAID OFF. IN AUGUST 1979, THE MONTANA DEPARTMENT OF FISH, WILDLIFE AND PARKS ISSUED ME A PERMIT TO HUNT THE CABINET MOUNTAINS SURROUNDING THOMPSON FALLS, MONTANA, AN AREA WELL-KNOWN FOR ITS SHEEP POPULATION.

I live in Missoula (which is about 100 miles southeast of this area) making it possible for me to hunt on weekends with my son Kenton. In the month before I began hunting, Kenton and I mapped-out the area and decided that Priscilla Mountain would be our central point.

Our first hunt was on September 23, 1979. After hunting four weekends, I was discouraged at not having seen more sheep. However, the opportunity to hunt bighorn sheep had come once in a lifetime for me, so I scheduled two full weeks of vacation to hunt. I hunted 12 out of 13 days of vacation.

It was November and Kenton was in school, so I hunted alone. The days were warm, to the mid-forties, but cooled quickly as the sun went down. I decided that my camp trailer would be much more comfortable than camping-out for two weeks. On

November 9, I pulled the trailer up the Thompson River to the West Fork and parked it in a camping area. This would serve as my home for the duration of my stay.

The next morning I began an expedition which spanned ten days that I will never forget nor tire of telling. The mountains the sheep inhabit are rugged and rocky, with shale rock and steep ledges covering Priscilla Mountain. I glassed the area surrounding this mountain every day. That first day, I saw a ram with a 3/4 curl. It was exciting for me because I knew the sheep were there; it was just a matter of finding them.

I met a hunter who told me of a bunch of sheep at a log landing near the highway. I went back to the Jeep and, after reaching the site, discovered the hunter wasn't exaggerating. There were at least 50 sheep, just 50 feet away from me. I recorded their activities with my camera, watching for hours with awe.

The morning of the 12th, I glassed four rams a mile above me. I climbed through the shale rock and ledges to get a closer look. However, when I got to a vantage point they were gone and I didn't catch sight of them again. Across another ridge, I spotted a 3/4-curl ram. I watched as he worked his way across the ledges to within 50 yards of me. Quietly, I waited until he moved on. I hadn't moved when I saw a little ram coming toward me, using the same route. He got within 40 feet of me and then just stood there. It seemed as though he had been run out of a bunch and was merely looking for a friend. He stayed with me as I worked my way down the ridge.

The next few days I observed several sheep in their natural habitat, fighting, feeding, and bedding down. I spotted a couple of 3/4-curl rams and a few that were better than 3/4, but I decided to take pictures rather than shoot as I had plenty of hunting time left.

Tuesday, November 13, I called home. Kenton needed help packing out a spike elk he had shot, so I returned home.

I resumed my quest on Thursday morning, climbing the ledges and shale rock where I had seen a big ram a few days earlier. I had no luck, but I continued searching.

Saturday was rainy and foggy, with visibility only about 100 feet. I climbed the slide rock to a small bench. The fog wasn't lifting, and it was so cold that I built a fire, quite a feat since all the wood was wet. Just after noon the fog lifted, allowing me to glass the ridges. However, the sheep were under cover from the weather also.

The rain held through the next day which meant fog again. By noon the dreary gloom started to move out of the valley but it was too late to climb into the canyons. I tried a trail I had used earlier that week, seeing a couple of 3/4-curl rams with a group of ewes and lambs. Darkness set in before I could reach the Jeep. The main ridge along this trail changes directions several times, going up and down. Because of the rain clouds I was unable to use the moonlight to see. After both sets of flashlight batteries had gone dim, and I had crossed my tracks in the half-inch of snow now on the ground, I decided it was time to build a fire and spend the night.

I cut pine boughs and built a shelter between the fallen timber to stop the wind. I then cut more boughs to lie on, but this proved very uncomfortable due to the icicles frozen on the needles beneath me. The temperature had already dropped to about 20 degrees, so I kept a fire going and took short cat-naps throughout the night.

Dawn was a welcome sight. I started walking at about 7:00 a.m., and found I was only about 100 yards from the ridge that led into the main ridge. I went back to the camper to eat and fix a lunch, starting again about 11:00 a.m.

I drove east, following a four-wheel drive road. Then I followed sheep trails on foot which led me into the steep slopes and ledges the sheep love. Below me, I saw some sheep grazing in a meadow. I took off my pack board and set-up the spotting scope. I studied a couple of 3/4-curl rams in the bunch. Falling rocks above me turned my attention to a fairly nice ram coming down the trail. He came close to me and watched me for a few seconds, then turned and looked out over a ledge. I picked up the camera and rifle, hoping to see the large ram that had been so elusive. The rocks above me again stirred. This time another 3/4-curl ram and a ewe followed the trail. A few minutes later, the rocks started falling and a big ram followed where the other three had come down. I could see that his horns were better than a full curl, protruding well below his jaw. He was in no hurry, and luckily he hadn't seen me.

When he reached the trail the others had taken, he stopped and looked at me. Again I could see that he had exceptionally large horns. I wasted no time; this was the ram I had seen, and I didn't want to risk losing him again. I shot, felling him instantly.

I knew he was a very good ram, but he was better than I had anticipated. On November 20 I returned to Missoula and called Jim Ford, Montana Fish, Wildlife and Parks District Supervisor, because he is an Official Measurer for the Boone and Crockett Club. Jim's green-score of my ram was: left horn - 46 inches long, 16-5/8 inches around the base; right horn - 44-6/8 inches long, 16-4/8 inches around the base. The total green-score was 200-6/8 points by the Boone and Crockett scoring system.

On January 22, 1980, Jim Ford measured the horns officially after the 60-day drying period required by the Boone and Crockett Club rules. His scoring showed my ram to be the largest recorded in Montana since 1955, and the biggest ram taken by a hunter since 1924. It was also a dream come true for me. 🦌

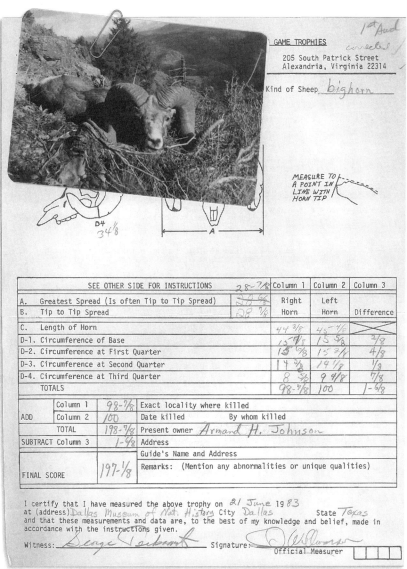

GAME TROPHIES

205 South Patrick Street
Alexandria, Virginia 22314

Kind of Sheep _bighorn_

MEASURE TO
A POINT IN
LINE WITH
HORN TIP

D4
34 1/8

SEE OTHER SIDE FOR INSTRUCTIONS	28-7/8	Column 1	Column 2	Column 3
A. Greatest Spread (Is often Tip to Tip Spread)	28	Right	Left	
B. Tip to Tip Spread	28 7/8	Horn	Horn	Difference
C. Length of Horn		44 3/8	45 4/8	✕
D-1. Circumference of Base		15 7/8	15 5/8	2/8
D-2. Circumference at First Quarter		15 6/8	15 2/8	4/8
D-3. Circumference at Second Quarter		19 2/8	19 1/8	1/8
D-4. Circumference at Third Quarter		8 5/8	9 4/8	7/8
TOTALS		98-7/8	100	1-6/8

	Column 1	98-7/8	Exact locality where killed
ADD	Column 2	100	Date killed By whom killed
	TOTAL	198-7/8	Present owner _Armand H. Johnson_
SUBTRACT Column 3		1-6/8	Address
			Guide's Name and Address
FINAL SCORE		197-1/8	Remarks: (Mention any abnormalities or unique qualities)

I certify that I have measured the above trophy on _21 June_ 19 _83_
at (address) _Dallas Museum of Nat. History_ City _Dallas_   State _Texas_
and that these measurements and data are, to the best of my knowledge and belief, made in
accordance with the instructions given.

Witness: _George Carbanet_   Signature: _____
                                          Official Measurer

Image from B&C Archives

*Original score chart for Armand H. Johnson' bighorn sheep, which
scores 197–1/8 points.*

Photo from B&C Archives

Bighorn Sheep, Scoring 200-7/8 points,
Taken by Lester A. Kish in Deer Lodge County, Montana,
in 1990.

Old Flare

By Lester A. Kish

21st Big Game Awards Program

To say that hunting is a sport of luck is an under-statement. In 1990, I had the good fortune to draw a bighorn sheep permit in Montana's Unit 213, near Anaconda. With odds exceeding 100 to 1, just drawing the permit was an incredible stroke of luck.

Unit 213 has a transplanted herd that originated from sheep trapped in Montana's Sun River area. In a little over 20 years, the herd had become a producer of super rams, with the herd consisting of over 400 sheep.

Then, late in the summer of 1991, the population crashed due to an epidemic of pasteurella pneumonia. Writer Duncan Gilchrist and I visited the area in February 1992. Range that sup-ported upward of 150 rams during the winter of 1991 contained only 22 sheep. While later counts were a little more encouraging, the total herd had been reduced to about 30 percent of pre-pas-teurella levels. In addition, the majority of the big rams perished during the epidemic.

I would not be able to write this story if my permit were for 1991 since most of the big rams had died prior to the hunting season. What a difference a year makes.

During August and September of 1990, I made several scouting trips to the area. Sheep were plentiful, and I was able to find the favored haunts of the rams. One day, more than six hours were spent watching a group of 14 rams. Two of the rams were huge. One sported a massive, deeply dropping, heavily broomed set of horns. The other ram was even more incredible. He had it all. Built like those of an argali, the horns were long, massive, relatively unbroomed, and flared. I would later learn that this ram had been observed, photographed, and even videotaped by Duncan Gilchrist and others during previous winters. The ram had aptly been nicknamed Flare. The shadows lengthened and darkness fell as I walked off the mountain. Sheep season was still three sleepless weeks away.

September 15, 1990, finally arrived and with it the opening of the Montana sheep season. Ironically, I had scheduled my vacation for this date. Imagine, nine whole days to hunt ram.

The weather was superb, though actually too warm during the first days of the season. My hunting partner, Jo, accompanied me the first two days. We saw lots of country and quite a few sheep, but nothing exceptional, so the hunt continued. I was glad that Jo had the opportunity to share the thrill of glassing for rams in the high country. Few people have been so fortunate.

From the third day on, I would be hunting alone; Jo had to go back to work. Early that third morning, I climbed out of Lost Creek Canyon. From my vantage point, I could see an expanse of rock and timber. Occasionally a ram or two would appear briefly in an opening and then disappear. Some rams were respectable yet not tempting enough to make me want to end the hunt of a lifetime. Vivid memories of those giant rams seen during preseason scouting kept me from getting too excited about taking an average ram.

That afternoon, I hiked out and moved camp to another area. I would concentrate on the area where I had earlier seen

Flare. With camp moved, I did some hiking and scouting. Around dusk, several rams were spotted, miles away. While I could not be sure, I had a feeling that they might be the same bunch I had watched for six hours during the preseason. Would the big rams still be with them?

For some reason, I did not get any sleep that night. I almost wore out the switch on my flashlight by checking the time every few minutes. At 4:00 a.m., I couldn't stand the waiting so I got up and made some coffee.

Soon after, flashlight in hand, I was hiking up the ridge toward the rams, hoping they were still bedded. I knew my intended approach well. I had worked and reworked the stalk during the sleepless night. The rams were approachable, provided that they stayed put.

What were the odds that this was the same bunch of rams that I had glassed for hours during the preseason? Better yet, what were the odds that the old argali named Flare would be with them? It just had to be the same bunch. I knew it was the day for a big ram.

The sky brightened. Soon, the first rays of morning sunshine would illuminate the neighboring peaks of the Pintlars. Spectacular scenery is usually available on demand when sheep hunting, and the Pintlars obliged each time I looked over my shoulder.

Only the sheep hunter knows the inexorable lure of hunting the high country. While I had spent years stalking the Rockies for other mountain game, those experiences paled in comparison to this hunt. The sheep hunting mystique was real; Jack O'Connor was right. Once you contract sheep fever, you are a goner.

At first light, I reached a vantage point overlooking the head of the drainage. Out came the spotting scope. Were the rams still there? You bet! There were 12 rams in all, with the big argali lying in the center. It was a most incredible sight.

I packed away the scope. It was crunch time. The rams were a little over a half-mile above me. I backed out of sight, threw the old legs into gear, and headed up the mountain.

I soon reached the lodgepole timber. Continuing on, I made sure that I was well above the rams. Then I cut across the slope in their direction. Eventually, I reached the drainage head. Grass appeared through the timber but I saw no rams. Like a snake in the grass, I bellied down the slope. A single horn appeared. More slithering, and more horns popped into view.

They were only 70 yards away. From a prone position, I could not see the rams. The grass was too tall. Up on my knees, I could only see heads and necks — not enough for a shot.

The biggest sheep on the mountain was right in front of me and I could not do anything. Man, was I nervous. I waited an honest 20 minutes as rams started getting up to feed. Finally, the big one got up. Caught in the open, I had to shoot offhand. Deer and elk running through the timber seem to be easy targets to me, but a huge ram, standing in the open, was almost impossible.

Every ram but Flare was staring at me. I shot, missed, and all hell broke loose. The stampede was on. Just as he was about to disappear into a gully, I broke his back. I could hear rocks rolling. Then the ram appeared down below, and he was trying to get up. I put two more shots into the rolling ram. All was quiet.

When I reached the ram, I was shocked. He was the most incredible animal I had ever seen. Unfortunately, I did not take much time admiring him. It was only 7:45 a.m. but the sun was already starting to feel hot. Hastily, I took some pictures and set about the caping and boning chores.

The next 12 hours were pure hell. It was hot and dry. I ran out of water. I wanted to get the meat and cape off the mountain in a hurry. By maintaining a relentless pace and leapfrogging loads of meat and the head for short distances, I got closer to the car with each load. That way, I did not have to hike all the way back to the kill site once any one load was all the way out.

I got back to camp with the last load just as it was getting dark. Rather than spend the night, I packed up my gear and drove home. When I pulled in late that night, Jo was up in a flash. The smile on my face said it all. Yes, I got one, a pretty good one.

"You look worse than the sheep," Jo said. "You certainly smell worse."

I was all scratched up and had a chunk of hide rubbed off my back from the friction of the pack frame. In addition, I had lost 10 pounds in 4 days of hunting.

Next morning, I went down to Montana Fish, Wildlife and Parks headquarters to get the horns plugged. Fred King, an Official Measurer for Boone and Crockett, was in the lobby. When I walked in, he asked how the sheep hunting was going. "Come out to the car and take a look," I said.

The reaction when I opened the tailgate was, "Oh my God!" We carried the head into the lab. Soon, people were popping out of the woodwork to admire the sheep.

"Is he a big one?" someone asked. "Yes, he certainly is. Maybe a new record!"

He was plugged as 80 MT 361. When the tape hit the left horn, it stretched to 20 inches, 30 inches, and then 40 inches, with more to go. The tape finally stopped at 49-2/8 inches. Even the short horn measured 45-5/8 inches. Geez, what a sheep!

Sixty days later, he scored 200-7/8, thus making him the new state record for Montana, the land of the giant rams.

Friend and taxidermist Dale Manning from Missoula, Montana, did a superb job on the shoulder mount. Now, when I look at old Flare (or Oscar, as I prefer to call him), I relive the excitement and rigors of the hunt. I also dream of the day when I can again pursue great rams in the high country.

Photo from B&C Archives

Desert Sheep Scoring, 197-1/8 points,
Taken by Arthur R. Dubs in Graham County, Arizona,
in 1988.

Desert Oasis

By Arthur R. Dubs

21st Big Game Awards Program

AT THE AUCTION OF THE FOUNDATION FOR NORTH AMERI-CAN WILD SHEEP IN FEBRUARY OF 1988, I OBTAINED A PERMIT TO HUNT DESERT SHEEP IN ARAVAIPA CANYON, AN EIGHT-MILE GORGE THAT SLASHES THROUGH SOME OF THE MOST RUGGED COUNTRY IN SOUTHWESTERN ARIZONA.

As I have done in the past, I wanted to capture the excitement and spectacle of the hunt on film. I could not wait to pack my camera, along with my .300 Weatherby Magnum rifle, and head for Arizona. I was determined to search out and take the largest desert ram in Aravaipa Canyon and to share the experience with my fellow sportsmen.

My guide, Floyd Krank, who lives in Globe, Arizona, had been hunting and scouting the area since the Arizona Game and Fish Department opened it to hunting in 1980. Three years prior to my hunt, Floyd had spotted a huge ram and named him Chiphorn, because a large piece was missing on the back side of his left horn. In succeeding years, while Floyd was hunting with clients, the old ram managed to escape all efforts to track him down. Floyd finally caught another glimpse of the ram on a scouting trip the previous summer, during the height of the rutting season. The ram was lean and haggard from running off young upstarts. At the time, Floyd had serious doubts whether Chiphorn would be able to make it through another winter.

I arrived in Aravaipa Canyon on December 1, 1988, and met Floyd a day before the season opened. He had already set up a comfortable camp, and we both had a serious dose of sheep fever. We sat up late that night, exchanging ideas on how we might be able to outsmart the ram. If he was still alive, we had 21 days to find him before the end of the season.

Five o'clock came early. Before sunrise, Floyd and I were dodging cactus and slipping on rotten volcanic rock as we made our way through the jagged rims overlooking the canyon. Soon, golden rays of sunlight spread a brighter path for us to follow along the canyon rim.

As we cautiously peeked over the edge, we were treated to a spectacular view of the canyon, and we could hear Aravaipa Creek bubbling 2,000 feet below us. A group of a dozen ewes and lambs grazed contentedly on an outcropping only a few yards from us. We skirted around them, leaving them undisturbed as we kept moving under cover of the rocks, glassing every draw and crevice. The sheep were scattered and we saw several small rams. We arrived back at our cozy camp two hours after sunset with new scratches and an accumulation of cacti.

After three days of hunting from daylight to dark, we ended up with no leads on Chiphorn. Floyd and I were beginning to wonder if the old ram was still alive. We had photographed and passed up several trophy rams that would have scored well up in the records book, but we saw nothing that approached the stature of Chiphorn.

It was a nice awakening when, at sunrise on the fifth day of the hunt from the top of the rim above Aravaipa Creek, we spotted a heavy-horned ram with a group of other sheep. They were more than a mile away, at the head of Javelina Canyon. The ram was on a talus slope, feeding on a barrel cactus.

We rushed to set up our 60x spotting scope. There was no question of identification. Even from the great distance, we could see the ram's massive broomed horns. We knew we were looking at one of the largest desert rams on the continent.

The ram had not only survived the summer's rutting season, but he had bulked up considerably and was robust and healthy. He was banging heads with two younger rams, showing his prowess in view of a half-dozen ewes and one small lamb. He looked out of proportion, holding up his huge load of yellowish horn. We were amazed by his ability to carry such a heavy set of horns with such agility.

We quickly took a series of telephoto film sequences. Then, we wasted no time in moving around the rocky rim to get closer to the old ram. After an hour of weaving around the heads of several scabrous side canyons, we still found ourselves 600 yards away, looking down on Chiphorn 1,000 feet below us.

We went around the last possible side canyon in the vicinity of the ram. Again, we were overlooking the ram, but the range was no more than 250 yards. Luckily he was still with the other sheep, continuing to dominate the herd and flirting with the same ewe.

I quickly placed my tripod and camera in position and ran off a few feet of movie film. Then, the thought struck me: I had an opportunity to bag the largest desert ram I would ever see, but how would we retrieve him if I shot him? We agreed that even if we had to resort to mountain climbing equipment, we were not going to pass him up.

I quickly chambered a cartridge and carefully crawled out as far as possible over the edge of the rim. I steadied my rifle on a rock. The crosshairs of my scope found the great ram, and I squeezed the trigger. As the rifle roared, the ram dropped in his tracks, never flinching.

Floyd yelled, "You got 'em!" as the echo of the shot bounced off the canyon wall below us. The rest of the herd scattered and disappeared.

Congratulations were followed by the challenge. We had to climb down to the talus slope to retrieve the ram. After attempting to backtrack through several side canyons and changing our route several times, we discovered a faint trail that revealed fresh sheep tracks. I have taken several bighorn sheep, but the tracks Floyd and I found were as large as any we had ever seen. We knew they had to have been made by Chiphorn and his band. We followed the tracks through a narrow passage hidden by boulders and continued by crawling through a jungle of undergrowth. We knew that if Chiphorn and his entire band, including the small lamb, had made their way through the canyon and onto the talus slope, we had a chance to do so as well.

We continued our descent through the rocky passage and finally broke out into some of the most beautiful terrain we had encountered in Aravaipa. There were several water holes. The canyon was an oasis, a paradise for birds and sheep and rattlesnakes too, for we met some of them.

It had been almost three hours since the shot. Soon, we rounded the last talus slope and saw the fabulous desert ram.

I broke out my measuring tape. Both of the horns measured more than 42 inches in length. More impressive still was the massiveness of the horns. They were broomed off as big as coffee cups, with 11-inch third quarters and bases of more than 16 inches. He had only four teeth left and all but one were extremely loose. We aged him at 12 years old. Yet the muscles still rippled over his dark-furred body. We concluded that his enormous front hooves were essential to support the weight of his horns.

We took a complete set of field measurements before fielddressing him. I wanted the end result to be the truest representation possible of a ram in a full mount, as he appeared in the wild.

A few days later, the horns green-scored 198-5/8 when measured by a Boone and Crockett Official Measurer in Tucson, Arizona. On May 20, 1992, I was informed that a panel of Boone and Crockett scorers had officially confirmed the score at 197-1/8 points. I was delighted that I had shot the largest desert ram ever taken by a modern-day hunter in fair chase.

Photo from B&C Archives

Stone's Sheep, Scoring 176-4/8 points,
Taken by James M. Peek near Tuchodi River, British Columbia,
in 1993.

Play Hooky Ram

By James M. Peek

22nd Big Game Awards Program

I SENSED IT WAS ABOUT TIME TO HEAR FROM ROSS PECK OF FORT ST. JOHN, BRITISH COLUMBIA, ABOUT A HUNT FOR STONE'S SHEEP. WE HAD INVITED HIM INTO THE TAYLOR RANCH IN THE CENTRAL IDAHO WILDERNESS LAST WINTER TO SHOW HIM A BIGHORN, BUT TIME AND WEATHER PREVENTED HIS VISIT. HE ASKED ME UP TO THE TUCHODI RIVER AREA OF BRIT-ISH COLUMBIA FOUR YEARS AGO, BUT I DECLINED BECAUSE OF TEACHING COMMITMENTS. IF HE TOLD ME HE HAD SPACE THIS TIME, I KNEW I WAS GOING, COME HELL OR HIGH WATER.

At 57, my knees were beginning to go, and there weren't too many 60-year-old sheep hunters rattling around on a mountain. I couldn't be certain of health or another sheep hunting invitation. So when Ross extended another invitation, I accepted.

The hunt began on Ross' landing strip. The pilot circled the sky to see which way the wind sock pointed and to make sure no horses were in the vicinity He pulled his flap lever and smoothly landed his Cessna 185. As we taxied to the corrals, my eyes wandered towards those high, sharp-sculpted crags in the distance that sheltered sheep. I had just arrived, and the trip was a success. The country is honest-to-God, bona-fide, top-quality, big-game country!

Our pack outfit left the horse camp and pulled out onto a series of parks or grassy meadows that paralleled the high ridge we were to hunt. We camped where there was no sign of a previous camp. A small group of ewes on one side kept popping over the ridge so we knew we'd see sheep tomorrow.

The next morning our horses carried us through wet brush up a forested section of the slope until it became too steep. I worked hard and stopped often. I gradually got my legs under me and caught my breath as we broke out into the alpine tundra. Rain became heavier, and we saw a series of snow squalls coming our way from the northwest. We walked up the hill through the squalls.

"Well, let's see what the ridge top looks like. This light snow won't hurt us," Ross said.

We trudged out of the scrubby spruce onto the ridge in 10 centimeters of new snow to look for sheep. No self-respecting sheep were loitering around on the windy side of the mountain; only dumb hunters.

"Now, keep your head down or the sheep will see you!" Ross said quietly

Crisp air created some image distortion as the sun's heat waves wafted from the melting snow on the black rock. Ewes and lambs were below us. I wasn't pleased because ewes and big rams usually don't mix this time of year.

"Don't forget to watch the brush below us on that slope," he said. 'They're apt to be down in the brush on a day like this."

Ross has the eyes of an experienced hunter. As we examined the country he pointed out three groups of ewes and lambs. Elk were below us in the spruce. I focused on big game with the binoculars but Ross pointed them out using only his eyes. Then I saw the first ram bedded in a little shady shelf below a ridgeline. We studied the curls and determined it had horns that ended below its nose. Were there more rams?

We found a game trail the next day that wound up the ridge. The sky was clear, and we walked to the ridge. We examined the other side of the ridge and went to the same ledge where we saw the sheep. Ross motioned me to stay down while he slowly looked over the ridge.

He instantly ducked and whispered, "Rams!"

We raised up and Ross motioned to the ridge where seven adult Stone's sheep rams were resting or feeding. We set up our scopes and examined their horns. They were about 1,000 meters away, but all were less than fill curl.

None of the rams were full-curl (the magic size), but we started to whisper about what to do next, realizing we hadn't seen all of the drainage from this vantage. We moved slightly and I got bolder about appearing above the ridgeline. Ross pointed to the birch below where he spotted four rams slowly moving away from us. I couldn't be sure if we had disturbed them. Ross studied them and I tried to get my scope set up. We did not think they were spooked.

We spent an hour walking across the cliffs and rocky side of the ridge. Every now and then we'd walk up to see over, then drop back down. We had to keep from disturbing any of the sheep in the drainage, knowing their sharp eyes were looking in all directions. When seven sets of sheep eyes are on a ridge, you can bet they'll notice any move. Whether or not movement disturbs sheep is another matter, but once you're spotted, they may stare at you for a long time.

Ewes and lambs were below, but there was no evidence of rams. We found more ewes but the rams were on the other side of the drainage. A rough mountain ridge has a million places for sheep to bed, so we had to examine every bit of the broken terrain; no rams. We moved down the ridge.

We continued this pattern, and I wondered if the rams had hightailed it out of the area when they first walked over the ridge. We decided to move where we last saw them. We slowly inched to the ridgeline, the last place to try to locate the rams today.

Ross doffed his hat looked over the ridge and ducked back down. He saw them. He put his fingers to his lips in the shush signal, and we slowly looked over the ridge. Below in a muddy bank lay a Stone's ram. The angle was steep, and we couldn't determine whether it was full curl or not, but it was at least close. Where were the others?

We studied the ram in silence. It moved its head a little one way and then another, but we were never sure whether those big horns crossed the bridge of its nose or not

"He's legal," Ross said "Slip down to that green spot when I tell you. Wait!"

I had moved. "If I whistle, stop. Now go!" he said.

I inched down on my back, rifle resting on my chest, hugging the ground. I slid into a solid prone shooting position. Ross whistled, a bit too loud I thought, so I froze. The ram turned its head toward us, but didn't move. As the ram looked away I settled into a solid rest, slipped off the safety of my rifle and viewed the ram through the scope.

I knew shooting downhill meant different trajectories than if I shot across level ground, so I aimed low. The rifle was dead still. I concentrated on squeezing the trigger. At the shot the ram got up and ran over the crest of the spur ridge above it.

"You shot in front of him!" Ross said.

I snapped off another shot but knew it missed, too. Hunting, like any sport, is a series of highs and lows. The absolute low is missing a shot. This missed shot was the lowest point in my 45 years of hunting experiences.

"Well, let's go down and look. You may have nicked him," Ross said.

I couldn't figure what went wrong. I thought I had compensated for the steep angle, but I knew better than to blame the rifle. I was wondering what to do next. I asked my friend to expend a considerable amount of time and energy on my behalf, and he had done more than I expected.

We needed to check if the ram was hit or not. We dropped down the hill to scout out its tracks for any signs and examined the bed. I wondered why we hadn't heard the ram clattering across the slide rock.

"There he goes, right beneath us! Get down here! Get down here!" Ross yelled.

Ross was disgusted with the events. The ram had gone below some low ledges on the ridge and stopped. I saw it running and headed directly to the ridgeline for a shot. I was concentrating on the ram and my footing. I got to a spot where I could get into a solid sitting position but the first two shots missed. The ram was scuttling along the far side of the draw, and there would be time for one more shot. I took a deep breath and squeezed the trigger. At the shot, the ram was down.

I bought my .30-06 Winchester, Model 70 rifle in 1959. Since the rifle has so many good experiences attached to it, it's an important part of my history. The rifle shoots a minute-of-angle group with several weights of bullets, and I chose the 150-grain Hornady for sheep hunting. I was haunted that I missed.

These old eyes were moist as I realized I had just finished an experience backed by about 40 years of anticipation, in an extraordinarily beautiful and wild country. The "Play Hooky Ram" was working its magic, and it would again and again.

I realized I would look at him at least 250 days or so out of each year.

I fell into bed, listening to the elk bugle, waking only when the lights of the generator went on at 5:45 a.m. We were on the tail end of the trip, and I was relaxed. The clouds brought snow delaying my flight to Fort Nelson. The elk bugled each night, and I had time to examine the ones that fed on the slopes around the camp.

I took the stolen time to visit, write, wander, and reflect. On the last night; I heard wolves on the slopes, probably examining the elk just in case one might be vulnerable. The unmistakable howl of the gray wolf floated across the ridges in the night air. Hunts are for memories, and I've my share of the best. 🦌

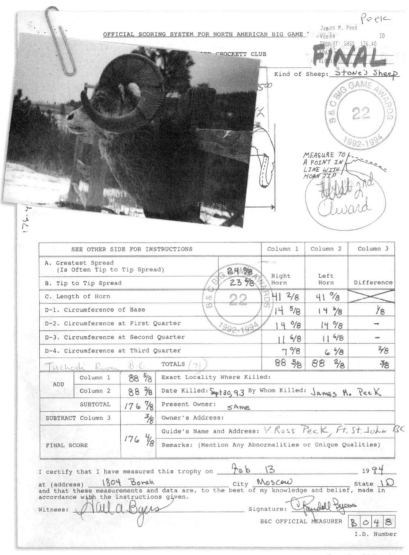

OFFICIAL SCORING SYSTEM FOR NORTH AMERICAN BIG GAME

...AND CROCKETT CLUB

James M. Peek
Viola   ID
TROPHY: SHSS 176.40

Peek

FINAL

Kind of Sheep: Stone's Sheep

22
1992-1994

MEASURE TO
A POINT IN
LINE WITH
HORN TIP

2nd
Award

SEE OTHER SIDE FOR INSTRUCTIONS			Column 1	Column 2	Column 3
A. Greatest Spread (Is Often Tip to Tip Spread)		24 1/8	Right Horn	Left Horn	Difference
B. Tip to Tip Spread		23 5/8			
C. Length of Horn			41 2/8	41 0/8	
D-1. Circumference of Base			14 5/8	14 6/8	1/8
D-2. Circumference at First Quarter			14 0/8	14 0/8	—
D-3. Circumference at Second Quarter			11 4/8	11 4/8	—
D-4. Circumference at Third Quarter			7 0/8	6 5/8	2/8
Tuchodi River B.C. TOTALS (71)			88 5/8	88 2/8	3/8
ADD	Column 1	88 5/8	Exact Locality Where Killed:		
	Column 2	88 2/8	Date Killed: Sept 30, 93 By Whom Killed: James M. Peek		
	SUBTOTAL	176 7/8	Present Owner: same		
SUBTRACT Column 3		3/8	Owner's Address:		
FINAL SCORE		176 4/8	Guide's Name and Address: V Ross Peck, Ft. St. John BC		
			Remarks: (Mention Any Abnormalities or Unique Qualities)		

I certify that I have measured this trophy on _Feb 13_ _19 94_
at (address) _1804 Borah_ City _Moscow_ State _ID_
and that these measurements and data are, to the best of my knowledge and belief, made in
accordance with the instructions given.

Witness: _Paul A Byers_   Signature: _J Randall Byers_

B&C OFFICIAL MEASURER | B | 0 | 4 | 8 |
I.D. Number

Image from B&C Archives

Original score chart for James M. Peek's Stone's sheep, which
scores 176-4/8 points.

Hunting party
in the Sierra madre Mts.
Chihuahua Mex
photo by Ed Irwin

Irwin Brothers Collection – Arizona Historical Society

At the turn of the century, market hunting was decimating wildlife
populations. By establishing our nation's first game laws, bag limits, and
ethical code of conduct for sportsmen, Boone and Crockett Club members
mobilized sportsmen as conservation leaders.

Fair Chase and Conservation

By Keith Balfourd

Boone and Crockett Club

THE ABUNDANCE OF FORESTS, PLANTS, AND WILDLIFE SEEMED INEXHAUSTIBLE TO EARLY NORTH AMERICAN SETTLERS. BY THE END OF THE 19TH CENTURY, HOWEVER, NORTH AMERICA'S WILDLIFE AND WILD HABITAT WERE IN SERIOUS JEOPARDY. OUR NATION'S POPULATION WAS GROWING, AND ALONG WITH THIS GROWTH CAME A THIRST FOR TIMBER, AGRICULTURAL LAND, MINERALS, FUELS, WATER, AND WILD GAME. THERE WERE NO LAWS, RULES, OR REGULATIONS REGARDING THE TAKING OF WILDLIFE, THE CLEARING OF LAND, OR USE OF OUR WETLANDS. IN ADDITION, THERE WERE FEW POLICIES AND LAWS GOVERNING THE USE AND PROTECTION OF THESE PRECIOUS RESOURCES.

The cattle industry was in its infancy and unregulated market hunting and extensive subsistence hunting were taking a heavy toll on big game populations. In the West, the U.S. Army had slaughtered entire herds of game in an effort to deprive the plains Indians of their nomadic lifestyle and force them onto the reservations. The railroad was also moving west. Along with it came the need for meat to feed the rail crews, and unregulated hunter access.

What was left of the big game herds of the Plains and the Rocky Mountains continued to dwindle in numbers. This same western expansion resulted in the clearing of forests and tilling of prairies, altering entire ecosystems. Something had to be done!

WISE USE

Theodore Roosevelt, a dedicated sportsman and visionary, founded the Boone and Crockett Club in 1887. In 1883, Roosevelt, an avid hunter, outdoorsman, and explorer returned from his ranching days in North Dakota with a mission. He had witnessed first-hand the negative affect on big game populations from unchecked exploitation. He called a meeting of several of his friends who shared his passion for the outdoors. One of these gentleman hunters, George Bird Grinnell, described this gathering as "an association of men bound together by their interest in game and fish, to take charge of all matters pertaining to the enactment and carrying out of laws on the subject."

Successful men of science, business, industry, and politics, had joined together out of their common concern for dwindling wildlife populations and irresponsible land use, to conserve wild resources for the future. Because of the dedication of these respected leaders and hunters, this meeting eventually resulted in the foundation for the greatest conservation revolution in the history of mankind and the survival of our hunting heritage.

B&C FIRST FOR CONSERVATION

When Roosevelt took office in 1901, the contemporary thinking on natural resource matters was that of "protection" and "preservation." Through his discussions with Grinnell, "conservation" became the keynote of his administration. The word soon appeared in dictionaries defined as "prudent use without waste." Roosevelt's administration produced a federal natural resource program that was balanced between economic development and aesthetic preservation, setting aside and protecting 150 million acres of national forests. In seven years, more progress was made in natural resource management than the nation had seen in a century, or has seen since.

Throughout the 19th century, Roosevelt and the hunter/conservationists of the Boone and Crockett Club continued to make significant contributions to wildlife and environmental welfare. Some of these early accomplishments of Club members include:

- The establishment of game laws and the enforcement of hunting seasons and bag limits;
- The abolishment of market hunting practices;
- The protection of Yellowstone National Park and the establishment of Glacier and Denali National Parks;
- The establishment of the National Park Service, National Forest Service, and the National Wildlife Refuge System;
- Passing of the 1894 and 1900 Lacey Acts, Federal Aid to Wildlife Restoration (Pittman-Robertson) Act, the Fish and Wildlife Coordination Act, Migratory Bird Act of 1913, the Migratory Bird Hunting Stamp Act of 1934, and the Cooperative Wildlife Research Unit Program.

Boone and Crockett Club Members were so effective that their conservation history, commissioned to be written in 1960, was so nearly a complete history of the conservation movement that it was expanded to include non-Club related items. This history was detailed in James B. Trefethen's book, *An American Crusade for Wildlife*, which has been accepted as a landmark text for conservation.

THE RULES OF FAIR CHASE
In a land of abundance, free-spirited pioneers and outdoorsmen

were naturally resistant to change, new laws, and limits. Early European law mandated that all wildlife belonged to the crown; therefore, American pioneers shunned anything that resembled old-world restrictions.

As indicated in Roosevelt's master plan, a set of guidelines had to be established. An ethical code of conduct for all sportsmen was required. If wildlife was to survive, and for "conservation" (wise use) to prevail over "preservation" (no use), sportsmen needed to lead the charge. With the leadership of Roosevelt, the Boone and Crockett Club's "Fair Chase" tenets encouraged laws in the states and provinces to maintain sport hunting at a high level of sportsmanship and ethical conduct. This "Fair Chase" code directly engaged the hunter's conscience to enjoy hunting in an ethical fashion. Born from these efforts was the concept of public stewardship and the realization that wildlife did indeed belong to the people.

Throughout its existence, the Boone and Crockett Club never skirted thorny issues. Changing the culture and thinking of the American sportsmen was, perhaps, one of the most difficult, yet significant, accomplishments of the Club. The Club's Fair Chase statement provided the foundation for hunter ethics as we know them today. The public image of the hunter was raised to that of a sportsman – one who can kill, yet protect and conserve what is taken.

THEY BELONG TO ALL

One of the early challenges facing the Club, and a successful launch of the conservation movement, was the disconnect that existed between citizens and wildlife. This disconnect was held over from the old days of European rule – no public ownership of wildlife. To bring the public into the realization that wildlife in the "new country" did indeed belong to them and was in their care, the Club went into action with two major initiatives – the protection of Yellowstone National Park and the establishment of the National Collection of Heads and Horns.

From the Club's first formal meetings a plan was initiated to save Yellowstone National Park (the Nation's first national park) from poachers, mining and timber speculators, and the Northern Pacific Railroad, which was lobbying to gain a right of way west, through the Park. "Resolve that a committee of 5 be appointed by the chair to promote useful and proper legislation toward the enlargement and better Government of Yellowstone." A single resolution, in a single sentence, but it marked the beginning of the Boone and Crockett Club's conservation crusade.

Through a series of expose' editorials in Club member George Bird Grinnell's *Forest and Stream* magazine, the public was drawn into the cause. The dramatic telling of a bison-poaching incident within the pages of Forest and Stream was a national sensation that focused public attention and outcry on the serious plight of Yellowstone. Sportsmen, nature lovers, and those who planed to someday visit the Park finally said, "No more."

In 1894, the Yellowstone Protection Act (Lacey Act of 1894) was pushed through Congress by Club Member and Senator John F. Lacey. The new laws gave Yellowstone the staff, funding, protection, enforcement, and penalties for violations it needed to maintain itself as a pristine national treasure for all the people.

The National Collection of Heads and Horns was another brainchild of the Club and its members. It was a trophy exhibit opened for public display in 1922 at the Bronx Zoo in New York City, in cooperation with the New York Zoological Society (also founded and directed by several B&C Members) and the Bronx Zoo, of which Club member William T. Hornaday was its first Director. The inscription over the entrance to the exhibit read "In

Photo from B&C Archives

Grancel Fitz measuring the main beam circumference on the A.S. Reed Alaska-Yukon moose (240-7/8 points) that is currently in the Boone and Crockett Club National Collection of Heads and Horns. Grancel was on the committee that developed the Club's copyrighted scoring system that is used today.

Memory of the Vanishing Big Game of the World." The display sparked public interest in big game animals, elevated the concept of public stewardship of wildlife, and created the momentum needed to launch a conservation and recovery effort that saved many of these great animals, and hunting itself, from extinction.

Once the positive effects of the conservation movement began to pay dividends, the plight of big game animals was no longer as much of a concern. Interest in the collection had waned and the building, which housed the trophies, became used for storage space. After a burglary in 1974, the Club rescued what remained of the collection and found a temporary home for them at the national headquarters of the National Rifle Association in Washington, D.C. In 1981, the collection was permanently moved to the Buffalo Bill Historical Center in Cody, Wyoming.

Today, the National Collection of Heads and Horns is again being shared with interested sportsmen and the hundreds of thousands of people who visit the Cody Museum annually.

WHY KEEP RECORDS

The grave condition our big game species were in at the turn of the century had many responsible sportsmen wondering if these great animals would be resigned to the same fate as Audubon's bighorn sheep, and the eastern and Merriam's elk – extinction. Certain species of animal and bird life were vanishing and, before it was too late, a biological record of their historic range and mere existence was needed. The Boone and Crockett Club again accepted the challenge.

When the Club's Executive Committee appointed Casper Whitney, Archibald Rogers, and Theodore Roosevelt to the Club's first Records Committee in 1902, it wasn't to develop a scoring system for bragging rights, endorsements, or what fees to charge for the taking of a trophy. Their goal was a system to record biological, harvest, and location data on the vanishing big game animals of North America – a system that is still in use today.

With the publishing of the first edition of *Records of North American Big Game* in 1932, the Club set in motion a system that would continue to elevate our native big game species to an even higher plane of public stewardship. A by-product of this book was an increased interest in trophy hunting, which subsequently motivates more hunters to become interested in the conservation movement.

Records-keeping activities enabled the Club to promote its doctrine of ethical hunting by accepting only those trophies taken under "Fair Chase." Through prestige received from the success and acceptance of the Records Book, the Boone and Crockett Club had the ability to forge a new understanding of species biology and the need for the management of big game species.

When it was reported that the Club would reject cougar trophies entered into the records book from states that classified cougar as vermin under a bounty system, the result led to cougar being elevated to the status of a big game animal. This allowed the cougar both management and protection such a classification warranted. This same awareness and recognition became available to other species such as the Central Canada barren ground caribou found in north-central Canada. The declaration of a separate records book category allowed this caribou sub-species to become eligible for funding and management from the government. These territories received a vital boost to their economies from the sale of licenses, tags, and a new interest in these great animals.

In Quebec, when complaints were received from hunters about the practices of caribou outfitters and guides, the Boone and Crockett Club contacted Quebec's Game and Fish Department. If questionable hunting practices continued, the Quebec-Labrador caribou would no longer be accepted for the Records Book. As a result, ethical fair chase hunting became the norm rather than the exception.

THE GREATEST STORY YET TO BE TOLD

Most hunters know of the Boone and Crockett Club. Many know only part of the story. Trophies, scoring, and records-books are only a small part of the Club's mission.

"Walk softly and carry a big stick" was Theodore Roosevelt's way of getting things done. The Club never sought recognition or notoriety for its actions. It was rare to see the Club's name in headlines, but little happens in the conservation arena that is not based on the legal foundation for the North American Model of Conservation formed and maintained by the Club and its members.

LOOKING WEST

When Roosevelt organized the Boone and Crockett Club, its members were eastern gentlemen, primarily from New York and Washington, D.C. Its activities were focused in Washington to promote initiatives through Congressional legislation and Executive Prerogative (order). This was the Club's necessary battlefield where its influential members could best achieve their goals and objectives because they were primarily federal in character. Accordingly, the Club's executive offices were in New York and Washington.

The Club's headquarters were moved to Missoula, Montana, in September 1992, for three essential reasons. First, its membership was now diversely scattered across North America. Second, the Club recognized the major national resource issues of the country continued to evolve in the West. And third, the solution to these western challenges was no longer solely in Washington at the federal level, but rather had devolved to the local level where the wildlife and watersheds existed. It was recognized, moreover, that the immense private land holdings in the West presented a challenge and opportunity equal to the resource issues of the nation.

Befitting of a century-old organization, the Club's National Headquarters is now housed in the historic Milwaukee Railroad Depot building in the heart of downtown Missoula, Montana. In addition to administrative offices, the Club has planned an interpretive visitors center highlighting the history of conservation in North America.

INTO THE SECOND CENTURY

Throughout its history, the Boone and Crockett Club has supported science, research, and education. In recognition of the Club's 100th anniversary, Club members committed to expand this purpose by purchasing the Theodore Roosevelt Memorial Ranch (TRM) in 1986. This 6,600-acre working cattle ranch is located on Montana's Rocky Mountain Front adjoining the Bob Marshall Wilderness and other privately owned ranches. This region encompasses prime wildlife wintering grounds. Here, habitat research and land management practices present an example to community ranchers demonstrating that diversified populations of big game, even predators like grizzly bear and cougar, can be compatible with profits from ranching.

Open to the public each fall, the TRM Ranch, through a cooperative agreement with the State of Montana, allows people of all ages to hunt on the Ranch; however, special emphasis is given to youth hunters who must be accompanied by an adult mentor. Hunting traditions will be preserved in the future through hunter/mentor opportunities like those who enjoy the privilege of participating in Fair Chase hunting in natural, well-managed environments.

In 2001, the Boone and Crockett Club constructed the Elmer E. Rasmuson Wildlife Conservation Education Center on the Ranch. This Center serves as the headquarters for the Lee and Penny Anderson Conservation Education programs. Using the TRM Ranch as an outdoor classroom, the Club's K-12 Education Program helps students and teachers build lasting awareness, understanding, and appreciation for the living and non-living components of our natural world. Through the Conservation Across Boundaries (CAB) program, teachers from across the country are invited to participate in workshops where wildlife and habitat conservation curriculum models are taught, benefiting both teachers and their students.

NEW KNOWLEDGE

History has proven there is no better investment in the future than knowledge through education. In keeping with the Boone and Crockett legacy of leadership, the Club launched a pilot program in 1993. This program funds the research of university graduate students who have chosen wildlife or natural resources as their life's work. The first B&C Endowed Professorship Chair found its home at the epicenter of today's resource challenges – the Rocky Mountain West. Here, at the University of Montana in Missoula, the Boone and Crockett Professor of Wildlife Conservation plays a central role in the Club's Conservation Program. The Professor teaches, guides graduate student research, and offers public service in the fields of wildlife conservation and ecosystem management for sustainable development. By focusing on education at the highest level, the Club ensures that investments made today will continue to pay dividends for decades as these students advance in their careers.

In 2005, success of this program in Montana was replicated at Texas A&M University when a second chair was endowed. The focus of this program is the impact of state and federal environmental regulations on private lands and wildlife populations, the potential of consumptive and non-consumptive wildlife resource use on landowner income, and public perceptions of private land stewardship and resource conservation. Other endowed professorships are planned at other universities throughout the U.S.

SUSTAINABLE DEVELOPMENT — BEYOND SAVING ANIMALS

The paramount challenge for humanity in the 21st Century is sustaining healthy ecosystems. Why? Because, this is where we live. Our increasing population and needs affect every living and non-living thing. This pressure on wildlife and the environment comes from this simple fact: the places people use for living and commerce are or once were the habitats of other living things.

The concept of sustainable development is to bring together environments, economies, and communities of people in new and different ways. Early conservationists, including Boone and Crockett Club members, paved the way for sustainable development with many successes. Species were brought back from the brink of extinction. Pristine places were saved for wildlife and the ethics of people's relationship with wildlife were changed from exploitation to stewardship. This shift in perspective brought with it a new focus on research to find more productive ways to use lands and resources. From this learning the process of teaching and enlightenment began, and with it, a social buy-in to rational practices for wildlife and habitat management. All of this was and is still necessary, but is it enough?

Today, most wildlife no longer lives in pristine places without people. Humans carrying out activities necessary for their lives now affect all populations of wild things, even those in the more remote areas. Therefore, the Club believes the future health of life on earth, human life included, depends on broadening our concepts of wildlife conservation and stewardship to a level that includes the perspectives of entire ecosystems, not just one particular species of animal or plant.

Humanity faces a dilemma. It's inevitable that future improvements to the quality of human life will draw more heavily on the earth's habitats and resources, displacing even more wildlife. The irony is that these improvements cannot take place in environments that continue to lose wildlife diversity and decline in the quality of water, air, and soil.

SOUND MANAGEMENT BACKED BY SCIENCE

The Boone and Crockett William I. Spencer Conservation Grants Program is one way the Club keeps pace with changing environmental issues and needs. For over 55 years the Club has supported classic studies in wildlife ecology and conservation, including pioneering work on wolves and moose in Michigan's Isle Royale National Park, grizzly bears in the Rocky Mountains, cougar in Idaho, and sheep, elk and deer throughout the west. B&C Grants continue to provide the stimuli for innovative wildlife research leading to responsible decisions backed by this research.

DEFINING AMERICA'S CONSERVATION POLICY

The Boone and Crockett Club has always nurtured partnerships and collaboration. This work has brought about policies that benefit both wildlife and natural resources. An example of this collaboration is a summit facilitated by the Club, which brought together for the first time the leadership of 35 wildlife organizations in August of 2000. This meeting resulted in the formation of the American Wildlife Conservation Partners (AWCP). Today, the AWCP is a confederation comprised of 40 wildlife conservation organizations representing over 6 million sportsmen conservationists. This partnership was formed to build unity and to harness our collective strength to address present and future wildlife conservation chal-

Photo from B&C Archives

Students and educators build lasting awareness, understanding, and appreciation from field-based studies. The Boone and Crockett Club's Theodore Roosevelt Memorial Ranch and Elmer E. Rasmuson Wildlife Conservation Education Center – pictured in the background – provide an outdoor classroom for these field-based studies.

lenges. The AWCP has provided the hunter/conservationists a stronger voice in conservation policy issues now and in the future.

Indicative of the progress that has been made is the response AWCP has received from the Bush Administration. In December 2003, President George W. Bush met with AWCP representatives at the White House to discuss critical issues related to wetlands and other conservation initiatives. President Bush followed up with AWCP representatives at his ranch in Commerce, Texas, in 2004 to continue those conversations. Secretary of the Interior, Gale Norton, met in May 2005 with the AWCP to discuss conservation issues that AWCP has determined priorities for the next four years with respect to the Department of Interior (DOI). Senior DOI officials and heads of different land management agencies also participated in this meeting.

As we look to the conservation challenges of the future, the Boone and Crockett Club will continue to form new partnerships and collaborations to better define America's conservation policy. The Club's members are key to the Club's success. Through their passion for the outdoors and respect for hunting and wildlife, members provide financial support and donate countless hours for this noble cause. Working with state and federal agencies, conservationists, corporate sponsors, and avid sportsmen, the Boone and Crockett Club will continue to be a conservation leader far into the future.

INTO THE 21ST CENTURY
Two Significant Issues: Critical Habitat and Public Perception
These issues will be paramount in the focus of the Boone and Crockett Club going forward. Negative perceptions and habitat loss are threats that will severely impact the future of wildlife and hunting traditions.

Loss of habitat – The loss of critical habitat is a core threat affecting everything. It is a symbiotic chain – reduced habitat means a reduction in wildlife numbers. This means fewer hunting opportunities and limited enjoyment of the outdoors. With a decrease in the number of hunters comes a reduction in funding for conservation, management, and enforcement, which in turns leads to even more loss of habitat. Inherent in this loss is the tradition of American game management.

Public Perception – In general, the non-hunting public accepts or tolerates hunting as long as the activity is viewed as fair, ethical, respectful, and within the cultural context in which hunting occurs. This attitude can, and is, shifting when hunting is seen or portrayed as unfair, unethical, and disrespectful of wildlife.

With anti-hunting efforts targeting the non-hunting public (voting majority) it is more important now than ever before to strengthen the public perception and acceptance of hunting.

HUNT FAIR CHASE

In keeping with the issue of public perception, the Boone and Crockett Club launched the Hunt Fair Chase program in 2004. This program brings together the hunting and conservation communities to deliver a unified message of positive hunter ethics to all hunters.

At the turn of the 20th century, the Boone and Crockett Club promoted the importance of ethical hunting and sportsmanship as a way to save wildlife from pending disaster. One hundred years later, Hunt Fair Chase reached over 5 million hunters, reaffirming their role as conservationists. As individuals making ethical choices these hunters will continue to positively affect the image of hunters as perceived by the public.

Since the message of ethical hunting has no sunset, the web site created by this Program (HuntFairChase.com) remains as a portal of information providing resources about the origins and importance of hunting ethics to the North American Model for Conservation.

The success achieved by this Program provides a foundation for our continued effort in perpetuating the highest ethical standards among all hunters. The extension of the Hunt Fair Chase program focuses on informing those unexposed to hunting, affording them a clearer understanding of the cultural context in which hunting occurs.

The delicate ecosystems in North America benefit from hunters and hunting in numerous ways, including untold conservation dollars that are spent by the hunting community. This support will ultimately lead to healthy wildlife populations and science-backed conservation systems that work. It is imperative that we, as hunters, hunt ethically, and that we do our part in changing negative hunting perceptions.

A JOB WELL DONE

The history of the Boone and Crockett Club is a tale of over a century of a measured and thoughtful commitment by hunters for conservation. This is a commitment that balances human needs with wildlife needs; a commitment that sees deep value in preserving the hunting tradition, as well as in conserving wild lands and wildlife; a commitment that grows out of a powerful love of wildlife, but that is also shaped by a common-sense, business-like approach to managing natural resources.

History has proven that the path Roosevelt and the Boone and Crockett Club took was the right path – creating, supporting, and enhancing what has evolved to become the most successful natural resource conservation system in the history of mankind. Habitats have been preserved and enhanced, game populations are at all-time highs for many species, and the infrastructure to support these programs is in place. People have come from all over the world to marvel at, study, and learn from our country's conservation programs.

In time, other conservation organizations have taken up the charge. Some were formed by Boone and Crockett members and others were patterned after the B&C Model. Organizations focusing their effort on a specific wildlife species have made tremendous strides in preserving, protecting, managing, and expanding the range of these species. Other groups exist today, which focus on habitat; others focus on the activities of state and federal agencies and national politics. But, are we doing enough?

OUR WORK HAS JUST BEGUN

Mankind is a destructor by our mere existence, and our population is growing. By 2050, the nation's human population is projected to be more than 400 million, about 43% greater than today. As a result:

- Demand for most natural resources, especially those on public lands, will increase dramatically
- Nearly all natural resources will likely become scarcer relative to demand
- Intense competition especially for public natural resources can be expected, as private land is developed and becomes less available for public use
- Remaining private land habitat will become increasingly important to wildlife conservation
- Advocates for exclusive use of public resources – both preservation and development – will likely increase their efforts
- Special interest groups and advocacy can be expected to increase
- Wildlife and opportunities for hunters will increasingly be caught in the crossfire between development and preservationist forces

The decade of 2005-2015 is recognized as critical for

wildlife as the die is being cast for its future.

It should not come as a surprise that, in spite of the great successes in restoration of wildlife over the past 119 years, the changing structure of our society makes it more important than ever before for wildlife managers and hunter/conservationists to work together more effectively in order to build on the successes achieved in the past.

PARTNERSHIPS — You and B&C

The Boone and Crockett Club has been forging partnerships since 1887, when the challenges were to protect wildlife habitats, restore depleted populations and stop excessive use of native plants and animals. The challenges of today are not unlike the challenges of more than a century ago as we look to the future of hunting and conservation issues in North America. The value of unity among hunter-conservationists is more apparent today than ever before as we work together to meet the challenges of the coming years.

In August 2000, the gathering of what is today the American Wildlife Conservation Partners representing 5 million hunter/conservationists was the precursor of what will be required as we look to the future. Now the task is even greater than that of a century ago, and the need for partnerships and collaboration are greater still. It is imperative that we unify our collective strength and apply it to common challenges and opportunities to protect wildlife, habitat, hunting traditions and the way of life it represents.

By joining Boone and Crockett as an Associate or Lifetime Associate Member you will add the strength needed to ensure the B&C remains visionary in its efforts to identify and work around new threats to conservation and our sporting way of life

The Boone and Crockett Club welcomes you to become a part of this continuing legacy and to add your name to a long and distinguished list of Boone and Crockett partners in conservation. 🦌

Acknowledgments for
Legendary Hunts

**Stories selected from the Boone and Crockett Club's Awards
book series – 18th Awards through the 25th Awards – by:**

Keith Balfourd

Mark O. Bara

Eldon L. "Buck" Buckner

Richard T. Hale

Robert H. Hanson

Ryan Hatfield

Julie T. Houk

Marie Pavlik

Remo Pizzagalli

Jack Reneau

Mark B. Steffen – Editor

Paul D. Webster

Copy Editing and Proofreading by:

Jack Reneau

Julie T. Houk

OCR Specialist:

Sandy Poston

Cover Photograph by:

Denver Bryan

Legendary Hunts was designed by Julie T. Houk,
Director of Publication, Boone and Crockett Club
using Adobe Caslon Pro typeface

Paperback printed and bound by Sheridan Books of Ann Arbor, Michigan
Limited Editions bound by Roswell Books of Phoenix, Arizona